FOREWOR

BY SIR HEW STRACHAN

The title by which we now know the Great War of 1914-18, the First Worlc
was known while the fighting was going on or in its immediate aftermath.
After all it would require a second and even greater conflict to make the Great War the first and not the
last of its kind. When in 1920 The Times's military correspondent, Charles à Court Repington, provoca-
tively called his war memoirs The First World War, he did so precisely because he recognised that pos-
sibility.

Stranger than the use, or non-use, of the word 'first' was the reluctance to call the war a 'world war'.
While it was going on, Germans frequently described it as 'ein Weltkrieg' – a world war; Britons rarely
did. And yet Britain's belligerence was one of the reasons why the war, which had begun as a limited
and local conflict in the Balkans, so quickly became a global struggle. All the powers which entered the
war by early August 1914, with the exception of its original protagonists, Austria-Hungary and Serbia,
ruled territories outside Europe – in Africa and in Asia, and on coasts abutting the world's two principal
oceans, the Pacific and Atlantic. However, only Britain – unlike Belgium, France, Germany and Russia - expressed its military power primarily at sea rather than on land, and only Britain also hosted the
shipping, banking and insurance services which created a globalised commercial network. In 1914 war
in Europe meant war for the world.

The impact on the Caribbean was as immediate as anywhere else. As major producers of sugar its islands depended on global – and especially European – markets. The waging of economic war closed
off those in Central Europe, in Germany and Austria-Hungary, but opened or widened others. One of
the points made in this admirable introduction to the war in the West Indies is that, while sugar sales to
Europe declined, demand for rum rose – not least because the newly expanded British army instituted a
rum ration to go alongside the tot issued to naval ratings. A medical officer of the Black Watch told the
War Office's committee on shell shock in 1922 that 'had it not been for the rum ration I do not think we
should have won the war'. That assertion is as questionable as is the idea that the expanded issue of rum
off-set the other constraints suffered by the sugar industry, especially when the ration was only a quarter-
gill – or about a tablespoon-full per man per day.

In 1914 Britain's dependence on its sea lines of communication put its colonies and their ports under
direct threat. The German navy had concentrated on creating a High Seas Fleet for use in the North
Sea, and had neglected the development of ships for oceanic warfare. However, it had formed a cruiser
squadron based at its colony on the Chinese coast, and it deployed light cruisers in the western Atlantic.
In early December 1914 the East Asiatic Squadron left the Pacific, rounded Cape Horn, and entered the
south Atlantic. The dangers to the islands of the Caribbean seemed to be about to become direct. In
the event the German squadron was destroyed on 8 December 1914 in the battle of the Falkland Islands,
and by the year's end the world's trade routes seemed to be secure once more. When the threat of cruiser
warfare was renewed, this time by submarines and not by surface ships, it affected Atlantic routes but it
did not pose a direct danger to the islands of the Caribbean.

As a result the local volunteer units formed for the defence of the British West Indies had little immediate function for the rest of the war besides that of making local worthies feel that they were doing their bit
for the imperial war effort. Britain needed men not on the western Atlantic seaboard but on the eastern,
and not just in France but also in the Middle East and sub-Saharan Africa.

The so-called 'white' dominions of Australia, Canada, New Zealand and South Africa were uncertain about, and in most cases other than in New Zealand downright opposed to, the enlistment of 'men of colour' for imperial service. While New Zealand enlisted Maori in 1915, it did not go on to conscript them as it did Pakeha (or whites), and all of the other three sought ways to redefine the race or qualifications of aboriginals or 'first nationals' rather than admit their right to take up arms. South Africa raised a Native Labour Corps, so effectively denying the hopes of the African National Congress who saw the war as an opportunity for blacks to stake their claim to civic rights through active fighting.

By the end of 1914 the British army's losses had outstripped the original strength of the expeditionary force sent to France and Flanders, and the urgency of the demand for fit men capable of joining the army outstripped the racial and social prejudices of settler communities. London pressurised its far-flung fiefdoms to relax their prejudices so as to respond to the military need. The other major colonial power in the Caribbean, France, had already understood before the war that the peoples of its empire constituted a reservoir of men to offset its own declining birth rate in the era of mass armies. One calculation is that over 4 million non-Europeans fought in this war: these armies, especially those of the Entente powers, were as multi-ethnic as those of the Caribbean more specifically.

The conventional historian's narrative – that the First World War proved to be a false down in the emancipation of colonised peoples and that it required the impact of the Second to prompt the collapse of Europe's empires – is one overwhelmingly shaped by sub-Saharan Africa and south Asia. Like South Africa's ANC, those who joined up in 1914 because they took seriously the view of the Enlightenment, that citizenship was the corollary of a readiness to defend the state, were often doomed to have their hopes dashed. They were in any case a minority. Most of the soldiers who served in the West African Frontier Force, the King's African Rifles or the Indian Army came from peasant backgrounds and were illiterate. Just as they have left us with few records of their service, so they seemed rarely to have seen military service as a route to political representation.

The story told in The Caribbean's Great War is very different. Its authors see the First World War to be a moment of emancipation to rank alongside the abolition of slavery a century previously. Britain's nineteenth-century record in the subsequent world-wide campaign against slavery kept that memory bright. In 1914 West Indians of every ethnicity believed that the empire's cause was one epitomised by a commitment to democracy and freedom, just as propagandists declared. When they enlisted and crossed the ocean to Britain some illusions were shattered: they themselves were discriminated against on racial grounds and they found a country that was depressed, too many of its workers rendered unfit for military service by factory conditions and slum dwelling. The trajectory of their political beliefs changed, ultimately from a commitment to empire to a demand for independence. Some of the founding ideas of Caribbean politics, and several of the West Indies' greatest leaders of the twentieth century, emerged from the forcing ground of the First World War.

The Caribbean's Great War has many strengths; it is succinct, clear and beautifully illustrated. It is also objective without being dispassionate. But its greatest quality is its determination to put the epoch-making events of 1914-18 in context, setting them against the longer course of history. It is only thus that the true significance of the war can be made clear. In smashing the globalised order of 1914 the Great War changed the world; it also fundamentally altered the lives of those who lived on the islands of the Caribbean archipelago.

Published by the West India Company

The West India Company Limited,
The West India Committee Rooms,
Clutha House,
10 Storey's Gate,
London,
SW1P 3AY

www.westindiacommittee.org

Copyright © 2017 The West India Committee

A catalogue record of this book is available from the British Library.

First Edition

Compiled by Blondel Cluff

Written by Blondel Cluff, Lord Ashcroft, David Wells, Barnabas Wale, Leah Alexander, Stacey Dehaney and Georgia Topley.

Designed by Georgia Topley

Edited by David Wells

ISBN 978-1-911233-02-2

Printed by CPI Group UK (Ltd)

The Caribbean's Great War

Compiled by the West India Committee

Written by Blondel Cluff

PREAMBLE

The story told in this volume draws upon the archive and collection of The West India Committee, which holds significant primary source material on the history of the Caribbean and its peoples amassed since its foundation. The West India Committee is a Royal Charter institution founded in London in 1735 whose roots lie firmly in the Eighteenth Century, when the relationship between Britain and the Caribbean was dictated by the inhumanity of trade based upon slavery. The West India Committee began as a trade association of planters and sugar merchants that rapidly evolved into one of the most pre-eminent charities of the Caribbean. Its meticulous record-keeping and timely publications throughout the centuries provide us with one of the few surviving contemporary accounts of many little known episodes in the history of this extraordinary region.

The charity's archive has recently been inscribed by UNESCO as a Memory of the World, attesting to its importance and relevance for those who seek to comprehend the Caribbean, a crossroads of world heritage. The West India Committee was itself complicit in many defining moments in Anglo-Caribbean heritage that have positively affected Britain, the Caribbean and the wider world.

Milestones in the history of The West India Committee include the infamous voyage of *HMS Bounty* in 1767 under the command of the notorious Captain Bligh; founding the Thames River Police in London in 1798, the oldest continuously serving police force in the world, making The West India Committee a forefather of today's Metropolitan Police Service; and opening West India Quay in 1802, marking a step change in London's first purpose-built wet dock and the longest brick building in the world at the time, improving London's proficiency as one of the world's leading ports. Each evinces the important contribution made by this unique institution, and the people of the Caribbean whom they have served for almost three centuries.

The Caribbean's Great War tells the story of the valiant contribution made by thousands of West Indian volunteers to a global conflict that would change the face of modern warfare and ultimately the world itself. Here we reveal the experiences of a people freshly liberated from the chains of slavery who chose to come to the aid of their King and Mother Country and who had to combat the British establishment in order to do so. It is therefore a story of a victory of patriotism over colonialism.

We trust this work will lead you to a better understanding and appreciation of the fine people of the Caribbean, one of the most diverse and fascinating places on Earth.

CONTENTS

THE CONTRIBUTORS

Blondel Cluff

Blondel is CEO of the Committee and focuses on protecting the heritage of the region to engender a better understanding of the Caribbean and it people. She is a Fellow of King's College London and Representative of the Government of Anguilla and also chair of the Heritage Lottery Fund, London Committee.

Lord Ashcroft KCMG PC

Lord Ashcroft is a businessman, philanthropist, author and pollster. His five books on gallantry include Victoria Cross Heroes. For more information, visit www.victoriacrossheroes.com. For more information on Lord Ashcroft's work, visit www.lordashcroft.com.

David Wells

David is a Research Fellow of the West India Committee and was a researcher for the Caribbean's Great War. He has a background in Ancient History with a BA and MA from Durham University and also holds a Graduate Diploma in Law. He has edited the book and authored and co-authored several chapters.

Captain Stacey-Marie Dehaney

Captain Dehaney is Curator of the Jamaican Military Museum and Library. She holds a Bachelors , MA, MBA and a Certificate in Paper Conservation. Prior to joining the Jamaican army, she was the Director of the Museums of History and Ethnography, a division of the Institute of Jamaica. She has told the story of Private Herbert Morris.

Leah Alexander

Leah is a History graduate of Grenadian heritage who in 2016 became Project Manager for the Committee's heritage project on the origins of modern policing. Her research explores the link between WWI and the growth of Caribbean Nationalism.

Georgia Topley

Born and raised in London and the Caribbean Georgia is the West India Committee Scholar for 2016. An English Literature Graduate from King's College London, she was lead designer for the book.

Barnabas Howard Wale

Barnabas has a background in Public Relations and the Language sciences. As a trained linguist, in 2016 he completed his MA in Politics & International Relations with the support of the West India Committee. His research contribution includes the enduring relevance of the BWIR to contemporary West Indian Culture and Polity.

Andreas Persson

A History Graduate, Andreas was the Project Manager for the Caribbean's Great War project and also did some of the research. Without him, this book would not have been possible.

The West India Committee would like to thank Mrs Helen Wells for her assistance with the book.

INTRODUCTION

An adaptation of Josiah Wedgwood's abolitionist slogan.

At the beginning of the Nineteenth Century Europe was experiencing its own social revolution. The abolition of the slave trade and ultimately the abolition of slavery itself, as initiated by the British after years of intense debate and lobbying, was part of that revolution. The abolition of the slave trade was not, however, one and the same as the abolition of slave labour. Indeed abolitionists such as Wilberforce refrained from challenging the use of slave labour, concerning themselves primarily with the manner in which slaves were traded. It took the unlikely figure of the twenty-six years old Third Duke of Northumberland during his maiden speech in the House of Commons to question why the Abolition movement would not take their campaign to its natural conclusion - the abolition of slavery itself. The timid Duke, whose nerves rendered his voice a barely audible whisper, debated face to face with Wilberforce himself. The simple fact that there were insufficient Members of Parliament present to pass a vote enabled the Speaker of the House to end the awkward debate, as reported in *The Sun* newspaper of the time, leaving hundreds of thousands of slaves to continue to suffer the indignity of slavery for almost a generation after the initial anti-trade legislation, for which Wilberforce had fought, was passed by Parliament.

The West India Committee was driven by a desire to remove any economic advantage Britain's slave-owning competitors may have enjoyed after Britain's revolutionary change in attitude towards the trade. Having secured over twenty million pounds in compensation for former slave owners throughout the British Empire, members of The West India Committee, which included over forty Members of Parliament, lobbied long and hard for Britain to secure a worldwide ban on the slave trade. This resulted in the Royal Navy policing the African coastline to apprehend slave ships of all nationalities.

The Abolition movement, although not all it seemed, marked a step change in the British attitude to human rights, inadvertently serving as a catalyst for the advancement of over half the British population through the emancipation of women. Whilst many had no knowledge of the West Indies, let alone the realities of slavery, they were nonetheless inspired to achieve their own liberation from an environment in which every married woman lost most of her personal liberties and all of her personal property to her husband upon entering the institution of marriage. Britain changed dramatically as it entered the Edwardian era after the demise of Queen Victoria. During this time visionaries like Coco Chanel freed women from the corset, clad them in jersey, and legitimised the notion of the independent woman capable of keeping herself. The work of the Wright brothers in achieving the first powered flight in 1903, and Henry Ford's Model T car, *"a car for the common man"*, allowed the average man in the street to broaden his outlook – the sky was no longer the limit of his expectations, with modern technology being made available to the masses. All of these fast-developing changes meant that conventional boundaries were no longer accepted as absolute barriers in peoples' lives.

This era of change was led by King Edward VII during his popular, albeit brief, reign. Like his mother and his son, Edward VII had a liberal attitude towards race, being more enlightened than most colonial officers. On visiting India as the Prince of Wales, he remarked, *"Because a man has a black face and a different religion from our own, there is no reason why he should be treated as a brute"*. His more conservative son, George V, maintained this trait during a reign that witnessed the most significant conflict Europe had experienced in almost a century. Europe, whose civilisation had originally lagged behind that of Asia and the Middle East, now stood at the epicentre of world power, at the heart of which were a small group of competing countries – 'the Great Powers' – France, Russia, Britain, the Austro-Hungarian Empire and the eager newcomer, Germany. America was not as yet the global power it would one day become and, with the advantage of its geography, was in a position to be circumspect about its role in what was initially a purely European dispute. Alongside America sat its neighbour, the Caribbean, whose role in the war could only ever be at the invitation of the European colonial powers that controlled it. The existence of the European empires magnified the impact of the conflict, augmenting the strength of small military powers such as Britain, whose real might had always resided in its navy. Britain had operated within the Caribbean for centuries, the Caribbean being described as *'the cradle of the British Navy'*. By the outbreak of war, despite having one of the smallest armies in Europe, the British Empire was the largest the world had ever known.

The social realities of Europe meant wealth, power and influence were concentrated in the hands of a select few. With women and the lower classes denied the vote, the fate of the majority of the world lay in the hands of a small band of men. Amongst these men were members of The West India Committee which, since its inception during the early Eighteenth Century, had maintained close ties with both Parliament and the City of London, having many influential members of both institutions firmly within its orb of influence.

The direct descendants of Queen Victoria, whose numerous progeny populated royal dynasties throughout Europe, rendered the conflict, for some, little more than a glorified family argument. Kaiser Wilhelm, Victoria's oldest grandchild, in whose arms she had died at Osborne House in 1901, waged war against his first cousins, King George V of Britain and Tsar Alexander of Russia, with a myriad of distant cousins and relatives playing their own parts in leading this struggle for territory and influence in Europe and the wider world that it controlled.

Four generations of the British Monarchy: Queen Victoria, Edward VII, George V and the Prince of Wales, (the future Edward VIII).

King George took great pains to travel throughout the British Empire, which encompassed a third of the world's population and landmarks, during his time on the throne. On a tour of India he, like his father, noted, with regret, the disdain with which the British treated native Indians. The relevance of European empires was economic, with millions of people in far-flung countries generating commercial outputs that would fuel Europe's evolution from rural economies into the industrial successes they would eventually become, in so doing causing the supporting countries to deteriorate economically. The great significance of these countries meant that they themselves were often the theatres of war, as European rivals fought for control of these economic engine rooms. The First World War was the first global conflict to take place on European soil in almost a century following the Battle of Waterloo in 1815. For generations, Europeans had played out their disputes in other lands. As a result of this tendency, military legends came to know the Caribbean region intimately. Nelson, who referred to Antigua as *that infernal hole*, was not only stationed there beside his close friend, the future King William IV, but married into a Creole family from Nevis; whilst his nemesis, Napoleon, also married a West Indian, the Empress Josephine, who was born a British West Indian on the island of St. Lucia. In this yellow fever and malaria riddled corner of the Empire, Nelson was to play out some of his most daring strategies, leading the West India Committee to correspond with the Admiral to enquire about the security of the islands. Nelson's reply to the West India Committee is recorded in the West India Committee Circular of November 1914.

An extract from The West India Committee Circular 17th November 1914.

The declaration of war between Europe's Great Powers in 1914 exposed the borders of the British Empire to invasion. India, which had replaced the Caribbean as the jewel in the Imperial Crown, was a particularly attractive target for invasion by Germany, although a standing Indian Army of over one and a half million men meant this would not be an easy task. It was nonetheless important to safeguard the British interest in India and troops from elsewhere in the Empire were deployed there accordingly. Slighted by Britain joining the conflict as a consequence of their treaty with Belgium, Kaiser Wilhelm sought a means of hitting back at Britain where he felt it would hurt most. In his own words, he would *"rouse the whole Muslim world into wild rebellion against this hateful, mendacious, unprincipled nation of shopkeepers"*, going on to state that if Germans were to *"shed our blood, England must at least lose India"*. With this, he turned his focus upon Germany's ailing ally, Turkey, and its once great Ottoman Empire. It is in this quest that West Indian troops saw the most action and experienced their first role in battle during the conflict.

By the onset of war many West Indians were of Asian heritage as a result of large numbers of indentured labourers having migrated to the Caribbean from India and China during the late Nineteenth Century in search of prosperity, encouraged by their governments. Consequently, West Indians, unlike many Britons at home, had a wider understanding and appreciation of the world, as the Caribbean was then one of the most diverse societies on the planet, having accepted to its shores dispossessed Jews, indentured Celts, Asians, and the downtrodden African slave to live beside their own Carib tribesmen. On joining their Indian comrades under the command of Wood Hill and Chaytor, the West Indians' war effort extended to providing coconut oil for Sikhs to dress their hair, a practice known in the region, reflecting their understanding of and respect for the wider world. There was also a proliferation of religions in the Caribbean that included the Muslim faith. However, when the Turkish Sultan declared Jihad against the Allied forces in a vain attempt to encourage Muslims within the Allied forces to defect to his army, this appeal fell on deaf West Indian ears.

Hugh Percy:
The Third Duke of Northumberland.

King George V was raised in staunch naval traditions and made considerable efforts to understand the Empire over which he reigned. His passion for stamp-collecting ensured he knew each of the British Caribbean islands by name, and his desire to engender mutual respect between Britain and her colonies was reflected in his personal quest to ensure that the men of the Caribbean satisfied their expressed desire to fight for their King and Mother Country. This venture pitched the Monarch against the heavyweights of the military, including Lord Kitchener. The King was not alone in supporting Caribbean servicemen. Queen Mary who, like King Edward VII and his father Prince Albert, was clearly of Germanic origin, strived throughout the conflict to express her loyalty to Britain and its Empire as opposed to her birthplace, Germany. The Queen embarked upon direct involvement in the war effort and was said to have presided over knitting circles and postal work in the offices of the West India Committee on behalf of West Indian troops. Her son, the Prince of Wales and future King Edward VIII, was also active, presiding over the National Relief Fund based in Buckingham Palace which interacted directly with the Caribbean countries. The Royal Family, with members such as Queen Mary who, like her father-in-law, spoke with a strong German accent, suffered the same fate as many West Indians in being regarded by many as not being truly British. To resolve this stigma, in 1917 The Royal Family changed their name from the Germanic 'Saxe-Coburg and Gotha' to the more British sounding 'Windsor', founding the House of Windsor. Such an option was not as readily available to black and mixed race West Indians, although it is likely that some West Indians of European origin may have addressed the question of acceptance by simply distancing themselves from their Creole heritage.

WEST INDIES GIFTS.

The West India Committee have now distributed over 6,500 cases of fruit from the Dominica and Jamaica Agricultural Societies and the Trinidad Orange and Lime Committee. Among recent gifts from overseas have been 40 Imperial gallons of coconut oil from Trinidad for the Sikhs' hair, and 1,500 walking sticks cut from native woods in Jamaica for wounded soldiers. The people of Barbados and Trinidad have presented two more motor ambulances to the British Red Cross Society.

An extract from The West India Committee Circular detailing contributions to the war effort from the West Indies.

THE CARIBBEAN

Despite its name, the First World War was not the first global conflict driven by European colonial ambitions. The Caribbean had regularly hosted 'global' conflicts, and the islands themselves were fought over by the European countries that orchestrated these conflicts from the other side of the world, as if indulging in an enormous game of chess. The result was that Caribbean islands changed imperial hands many times, in extreme cases dozens of times over. With each change of dominion came new allegiances, languages, laws and codes of conduct. This mosaic of global heritage impacted greatly upon the culture of the Caribbean, with each island becoming a distinctive, complex cocktail of European, African, Asian and American influences. Consequently no two islands are the same, each possessing its own distinct heritage.

By the time of Archduke Ferdinand's assassination in the summer of 1914, life in the Caribbean had found its own post slavery order and rhythm. Planters still endeavoured to retain their position at the pinnacle of the Plantocracy in the hope of reliving the heady days when their kind were the richest, most powerful of their generation in the known world. However, European sugar beet put pay to such lofty aspirations and rendered the Caribbean a commercial backwater, with an unsavoury past that many in a progressive Europe preferred to forget.

The West India Committee, stalwarts of British West Indian trade, had evolved from a trade association in London into one of the most benevolent institutions in the region, often acting as a much-needed intermediary between the various assemblies of the islands and the British Government. In 1904, in recognition of its pivotal role in the region, The West India Committee was incorporated by a much-prized Royal Charter, making it directly accountable to the Monarch in Privy Council, a status bestowed upon a small number of elite British institutions.

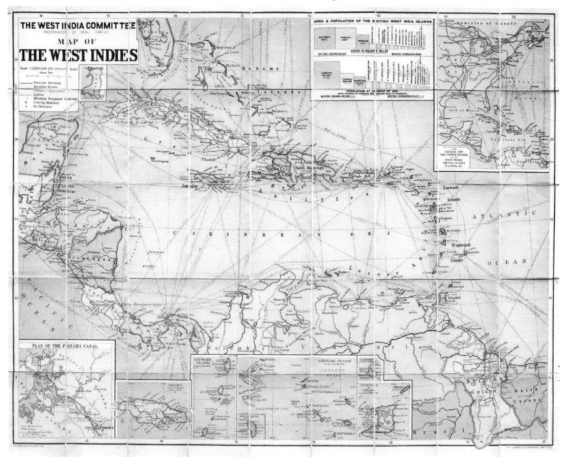

The West India Committee map of the Caribbean which includes the islands of the Caribbean Sea and the surrounding coastal countries of Belize, Columbia, Venezuela, Guyana, Suriname and French Guiana.

The annual bout of natural disasters, whether hurricanes, earthquakes or droughts added to the on-going burden of regionalised threats from insect-borne disease such as Dengue fever, yellow fever and malaria, each of which was rife in the Caribbean at the beginning of the conflict. Jamaica, Britain's largest Caribbean island, had lost its capital Kingston during a major earthquake in 1907, and despite the most valiant of efforts on the part of the West India Committee and its staunch supporters in the City of London, Kingston

A SCENE IN RUM STREET.
It seems remarkable that any people managed to escape.

VERANDAH AT THE MYRTLE BANK HOTEL.
Where Sir A. L. Jones and many of his party lunched on January 14th.

remained a mere shadow of its former self by 1914.

The larger islands of the West Indies, as Columbus historically referred to his 'discovery', started life in the Pacific Ocean, slowly gliding eastwards upon the quaking shoulders of groaning tectonic plates deep beneath the young Pacific. As if a flimsy garden gate, Central America closed behind the islands shutting off the Pacific. The islands, only 2% of which were ever inhabited, were then claimed by the Atlantic.

Although appearing as some 7,000 small, often-minute landmasses strewn like a chain across the Caribbean Sea, the islands are in fact the tips of a huge submarine mountain range in which some of the world's geographic extremities are found today. The steepest cliff in the world at three miles high demarks the edge of the Bahamas Bank, whilst the tiny islands of Turks and Caicos lie beside the Atlantic's deepest trench. The Leeward Islands, like Anguilla, were formed of a more ancient volcanic chain, which had eroded and is now covered by a build-up of coral. Despite man's ability to explore the depths of this world, life in the Caribbean remains largely unknown and unidentified, although now recognised as being home to a considerable proportion of the biodiversity of the European states that still retain territory there.

The female Aedes mosquito responsible for the spread of yellow fever, malaria and now suspected of carrying the Zika virus.

Images from The West India Committee Circular of 1907 of the destruction caused by an earthquake in Jamaica.

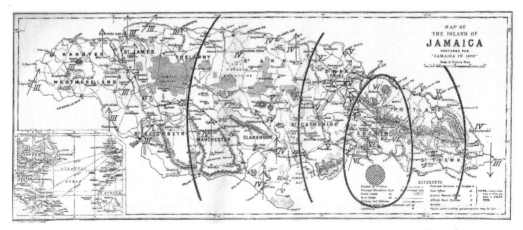

A West India Committee map showing the epicentre of the 1907 earthquake.

THE PEOPLES OF THE CARIBBEAN

Man's presence in the West Indies is less of a mystery than its ecology, although misconceptions continue to this day. It is now widely appreciated that the earliest evidence of man's presence in the Caribbean points to the stone-age settlements of the Saladoid peoples. Middens from this period reveal heavy reliance on clay pottery and a diet that was predominantly marine in content.

An example of indigenous ceramics.

Tribes from both North and South America gradually supplanted these, the first known West Indians. One such tribe, the Lucayan Indians of the Bahamas, who originated in North America, practised unique marine burials, and a tradition of skull deformation. This was achieved through

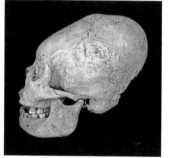

An elongated skull.

applying pressure to the foreheads of their young children by tying wooden planks to their heads until the head sloped back to an elongated peak, marking these people out from other American tribes. Their distant relatives from South America, the Arawaks, were a sea-going race that built enormous canoes from the giant trees of the Amazonian forest in which they originated. In craft transporting up to a hundred men, women and children, they navigated their way through the islands, respecting a tradition whereby offspring were obliged to find their own homelands away from the their birth-place, thereby ensuring security of food and water for the next generation. It is said that they were propelled on this quest by the pursuit of a warlike tribe who gave their name to the region – the Caribs. Demonised in early European accounts, the Caribs were notoriously aggressive, allegedly consuming their victims, contributing yet another word to the Oxford dictionary - cannibalism. It may well be that the Spanish labelled them as such to justify their subrogation of these, the true West Indians. We shall never know. What we do know is that the Europeans on first arriving in the West Indies met people who were both trusting and innocent of the ways of the European invaders, swiftly falling prey to enslavement and genocide far beyond anything the Caribs had meted out upon their docile Arawak cousins. As a consequence of these atrocities, many have laboured under the misconception that the Indians were 'wiped out' by the settlers when, in fact, many remain today, with some communities residing in reservations. These reservations were negotiated in the Eighteenth Century when the English tired of the stealth campaigns of guerrilla warfare waged so successfully by these accomplished tribesmen.

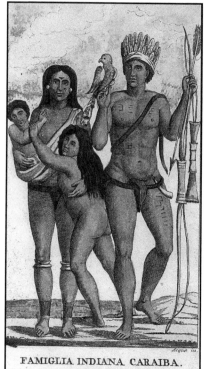

FAMIGLIA INDIANA CARAIBA.

An early depiction of an indigenous Carib family.

Islands such as Dominica, St. Vincent, Puerto Rico and neighbouring Anguilla remain home to peoples distinctively Carib in cultural origin and race. High cheekbones, straight hair and a hint of their long distant oriental lineage remain etched on the faces of many West Indians today, with over 62% of Puerto Rico's current population claiming Carib heritage, raising questions over the accuracy of the Afro-Caribbean label so prolific of late. Their culture did not embrace the written word nor were they builders of note, using perishable materials that invariably deteriorated leaving little trace. Carib culture was conveyed from one generation to another by folklore, song, petroglyphs and zemis, with rare ball courts providing insight into a lost sporting heritage. Carib words have long been absorbed into the English language and remain in common use today, as have key aspects of their lifestyle, such as their hammocks, barbeques and tobacco. Their custom of women using a separate language to their men kept the language of the conquered Arawaks alive.

Global awareness of the Caribbean region revolves around the story of the slaves, the plight of imported African labour whose experiences were undoubtedly some of the most brutal in humanity. The ancient institution of slavery had few examples of such prolonged and extreme brutality. The catastrophic extent to which the human rights of Africans and black Creoles were suffocated by this institution overshadows the experiences of so many other West Indians that are now consigned to a mere footnote of history, resulting in an incomplete awareness of the peoples of the Caribbean and the remarkable diversity that evolved at this crossroads of so many civilisations.

The African influx was in fact the third attempt at developing a sustainable slave work-force in the region. Columbus instigated the enslavement of the docile Indians, taking advantage of their naivety concerning the darker side of man's ambitions. Many preferred to commit suicide rather than be reduced to beasts of burden to satiate the greed of the Europeans and the violation of their lands. Following Columbus, the Spanish introduced a system known as the Ecomienda, a form of feudalism, and Queen Isabella proclaimed the native people to be free vassals of the Spanish Crown. The indigenous people were converted to Catholicism and received a rudimentary education, unlike their African successors. However, they could be forced to do harsh labour and punished if they refused. Many were also displaced from their lands and separated from their families.

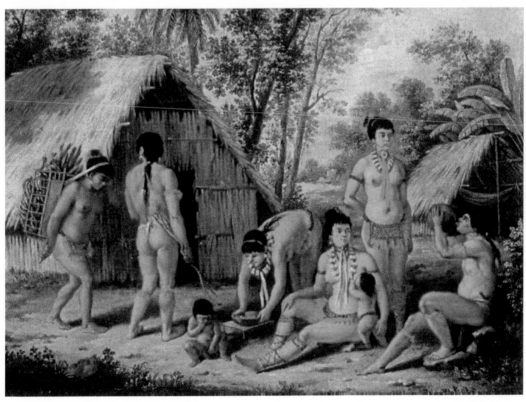

A painting of Caribs by Agostino Brunias, one of the leading artists to portray the Caribbean.

INDENTURED SERVITUDE AND SLAVERY

Before the advent of African slavery in the Caribbean and after a short-lived, failed attempt to enslave indigenous West Indians, the English looked much closer to home for a source of free labour. Often overlooked because of the sheer magnitude and brutality of the African slave trade, hundreds of thousands of Europeans comprised the first wave of foreign slaves in the region, who were transported to the West Indies in the early colonial period of the Seventeenth and Eighteenth centuries as a means of judicial punishment. A biased legal

A deed of indenture.

system often focused upon the poor in a society in which a man had no legal representation, cross-examination of one's accuser was unheard of and the death penalty could be meted out for the theft of a crust of bread by a starving man. Transportation to the New World was a lesser sentence, causing many to serve their sentences in the Caribbean long before Australia was 'discovered' by Cook in 1770 and penal colonies were established there.

The huge numbers of indentured convicts in the Caribbean were swelled by prisoners of Cromwell's Civil War and a lesser number of brave young men of all classes seeking their fortune in far distant lands. Like the convicts, these men were committed to labour for Caribbean planters for a number of years, but their contracts meant they also had to pay off their fares and their cost of living whilst saving to purchase land of their own at the end of the indenture. This took years of hard toil, but ultimately led to freedom from the complexities of class and religion in Britain and gave rise to opportunities in the New World far beyond those within their reach at home. Whilst extensive restrictions were placed upon their personal freedom, it was for an agreed number of years, unlike the African experience that could last a lifetime. Instead, voluntary European indenture was more akin to modern day economic migration, and even convicts chose to remain in the Caribbean after their sentence, becoming subsistence farmers and ultimately planters, benefiting from grants of land from the Crown designed to encourage colonisation by Europeans.

By transporting Irish, Scots and Welsh together with their convicts, the English not only secured a source of cheap agricultural labour to support their expansion into the newly-claimed lands, but also greatly reduced the population of their unruly neighbours at home. In 1625 alone, James II sent over 30,000 political prisoners from Ireland to Virginia and the West Indies to be sold as chattels. As a result, by the mid Seventeenth Century the slaves of Antigua and Montserrat were predominantly Irish. At the time a combination of Irish slaves and Catholic asylum seekers from surrounding Caribbean islands accounted for over 70% of the overall population of Montserrat. Between 1641 and 1652 Cromwell had succeeded in subrogating Ireland, selling over 300,000 Irishmen and women into slavery, amounting to over one quarter of the country's total population.

European slavery resulted in large numbers of white workers remaining in the Caribbean alongside the original planters. At the zenith of European migration, the slave trade of western Africa had only just begun and often African slaves were treated considerably better than their European counterparts, with abuse of the white slaves being fuelled by negative sentiments from home. Furthermore, African slaves were up to ten times more expensive than those from Europe, costing fifty shillings sterling on average, whilst Irish slaves could be purchased for as little as five shillings each. To ameliorate the disparity in costs planters began breeding mixed-race slaves known at the time as Mulattos. This practice was, however, soon terminated due to the financial impact it had on the lucrative transatlantic slave trade that evolved to meet demands in the Caribbean, which entailed European goods being sold to Africans in consideration for African slaves.

When African slaves became numerous in the Caribbean, the fate of the less valuable Europeans was placed at risk as, whilst indentured, there was no intrinsic value in their life other than the value of the work of which they were capable. Old, sick and injured indentured slaves could and were often discarded with no resale value to secure their future.

The white Creole descendants of European indentured slaves became known as 'red legs', or more simply 'red', owing to the effect of the tropical sun on their fair skins and, like the related Mulatto community, flourished, rendering the region one of the most integrated in the entire British Empire. With the prospects back at home in Britain far from attractive, the majority of the indentured labourers chose to remain in the Caribbean. As militia formed to protect the islands from the colonialist aspirations of other European powers, they found their place among the officer ranks, albeit beneath those of the planter class. However, the prevailing tendency to assume military postings on paper alone, meant that these 'red' Creoles were invariably left to their own devices, sitting at the top of the proverbial pile.

The caste system that inevitably arose as a consequence ordained that a person should be preferentially treated according to the strength of their European bloodline, with those of pure European heritage attaining higher social status. On the island of Montserrat, a recently discovered journal from 1834 stated that a person that is one sixteenth black is deemed white. This approach meant those of European extraction, who preferred to retain some degree of segregation from other sections of this complex society, had a means of surviving the risks attached to intense interbreeding. Ironically, it was the injection of black blood into the veins of white West Indians that literally kept them alive. The caste system of the Caribbean is very much alive today in certain countries, with little having altered from the days when complexion demarked potential and attainment. The darker skins were considered to be destined for unskilled work and manual labour, whilst those of a fairer complexion gravitated to the professions, politics and leadership. The system is, as ever, complex and riddled with nuances that the eye alone cannot discern. Inter-island competition added another dimension to the social hierarchy of the place. Inhabitants of bigger islands often regarded themselves as being more advanced and sophisticated than those of smaller islands, an attitude that sadly lingers today.

'Las Castas Mexicanas' by Ignacio María Barreda depicting the caste system.

The African slave trade was a Portuguese invention adopted by the British as early as Elizabethan times due to the enthusiasm of Hawke, one of Queen Elizabeth I's privateers, whose descendant was to beg for forgiveness from the African peoples almost four centuries later. The African continent was not, however, penetrated by Europeans until the mid Nineteenth Century, as so eloquently recounted by Thomas Pakenham in his book 'The Scramble for Africa', centuries after the Triangle of Trade had commenced. For the slave trade to have been so successful in displacing the many millions of Africans to the Americas, the collaboration of Africans was imperative and continued throughout the entire era. Along the coastline of West Africa were huge 'forts' and 'castles'. The Africans traders who participated in the Triangular Trade managed them as trading posts, much like those found in China in the Eighteenth Century. Here golden guineas,

Examples of the popular Toile de Jouy fabric.

silk parasols with tassels, bells, manillas, Toile de Jouy cloth, and countless other fripperies were willingly traded between Africans and Europeans for human flesh, to such an extent that upon the abolition of the infamous trade, several tribal economies along the continent's west coast promptly collapsed, including those of the Ashanti and Oyo whose power-base centred upon the Kingdom of Dahomey, that was economically dependent upon the conquest and enslavement of neighbouring tribes throughout the Eighteenth and Nineteenth Centuries. The respected and renowned African author of the time, Olaudah Equiano, commented on the African leg of the Triangle of Trade in his autobiography published in London in 1789, "*When a trader wants slaves, he applies to a chief for them, and tempts him with his wares. It is not extraordinary, if on this occasion he yields to the temptation with a little firmness, and accepts the price of his fellow creatures' liberty, with as little reluctance as the enlightened merchant. Accordingly he falls on his neighbour, and a desperate battle ensues.*"

A portrait of a freed African slave, by Allan Ramsey (1713-1784), thought to be Olaudah Equiano.

It may be argued that the Africans had no idea of what would befall their kinsmen once on board a slave ship, nor the terror that would meet them in the New World, if they were fortunate enough to survive the perilous voyage. What is clear, however, is that they were never expected to return, unlike the European slave traders who returned time after time to the African continent bringing news of the fatalities among their cargo, seeking more resilient stock from which they could profit. Yet this salacious, interracial trade continued unabated for centuries. The life expectancy of a West Indian sugar worker was on average a mere eight years, necessitating a constantly renewed labour force. In reality, it is unlikely that the slave trade could have taken such a toll had Africa itself not been complicit. The lack of respect shown by Africans to their fellow Africans by incarcerating the people they had captured for sale in the forts and castles strung along Africa's coastline, and trading them for such valueless goods, is likely to have 'set the bar' for European treatment of the human commodity. The sheer scale of the trade between Africans and Europeans reflected an immeasurable lack of respect for their fellow man, and devalued the black man in the eyes of the world; a position of inequality society continues to combat globally.

'To the Friends of Negro Emancipation', an engraving by David Lucas.

Back at home, Europeans were past masters at disrespecting the human rights of their own people. Women in particular related to enslavement, suffering restrictions akin to an open prison. Wedgwood's iconic motto – *"Am I not a man and a brother"* was soon being worn on evening bags amongst upper class British women, with the necessary revision: *"Am I not a woman and a sister?"* Married women were legally the chattels of their husbands and a woman's possessions automatically became those of her spouse, meaning many heiresses became personal paupers upon uttering the immortal words, "I do". Moreover, they did not have the vote, having to wait until 1918 for formal recognition of their entitlement to it, whilst the women of the Caribbean were to wait as late as the 1960s to attain their democratic freedom. Ironically, the first women in the British Empire to secure the vote were ex-slaves that were liberated and sent to Sierra Leone in 1819. Meanwhile, young children in Britain were being lowered into gas-filled mines, or forced up sooty chimneys, many losing their lives in the process, a practice that endured long after the abolition of slavery in the British Empire, whilst Britons most closely linked to the West Indies, the mill workers of the industrial heartlands, were effectively enslaved by Deeds of Indenture for years at a time. Many were mere children, who were incarcerated in municipal workhouses owned and controlled by their employers, and were subject to conditions that compromised their health and often proved fatal. In a myriad of ways, the abolition of the transatlantic slave trade proved to be the catalyst that reflected badly upon man's lack of respect for his own, causing a step change in human rights globally.

The mix of peoples in the Caribbean was further enriched from the 1880s onwards when self-indentured Cantonese workers began to migrate to the Caribbean via the Empire's trading routes, as did the Hindus, Sikhs, Muslims and various other Europeans, together with a fresh influx of free Africans. This confluence of labour from across the globe was prompted by the oft times misrepresented economic opportunities arising from the abolition of slavery. Augmented by subsequent waves of migration, certain communities flourished. Migrants from the Indian subcontinent gave rise to robust Asian communities in Guyana and Trinidad, accounting for over 50% of the population of Trinidad today.

Having commenced with indigenous West Indian slaves, a combination of Europeans that were self-indentured, convicts and political prisoners held sway on the islands and were then replaced by the product of the lucrative African slave trade. The demise of the Triangle of Trade was then followed by the migration of Asian and African self-indentured labour. Complex and prolonged migration to the Caribbean meant the British West Indies Regiment, made up of men from every section of Creole society, became one of the few multi-racial regiments in the British Army during the First World War.

At the advent of the First World War, the commercial success of certain Caribbean countries served to entrench a social hierarchy demarked by race and nuanced by caste. In less economically successful countries this social order was less strict, with many red West Indians found languishing within the lower classes, whilst entrepreneurial blacks were elevated to positions of influence.

Trinidadian workers of African and Asian descent.

West Indians are now deemed Afro-Caribbean, predicated on the assumption that they originate from Africa and nowhere else. Today Africa is a continent personally unknown to the majority of West Indians. As such, the concept of a purely Africa identity proves difficult for many to embrace beyond the realms of ideology. Africans themselves, many of whom struggle to relate to their distant relatives in the Caribbean, often share this sentiment. Many in Africa, where the huge castles and forts used to trade slaves still exist, regard the mutual heritage they share with the Caribbean from a different perspective. Many question whether West Indians are as completely African as some may claim. These issues remain unexplored or fully rationalised, although the utopian idea of Pan-Africanism remains a popular ideology in the Caribbean and amongst its extensive global diaspora. Sadly these are questions few, if any, have answered. What we do know is the reluctance of Edwardian West Indians to be grouped with Africans. In one instance, members of the British West Indies Regiment openly complained of being made to dine beside their African comrades. Victorian West Indians were even more vocal with accounts from the West India Regiment scorning the less disciplined 'bushmen', whom they looked down upon as being less civilised and worst still, heathen. This prejudice arose despite many members of the West India Regiment being of direct African descent themselves. Attempts to repatriate ex-slaves to Sierra Leone in the early Nineteenth Century had not run smoothly, the émigrés finding life in the post-slavery Caribbean more palatable than life in Africa. The term 'Afro-Caribbean' so widely used today is arguably inaccurate in describing a people that comprise Jews, Asians, Europeans, Native Americans and Africans, all West Indians in their own right - red, yellow, black, white and brown people forced together in one of the world's most prolific and effective melting pots, for whom the Caribbean alone provides their creole identity.

These people were at liberty to integrate, unlike those of mainland America, where legislation prevented integration until 1968. The swathe of languages that had once separated them soon merged to form pidgin English and patoise, launching once of the world's most prolific creole societies where men that had originated in the four corners of the world knew each other as fellow West Indians.

A Hindu West Indian of Indian origin.

A scene from a West Indian port shortly before the First World War.

THE OTHER AFRICAN SLAVE TRADE

In the personal account of Asa-Asa, an African enslaved during the early Nineteenth Century, who may well have had grandchildren that served in the First World War, it was made clear that the slaves themselves recognised that their enslavement was facilitated by African tribes that preyed upon neighbouring tribes as a human commodity with which they could trade with the Europeans that flocked to their shores. This trade lay at the epicentre of Europe's commercial success at the time, funding the Industrial Revolution that took millions of Europeans out of abject poverty and their own brand of quasi-enslavement, which dominated their erstwhile rural economies.

Asa-Asa dictated his experiences to members of the Anti-Slavery Society. As he was competent at both reading and writing English, this account has been widely accepted as an authentic contemporary record of the circumstances in which many peaceful African tribes found themselves during the slave era. The narrative was concluded in his own hand, providing insight into how slaves may have well evolved so swiftly into patriots, less than a century after many were still being enslaved in their native Africa. It also offers some explanation as to the hostility that existed, and continues to some extent today, between Creoles of African descent and native Africans. This trait was recorded within the annals of the West India Regiment and was also recorded during the First World War, amongst members of the British West Indies Regiment.

In his account, Asa-Asa describes his personal experiences of enslavement at the hand of the Adinyes tribes and his life as a slave in both Africa and the West Indies. Asa-Asa eventually ended up in England as the French vessel, on which he was in service, was driven upon the Cornish shore at St. Ives in inclement weather. Once ashore in Britain, all slaves were effectively liberated as the British had not recognised slavery within their jurisdiction for centuries, a stance that prevailed despite Britain being one of the three points in the Triangle of Trade.

As Asa-Asa explained in his own words:

"My father 's name Clashoquin; mine Asa-Asa. He lived in a country called Bycla, near Egie, a large town. Egie is as large as Brighton; it was some way from the sea. I had five brothers and sisters. We all lived together with my father and mother; he kept a horse, and was respectable, but not one of the great men. My uncle was one of the great men at Egie: he could make men come and work for him; his name was Otou. He had a great deal of land and cattle. My father sometimes worked on his own land, and used to make charcoal. I was too little to work; my eldest brother used to work on the land; and we were all very happy.

A great many people, whom we call Adinyes, set fire to Egie in the morning before daybreak: there were some thousands of them. They killed a great many, and burnt all their houses. They staid two days, and then carried away all the people whom they did not kill.

They came again every now and then for a month, as long as they could find people to carry away. They used to tie them by the feet, except when they were taking off, and then they let them loose; but if they offered to run away, they would shoot them. I lost a great many friends and relatives at Egie; about a dozen. They sold all they carried away, to be slaves. I know this because I afterwards saw them as slaves on the other side of the sea. They took away brothers and sisters, and husbands, and wives: they did not care about this. They were sold for cloth or gunpowder, sometimes for salt or guns; sometimes they got four or five guns for a man: they were English guns, made like a master's that I clean for his shooting. The Adinyes burnt a great many places besides Egie. They burnt all the country wherever they found villages; they used to shoot men, women, and children, if they ran away.

They came to us about eleven o'clock one day, and directly they came they set our house on fire. All of us had to run away. We kept together, and went into the woods, and stopped there two days. The Adinyes then went away, and we returned home and found everything burnt. We tried to build a little shed, and were beginning to get comfortable again. We found several of our neighbours lying wounded; they had been shot. I saw the bodies of four or five children whom they had killed with blows on the head. They had carried away their fathers and mothers but the children were too small for slaves, so they killed them. They had killed several others, but these were all that I saw. I saw them lying in the street like dead dogs.

In about a week after we got back, the Adinyes returned, and burnt all the sheds and houses they had left standing. We all ran away again; we went to the woods as we had done before.------The followed us the next day. We went farther into the woods, and staid there about four days and nights; we were half starved; we only got a few potatoes. My uncle Otou was with us. At the end of his time, the Adinyes found us. We ran away. They called my uncle to go with them, but he refused, and they shot him. The rest of us ran on, and they did not get us till the next day. I ran up a tree, they followed me and brought me down. They tied my feet. I do not know if they found my father and mother, and brothers and sisters; they had run faster than me, and were half a mile farther when I got up into the tree: I have never seen them since.-------- There was a man who ran up into the tree with me. I believe they shot him, for I never saw him again.

They carried away about twenty besides me. They carried us to the sea. They did not beat us: they only killed one man, who was very ill and too weak to carry his load; they made all of us carry chickens and meat for our food; but this poor man could not carry his load, and they ran him through the body with a sword.-------- He was a neighbour of ours. When we got to the sea they sold us for money: and I was sold six times over, sometimes for money, sometimes for cloth, and sometimes for a gun. I was about thirteen years old. It was about half a year from the time I was taken, before I saw the white people.

We were taken in a boat from place to place, and sold at every place we stopped at. In about six months we got to a ship, in which we first saw white people: they were French. They bought us. We found here a great many other slaves; there were about eighty, including women and children. The Frenchmen sent away all but five of us into a very large ship. We five staid on board till we got to England, which was about five or six months. The slaves we saw on board the ship were chained together by the legs below deck, so close they could not move. They were flogged cruelly: I saw one of them flogged till he died; we could not tell what for. They gave them enough to eat. The place they were confined in below deck was so hot and nasty I could not bear to be in it. A great many of the slaves were ill, but they were not attended to. They used to flog me very bad on board the ship; the captain cut my head very bad one time."

"I am very happy to be in England, as far as I an very well;------but I have no friends belonging to me, but God, who will take care of me as he has done already. I am very glad I have come to England, to know who God is. I should like much to see my friends again, but I do not wish to go back to them; for if I go back to my own country, I might be taken as a slave again. I would rather stay here, where I am free, than go back to my country to be sold. I shall stay in England as long as (please God) I shall live. I wish the King of England could know all I have told you. I wish he may see how cruelly we are used. We had no king in our country, or he would have stopt it. I think the king of England might stop it, and this is why I wish him to know it all. I have heard say he is good; and if he is, he will stop it if he can. I am well off myself, for I am well taken care of, and have good bed and good clothes; but I wish my own people to as comfortable."

Quel Contrat infame, l'un Marchandes,   TRAITE
Ce qui n'appartient a Personne,

A 1791 engraving of a painting by George Moreland, depicting the sale of African slaves by African slavers to European traders.

NÈGRES. L'autre Vend la Propriété
De la Nature.

FROM SLAVES TO PATRIOTS

By the outbreak of the First World War, Britain had held territory in the Caribbean for almost three centuries, beginning with the settlement of St. Kitts in 1623. Colonists were keen to take advantage of the tropical climate, swiftly moving from subsistence farming to establish plantations. For agriculture on this scale, they chose to use slavery as a source of cheap labour to grow cash crops that included tomatoes, tobacco, indigo and the most successful of all, sugar. With the European fashion for the new bitter-tasting beverages - coffee, tea and chocolate, the demand for sugar grew exponentially and with it the significance

A TYPICAL CROWD IN PORT OF SPAIN.
RECRUITING SCENES IN TRINIDAD.

of the West Indies as a driver of Europe's economic prosperity. West Indian commerce funded a considerable proportion of the Industrial Revolution in Britain, ultimately changing the face of Europe forever. The value of the West Indies made these countries prime targets for the expansionist ambitions of Britain's European rivals and, as such, they were fiercely defended.

Agriculture was not, however, the original objective for slavery in the Caribbean, with the indigenous West Indians being enslaved by the earliest European settlers during the Fifteenth Century to pursue the quest for gold. Despite

West Indian sugar cane cutters.

high mortality rates, and in certain countries near extinction, many indigenous people survived throughout the region, and were regarded both by themselves and others as fellow citizens, albeit living beyond the edicts of European society. This recognition of citizenship and humanity did not extend to the slave population who were chattels in the eyes of the law, and thus were denied education and the right to practise a religion.

The main influx of Caribbean slaves arose from the transatlantic slave trade. The impact of the trade was felt both in Africa and the Caribbean, as millions were displaced and the African slave population and their Creole descendants soon outnumbered any other race in the Caribbean. This was not the case in North America where cotton was King and the less arduous work meant longer, safer lives for African-American slaves. Yet the African-American population never exceeded 10% of the country's population.

In 1807 the transatlantic slave trade was outlawed after years of debate and lobbying in Britain's Parliament, and in 1833 the resultant Emancipation Act effectively freed all slaves throughout the British Empire. Although this was only British law, spurred on by British commercial interests such as those of the members of the West India Committee, Britain sought to enforce the law internationally to ensure that competing nations could not undermine British sugar production by continued use of slave labour. Accordingly, the Royal Navy was deployed to police the African coast to prevent slave trading of any kind.

British cultural values were imbued into the West Indian consciousness through the colonial education system, and ground-breaking liberal policies such as abolition. Abolition undertaken in advance of its European neighbours enforced the notion that the British Empire was at the pinnacle of justice and human endeavour. In fact, Queen Victoria herself was personally heralded in the British West Indies as the architect of emancipation.

The legacy of centuries of slavery was the distortion of perceptions of racial and social worth. The issue of racial inequality was further complicated by the arrival of millions of indentured workers from elsewhere within the Empire, who saw an opportunity in the post-Emancipation Caribbean that suffered from a severe shortage of committed labour. This influx, largely from India and China, was augmented by a new wave of Africans who freely ventured to the Caribbean during the mid Nineteenth Century in search of employment. Many were not welcomed by the local black Creole population who frowned upon this source of cheap, ready labour which competed with the former slaves for paid employment. African recruits had also been used in the early formation of the West India Regiments, first founded in 1795, causing rifts within black society in the Caribbean. This was further aggravated by religious tensions between a largely Christian Caribbean population and the religions of the African migrant community which were perceived to be 'pagan'. Unused to the trappings of the European lifestyle found in the Caribbean, Africans were generally regarded by Creoles of all races as primitive.

By 1914, a mere eighty years after Emancipation, influenced by their perception of their relevance to the British Empire as its founding component, the very Creoles whose African ancestors had been enslaved by the British were eager to defend their former masters

"A patriot of St. Kitts" - The West India Committee Circular 20th October, 1914.

against another form of tyranny: German militarism. Caribbean patriotism was spurred on by a perception of what a German victory might have meant for the region. In an article in The West India Committee's Circular of 22nd August 1914, a few days after Britain entered the conflict, these fears were clearly articulated: *"It was alleged that should the German War Lords emerge from war victorious, a contingency which we [The West India Committee] are satisfied would not arise, one of his first acts would be to revive slavery in the West Indies."* This perception was one that had resounded throughout the Caribbean for centuries with European powers presenting the prospect of liberation from slavery, and during post-Emancipation, the hazard of the reintroduction of enslavement as a means of securing the loyalty of

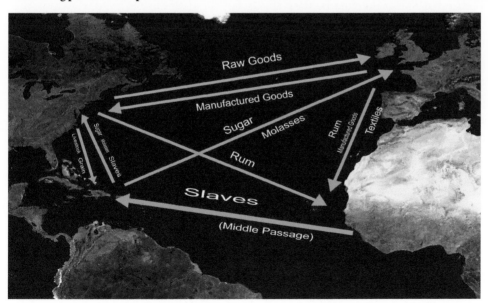

A map of the Triangle of Trade detailing the products exchanged for the lives of Africans.

the black population, who comprised the majority of the region's population ever since the plantation economy had taken a firm grip on the Caribbean. What was different about the First World War was that West Indians volunteered in their thousands, despite persistent rejection of their offers of service by the British War Office.

THE PLANTOCRACY

The Caribbean, like other plantation based societies, had its own class system – the Plantocracy. Drawing firmly from its European equivalent, the Aristocracy, meaning 'rule of the best', the Plantocracy was, by necessity, less rigid. Moreover, when compared to that of mainland America, the Caribbean's version of the Plantocracy, that had evolved in the absence of legislation demarking racial groups, was more fluid, permitting men and women of colour to straddle the classes, albeit in accordance with the unwritten conventions of the region's caste system. Necessity as the mother of invention made room for meritocratic undertones that allowed talent derived from a limited pool of educated, trained and skilled people to rise closer to the top although, on the face of it, the Plantocracy remained a mirror image of the European system. The fact that upper class Creoles were sent 'home' to Britain to be educated further entrenched the desire to mimic the Mother Country, although the more liberal lifestyle of the Caribbean had been enjoyed for centuries by the very same people.

The Plantocracy designated the social standing of various roles played in the plantation economy, whereby the working and slave classes of the Caribbean correlated with the working classes that had arisen in Britain during the Industrial Revolution. Paradoxically, both systems were more directly linked as the Caribbean supplied cotton picked by slaves to the mills of northern Britain where it was processed by indentured mills workers, often in their infancy living under similar conditions to their Caribbean colleagues.

At the head of both the Plantocracy and Aristocracy sits the reigning Monarch, under whom their representatives, the Governors and Governor Generals reside. Beneath them are the planters supported by the professional classes – doctors, accountants and attorneys. The lowest white class comprised the overseers who interacted directly with the intricate slaves classes below and, in the early days of the Plantocracy, may have started life as indentured slaves themselves. Amongst the slaves, status was dictated by the level of intimacy with the Planter and their family with house slaves, that included cooks, maids, butlers and footmen, ranking the highest on a par with those that had special skills and crafts, such as carpenters, blacksmiths, gardeners and coachmen. Those that worked outside were, however, generally regarded as lower class, although their ranking was dictated by their skills. For the slave classes the devil was in the detail, in that their value and therefore their standard of living and treatment within the plantation was dictated by their position within the system.

There is a direct correlation between the Plantocracy and the Colonial system itself, which could be said to be a super-sized version of the same pyramid system, whereby the work of the masses who benefit the least from their efforts, support an ever diminishing hierarchy above, who benefit progressively more. Notwithstanding the post war political advancement of the lower echelons of the Plantocracy, remnants of it are evident today, as is true of its supporting caste system, each continuing to influence the aspirations and attainment of millions of West Indians both within the Caribbean and amongst its global diaspora; a reality referred to by a leading Caribbean academic as *"the mental chains of slavery"* in support of an argument in favour of reparations for those that suffered under this unjust system.

The British Monarchs of Caribbean territories and their subjects.

THE COLONIALS

The aspirations of the relatively new German Empire upset a fragile balance and web of alliances that had been achieved by the Allied victory at Waterloo some ninety-nine years earlier with little foresight into the political alliances that would evolve. This created a domino effect by which country after country would become embroiled in the territorial disputes of the Great Powers, bringing with them their respective empires and the hundreds of millions of innocent people they controlled throughout the world. The influence of Britain had impacted upon the lives of Caribbean people for generations. This meant a common religious, social and political culture had developed between the Caribbean and Britain over time, manifesting itself in the trappings of empire. By the Twentieth Century regional government were more important than ever to the Caribbean. Most islands were run on the old system of representation, focusing upon the authority of the Governor. The regionally based Governor reported to the Secretary of State for the Colonies in London, and represented the Monarch, but was also answerable to the island's Council, an elected body consisting of local men invariably from the upper echelons of Creole society. During the war this administrative structure changed when the islands participated directly in the conflict.

West Indian children celebrated Empire Day, a festivity held across the British Empire. The first Empire Day was held on Queen Victoria's birthday, 24th May 1902. She died the year before and continued to be mourned globally. The celebration was made official in 1916, although it had been adopted by many West Indian schools years before. The children not only reflect the huge diversity of the British Empire in their costumes, but also that of the West Indies in their own diversity.

On 4th August 1914 as a result of alliances with Belgium, France and Russia, Britain was irrevocably committed and reluctantly entered the war. This war was made all the more treacherous by the modern technology of the day which accelerated the rate of human destruction to such a pace that by the end of 1914, less than six months into the conflict, over one million service men and civilians lay dead. The social impact of the war was magnified in Britain. For a country such as Britain whose army was considerably smaller than the forces of its allies or enemies and whose social hierarchy dictated that the sons of the 'good and the great' should be the first to face the foe, there were fatal consequences. With a large number of the heirs of Britain's leading families annihilated early on in the foolhardy belief that it 'would all be over by Christmas [1914]', the country was ill-prepared to proceed, and yet, with Germany fierce enough to bombard its shores at Scarborough by sea and London by air from huge Zeppelins, Britain had little choice but to press on with the war.

Greater recruitment from the lower classes, necessitated by the need for more infantry, exposed the military to the realities of the country's economic inequalities. Many men had been malnourished throughout their lives and forced to live and work in appalling conditions, meaning their health was too poor to pass the medical tests required for military service. Bantam regiments allowed some to serve in ancillary roles, but the need for 'fighting fit' men proved difficult to satisfy. Lord Kitchener, a hero of Khartoum, had his own personal prejudices against using colonial troops and, through the War Office, challenged the Colonial Office and the King until forced to accept recruits from the Empire.

A gathering of colonials in a typical colonial mansion.

The War Office was also forced to look further afield for men. In 1914 the acting Governor of Jamaica, William Manning, urged the Secretary of State for the Colonies, Lewis Harcourt, to begin discussions with the War Office on the issue of raising a West Indian contingent. When the War Office refused the service of West Indians, lobbying by the Governors of the Caribbean helped change the policy. A proposal to raise a contingent from the Caribbean region had also been tabled by Canada and although denied, the Canadians went on to create the first black contingent of the British Army. This was derived from the community of former slaves in Nova Scotia, which dated back to 1605, a place many slaves regarded as a route to freedom. Canada's more liberal approach resulted in the Reverend William White of Nova Scotia becoming the first black officer and the first black chaplain ever to serve in the British Army within a contingent that was later to be relegated to the No. 2 Construction Battalion of another regiment.

Back in Britain the West India Committee took up the cause of the Caribbean and applied pressure upon the War Office to accept the men of the region. The political dynamic proved finely balanced as reflected in the words of King George V's Private Secretary, Lord Stamfordham, who stressed *"rejection of offers of service would affect the loyalty of the black population and their existing attachment to the Empire"*, a sentiment apparently shared by the Monarch. This risk to colonialism was carefully managed by the Governors who encouraged support for Britain by passing on encouraging messages to islanders. In response to receiving an offer of sugar from Jamaica, Lewis Harcourt responded by announcing, *"His Majesty's Government heartily appreciate [this] patriotic and generous offer of [the] people of Jamaica, and would find a gift of sugar most acceptable"*. Statements of this kind were well-received in the region as direct acknowledgements of support and spoke to the West Indians' sense of loyalty and their desire for recognition as playing an active role in the conflict.

By the middle of 1915, the initial reluctance of the War Office to pitch men of colour against white Europeans was overridden by the King Emperor himself, supported by the Colonial Office. Patriotism was deemed by His Majesty to take precedence over colonialism and its implicit social hierarchy that placed the natives of one third of the world beneath the 'home-grown' Briton. In one fell swoop the order of things changed and the countries over which the Mother Country had presided for centuries were invited to her table. The administrative culture that had dominated the Caribbean had changed forever with the formation of the British West Indies Regiment.

Whilst the War Office had accepted the need to recruit non-white soldiers, and promoted the policy amongst the colonies and dominions, it did its best to ensure that they could not take up arms against whites, rendering black and mixed-race infantrymen little more than labour corps. The ostensible victory for the King in securing a place for patriotic colonial troops in the British Army was, as anticipated by Kitchener, to upset the colonial order once these men witnessed the poverty, lack of education, poor health, and disenfranchisement of those they had been indoctrinated to regard as their natural superiors. For the West Indians, whose remarkably high fitness levels stunned the British press, winning them the sobriquet, *"huge and mighty men of valour"*, disappointment lay ahead as they, along with almost 100,000 Chinese servicemen, were deployed as native labour corps, rather than fighting men.

EUROPEAN REVUE.
KILL THAT EAGLE.

Produced by 'Geographia' Ltd. 55 Fleet Str. London E.C.

A British Propaganda Poster of 1914, depicting the Allied Forces focusing their efforts on the German eagle supported by imperial troops seen wading in across the Atlantic.

COLOURED TROOPS OF

A depiction of the diverse range of colonial troops from the empires of the Allied Forces, including the British West Indies Regiment (far left).

BENEFICIARY TO BENEFACTOR

In the early Twentieth Century, the Caribbean was a relatively impoverished region as the victim of regular natural disasters and endemic tropical diseases. The West India Committee Circular continuously reported on the devastating impacts of the annual hurricane season, earthquakes, droughts and bush fires that beset the Caribbean. The Committee would often appeal successfully for aid in the Circular. The inability of the local population to rebuild and recover from these disasters without significant aid from Britain resulted in an on-going financial dependency.

The sugar cane plant in its raw state and sugar as we know it.

Sugar production was the driving force of the Caribbean economy for centuries. This in turn fuelled the development of Britain from the advent of the Industrial Revolution until the decline of the 'sugar' economy caused by the abolition of slavery. At the beginning of the Twentieth Century, the English-speaking islands continued to supply Europe with sugar, albeit in the face of fierce competition from European grown sugar beet. To combat the success of sugar beet, distinctively flavoured Demerara sugar was specifically invented for the British market. During the war, however, the British Government announced that Caribbean sugar should no longer be exported to Europe to avoid interception by enemy vessels, thereby further undermining the Caribbean's economy. Despite suffering an economic slump, the region continued to provide tens of millions of pounds worth of aid to the Allies as the conflict unfolded.

Caribbean sugar had also generated income for Europe by virtue of the high import duties that were charged upon its arrival in Europe. In 1913 alone, Britain levied over £15,145,000 in duties on Caribbean sugar. The embargo on Caribbean sugar imposed at the outset of war, and the consequential hardship suffered in the Caribbean, led the West India Committee to remark that it would have been better had the money raised for the war effort been spent on their kith and kin in the islands. This attitude led the West India Committee to redirect some funds to the earthquake victims of Antigua in November 1914.

As soon as war was declared in Europe, the British West Indies mobilised itself in support of the Allied war effort. Public donations were collected through various fundraising bodies and a collective £2 million in cash was sent, with an additional £54 million in kind in the form of local produce including rum, sugar, cotton, and much-needed oil, together with medical supplies, vehicles, machines, and various other necessities. These contributions went some way towards addressing the economic loss suffered in Britain from being detached from the West Indies as a result of the conflict.

WEST INDIAN GIFTS.

The people of Barbados, at the instance of Mr. F. A. C. Collymore, to whom much credit is due for his initiative in the matter, have now subscribed over £1,900 for two motor ambulances for the British Red Cross Society and their maintenance. The last remittance, received by the West India Committee, on this account amounted to £400, which has been forwarded to the proper quarter and has been gratefully acknowledged by the Society. Messrs. Elders and Fyffes steamers *Coronado* and *Cavina* which arrived at Avonmouth on November 22nd and December 6th, respectively, brought 406 packages of oranges, grapefruit, lemons and limes, besides preserves, clothing, cigarettes, books, etc., from the Jamaica Agricultural Society, and the Royal Mail Steamer *Magdalena*, which reached London on December 6th, brought 90 cases of oranges and limes, in addition to a large quantity of lime juice and some shaddock preserve sent by the Trinidad Orange and Lime Committee. The Dominica Agricultural Society sent 72 packages of limes, oranges and grapefruit. Mrs. Brodie, of Grenada, whose generosity seems inexhaustible, forwarded 3 barrels of fruit, and Mrs. Sworder, of Tobago, to whom the same remark applies, sent a further case of preserves, while Mrs. Spooner, of Antigua, sent another case of clothing for the Belgian refugees, and Mrs. Flood, of Barbadoes, a really enormous case of linen and bandages. In addition to the gifts already acknowledged mention must be made of 5 cases of guava jelly from the people of the Grand Cayman Islands, which arrived in the *Camito* at Avonmouth on November 7th.

The guava jelly from Grand Cayman was packed in 55 ten-pound tins and there were few members of the community who did not take some share in making the gift a success. Some persons gave sugar, some the money with which to purchase it,

The West India Committee published fortnightly reports throughout the conflict on the Caribbean's war effort.

SOME GRATEFUL RECIPIENTS.

Injured Belgian soldiers in a hospital in London spell out their thanks to the West Indies for recuperative fruit.

The Caribbean's contribution far outweighed the region's financial strength long after it had ceased being the richest economy in the world. In the case of the smaller and more impoverished countries, financial contributions were limited, yet acknowledged with the same level of gratitude as those of considerably more value to Britain. The diminutive island of Anguilla raised £48 4s 1½d in cash for the National Relief Fund, a tiny sum when compared to the many millions in aid submitted by Trinidad and Jamaica. All donations to the National Relief Fund received an acknowledgement and thanks from Buckingham Palace, where the Prince of Wales presided over the appeal.

Mindful of technical innovations in warfare, the Caribbean also set its sights on providing the Allied Forces with equipment that included some of the most advanced technology of the time. Eleven fully equipped motor ambulances were presented, together with nine aeroplanes less than ten years after the Wright brothers first took to the air.

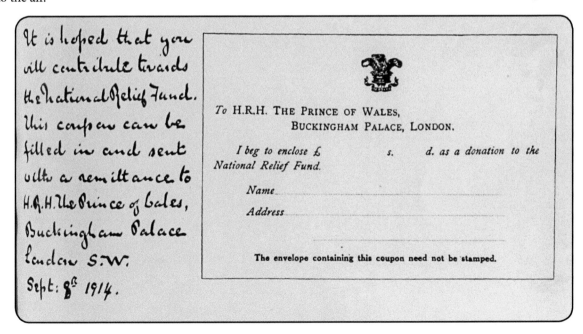

A coupon for donations to Britain's National Relief Fund, whose President was H.R.H. The Prince of Wales, found enclosed in a Circular with handwritten instructions from the West India Committee.

This bi-plane was named the 'Dominica' after the island that donated it to the newly established Royal Flying Corps, forerunner of the Royal Air Force. Various Caribbean countries together sent a total of nine planes to Britain throughout the conflict.

The people of Barbados, Trinidad and Tobago have donated two well equipped ambulances to the British Red Cross Society. They are inscribed "From the people of Barbados" and "From the Trinidad and Tobago Branch" respectively - The West India Committee Circular 21st September 1915.

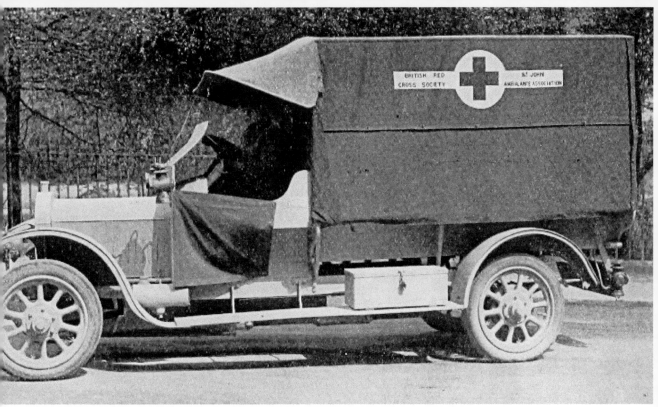

Eleven fully equipped ambulances were also dispatched by the Caribbean to Europe, addressing the complex needs of the wounded in the bloodiest conflict the world had ever known when new technology, such as barbed wire, machine guns and the use of chlorine gas inflicted wounds unseen until then.

he need for certain commodities spiralled, particularly when they formed part of Britain's military supplies, such rum, pictured above, which was a compulsory ration carried on all British naval vessels until as recently as 1970. e received in docks, such as London's West India Quay, supplies were distributed to the various military depots throughout Britain by rail. The rum ration was extended to the army during the conflict.

VOLUNTEERS OF EVERY CLASS, COLOUR AND CREED

Just as the conflict caused domestic factions that opposed the British Government, such as the Suffragettes, Irish Nationalists and trade unions, to pull together as one nation in the face of a common enemy, similar unifying forces drew disparate groups together in the Caribbean behind the flag of their Mother Country. The call in the Caribbean for men of *"every class, colour and*

The Second Trinidad Merchants' Contingent. Trinidad and Tobago was a colony with a large merchant community based around the city of Port-of-Spain, the colony's capital.

creed" to enlist to fight for King and Country was well received, and thousands of men and boys in the region did so voluntarily. Ultimately, however, their experiences during the war dispelled the myth of European superiority. Thereafter few could accept their position within the Empire without question and, upon returning from the war, many were set on the road to self-determination and, eventually, independence.

As was the case in Europe, volunteers in the Caribbean were initially from the upper echelons of Caribbean society. Patriotic fervour was, nonetheless, prevalent amongst all classes regardless of colour or creed with men from every level of society keen to fight as patriots and proud to present themselves to the world as British.

Local militias began to form throughout the West Indies as soon as Britain entered a state of war in anticipation of being allowed entry into the British forces. They comprised West Indians whose evident European descent allowed them to enlist in the British Army without question, long before the establishment of the British West Indies Regiment. Such groups included the Barbados Citizens' Contingent and the Trinidad Merchants' Contingent, who were invited to participate in the Lord Mayor's Show of 1915 in the City of London. Racial reservations in Britain meant many black volunteers that had made their own way to Britain were rejected and sent back to the West

2nd Lieutenant A.E. Thompson, British West Indies Regiment.

Indies. White West Indians, and those able to convince authorities of their 'pure' European ancestry, also arrived in England at their own expense, to enlist in Kitchener's volunteer army, a journey costing up to £25, often aided by contributions from the West Indian Committee.

The Atlantic island of Bermuda, whose administration was co-joined with the Caribbean at the time, was one of Britain's proudest and oldest colonies. Bermudans banded together to form the Bermuda Volunteer Rifle Corps and the Bermuda Militia Artillery. Serving from the very outset by adjoining their men to the Lincolnshire Regiment, Bermuda's volunteer forces suffered terrible losses at the Battle of the Somme in 1916, losing over half their men during one German assault. After the establishment of the British West Indies Regiment, black Bermudans were able to participate and did so by forming the Bermuda Militia Artillery. They too saw action at the Somme, Passchendaele, Vimy Ridge and at Messines Ridge. Field Marshal Haig lauded their service in a 1918 report in the *Gazette*: *"Physically and intellectually they are as fine men as any to be found in their Brigade and their conduct has always been exemplary"*.

These new troops were urgently needed after heavy Allied losses suffered on the Western Front in the early years of the war. The Secretary of State for War, Lord Kitchener, who was against inter-racial combat, established the British West Indies Regiment in 1915, as a necessity, despite an initial reluctance. Eventually over 16,000 men, every last one a volunteer, joined the Regiment from across the Caribbean, Belize, and Guyana. Thousands more joined other regiments in both the British and Indian armies and also the Royal Navy, whilst many served in the newly-established Royal Flying Corps. The West India Regiment, which was formed in 1795, also participated in the conflict in its own right.

Soldiers of the Barbados Citizens' Contingent.

Since the Napoleonic Wars, much of which were played out in the Caribbean, defence forces were active in the islands as a necessary means of defending the essential commercial interests of the colonial powers. They were made up of local men, who adopted European military practices. By 1914 every British West Indian country had its own defence force. As was the case for the army, the defence forces were multiracial, and reflected a class structure loosely based upon that practised in Britain, with the rules of the caste system and desires of the War Office dictating that only white or mixed race West Indians could secure the post of commissioned officer.

In addition to the challenges in Europe's theatres of war and despite being thousands of miles away from military action, the Caribbean faced defence challenges of its own. These arose as the Caribbean comprises seven thousand islands of which only 2% were inhabited. Opportunities for enemy shipping were therefore rife, particularly for restocking essential provisions, such as fresh water, and concealing their presence.

A West Indian 'Tommy'.

FROM TRINIDAD TO ENLIST

Party of 160 Now Joining British Regiments.

I had a chat, writes a correspondent, with Mr. Huggins, of Trinidad, who has accompanied to England a party of 160 young men, who are prepared to enlist in the British Army. For the time being they are staying at the Central Y.M.C.A., Tottenham Court-road, where they have made themselves quite at home.

"We recognised," said Mr. Huggins, "that just as men of the coloured races had enlisted in order to help Great Britain there were probably British-born young men who, if offered the facilities, would gladly answer the call. In order to cover all the expenses we raised £5,000, and then issued an appeal to those whom we thought might like to join the party.

"In three days we had offers from 160 men, who, we are assured, will be welcomed in various units of the Army. Many have already been accepted, and in the course of a few days we hope to get the whole of the party joined up to suitable battalions.

"We had a fine send-off, the Attorney-General for Trinidad and other leading men making appropriate speeches."

There arrived in London last night 120 young white men from Trinidad for the purpose of enlisting. They have come over at the expense of a committee of business and professional men at the instance of Mr. G. F. Huggins, of Port of Spain, and were met at St. Pancras by a band and marched to the Central Y.M.C.A. in Tottenham-court-road. To-day, headed by a detachment of the Royal Fusiliers and a band, they will march to the Mansion House, where they will be addressed by the Lord Mayor.

THEY CAME FROM TRINIDAD TO BE SOLDIERS OF THE KING.

These Creole men from the Trinidad Light Horse Regiment were among those who were able to fight at the outbreak of war. Britain was willing to accept their service because they were from the upper echelons of Caribbean society and clearly of European descent. These early volunteers posed no threat to the social hierarchy in the region and would also have gone largely unnoticed in England.

Trinidad and Tobago was strategically important to Britain, as the largest and most powerful wireless station in the region was located in Port-of-Spain, and the islands provided the Admiralty with millions of gallons of oil. Despite its value as a colony, the islands were poorly defended by Britain. As a consequence, tensions ran high when war began, resulting in defence forces of local men being formed to preserve stability and offer some form of defence should they experience enemy attack or invasion. The Trinidad Light Horse, Volunteer Force and Constabulary Force each pre-dated the First World War, and had over a thousand men in their ranks by 1914. These forces remained in situ throughout the conflict, protecting some of Britain's most important strategic assets in the Americas.

With the establishment of the British West Indies Regiment, West Indians took pride in the fact they had their own regiment to join, though many were disappointed by the conditions of their service as men were often denied the opportunity to fight and were invariably deployed as Labour Battalions, despite being officially designated infantrymen. In Britain they also endured poor conditions in training camps that claimed the lives of many, long before they set foot in a theatre of war. Extensive losses were suffered as a result of the cold climate, inadequate uniforms and poor medical facilities within the camps, which themselves offered substandard accommodation. Nineteen West Indian servicemen were buried at Seaford, victims of these unanticipated, yet avoidable, hazards.

2nd Lieutenant E. Lucie-Smith of Jamaica, 1st Royal Warwickshire Regiment.

Alongside the thousands of West Indians that volunteered to serve, British regiments that were stationed in the West Indies also travelled back to Britain. The Northumberland Fusiliers were based in Antigua when war broke out, returning in 1915, after a rapturous send off by the islanders as they marched through the streets of St. John's, the island's capital, and on to their troopship.

The excitement of the declaration of war and the ensuing patriotism was celebrated in music, based upon the traditional military marches so evident at the time and which used lyrics that spoke of the patriotic fervour that swept through the world.

OFFICERS OF THE BRITISH HONDURAS DEFENCE FORCE.

[Photograph] THE MONTSERRAT DEFENCE RESERVE. [Jose Anjo.

We're off to the front
We're off to the fight
For our noble King and Country.
We'll fight for the truth and right
We will not fear.

We're off to the front
We're off to the fight
Marching where our banner
leads us,
that noble Red White and Blue
We will not fear.

Bahamian Sheet Music of the First World War: 'A March Song' by Austin Destoup, sung by the Bahamas Contingent before leaving for the Front.

THE DRUMS AND FIFES OF A BATTALION OF THE BRITISH WEST INDIES REGIMENT.

An early contingent of the British West Indies Regiment comprising men and boys of Grenada.

The call to arms in the British West Indies was designed to appeal to all levels of Caribbean society, a complex society that had many dimensions to it and that sought to reflect that of Britain. It was not only a multifarious mix of race and religion, but also one that was stratified into a social hierarchy that had evolved from the old plantation economy into the Caribbean's own unique class system – the Plantocracy. Undoubtedly the Caribbean's patriotism and idealised view of the British Empire produced such a significant flood of volunteers during the First World War, enticing men to come to the aid of a place they knew as their Mother Country, a place from which they craved recognition and respect. These sentiments were, however, not solely responsible as many poorer West Indians saw an unprecedented opportunity to improve their prospects by serving in the British Army, an institution that ironically had once been the largest slave owner in British history. Upper class West Indians had always regarded themselves as intrinsically British, often returning there to be educated, constantly endeavouring to become fully integrated into and accepted by the upper echelons of British society with whom they readily mixed, whilst at the same time maintaining their ties with the Caribbean and status at the pinnacle of West Indian society.

As with much of the Empire, British authority in the Caribbean was supported by a myriad of local myths about the superiority of Britain and her people. However, poor treatment and conditions, racism and the generally underwhelming reality of British life that the troops personally experienced during their time in Britain led many Caribbean volunteers to re-think their connection with the country, which the majority had mistaken for an equal partnership.

Captain A.C. Ward, 2nd Lancashire Fusiliers.

The hierarchies of class and race were deeply entrenched in the Caribbean at the time of the conflict, the remnants of which remain in a surprisingly active caste system found in various larger Caribbean countries. Unlike other societies in the British Empire, including America, interracial integration was legally permitted and active, albeit within certain social constraints; however, integration provided no protection against racism. As a result, a robust and often affluent mixed-race community evolved throughout the region, separate and distinct from the larger black community, and more readily accepted by the influential white Creoles to whom they were related.

Men from the upper classes, who were often the descendants of white planters, were encouraged to enlist as officers together with men of mixed race. However, generally, on racial grounds, men of colour seldom rose beyond the rank of non-commissioned officer. Long before the Caribbean's legislatures were authorised by the War Office to establish a contingent to participate in the conflict, many Caribbean men made their own way to Britain to enlist in existing regiments in the British and Indian Armies. This option was not as readily available nor as attractive to the lower classes, largely made up of black Creoles that found the cost of travel prohibitive and would have encountered varying degrees of racism in the process. Despite this, there are many examples of black West Indians successfully enlisting in regiments throughout Britain.

YOUNG MEN
OF THE BAHAMAS

The British Empire is engaged in a Life and Death Struggle. Never in the History of England, never since the Misty Distant Past of 2,000 years ago, has our beloved Country been engaged in such a conflict as she is engaged in to-day.

To bring to nothing this mighty attack by an unscrupulous and well prepared foe, HIS MOST GRACIOUS MAJESTY KING GEORGE has called on the men of his Empire, MEN OF EVERY CLASS, CREED AND COLOUR, to

COME FORWARD TO FIGHT

that the Empire may be saved and the foe may be well beaten.

This call is to YOU, young man; not your neighbour, not your brother, not your cousin, but just YOU.

SEVERAL HUNDREDS OF YOUR MATES HAVE COME UP, HAVE BEEN MEDICALLY EXAMINED AND HAVE BEEN PASSED AS "FIT."

What is the matter with YOU?

Put yourself right with your King; put yourself right with your fellowmen; put yourself right with yourself and your conscience.

ENLIST TO-DAY

THE GLEANER CO. LTD., PRINTERS, KINGSTON JAMA'CA.

44

B.W.  I.R.

THE BOYS ARE DOING SPLENDIDLY
IN
EGYPT
MESOPOTAMIA
FRANCE

ANOTHER

BAHAMAS CONTINGENT

WILL BE SAILING SOON.

Roll up
Men  Make it
the Best

GOD SAVE THE KING!

The Gleaner Co., Ltd., Printers, 148, 150 & 152 Harbour Street, Kingston, Jamaica.

Rare early recruitment posters published by *The Gleaner* designed to appeal to all sections of Caribbean society, *'Men of Every Class, Creed and Colour'.*

THE CARIBS
SOLDIERS OF THE KING, ONCE MORE!

It is an unavoidable fact that history, as with so many aspects of life, has a way of repeating itself. For the Europeans, we could say that the First World War was initiated a century earlier when the continent was shared out between the victors of the Battle of Waterloo. The key role played by the Prussians in defeating Napoleon was the stuff of legends, with Napoleon's defeat by the then Allied forces of Europe marking an end to what had been a reign of terror comparable to the World Wars of the Twentieth Century. As the newly formed German Empire glanced amongst its neighbours, it no doubt felt a pang of inadequacy, and looked to the instability in the Austro-Hungarian quarter as a means of redressing this perceived imbalance of power. The erratic grandson of Queen Victoria, Kaiser Wilhelm II, led this quest, supported by an Imperial Army of over thirteen and a half million men that must have appeared invincible. With the vastness of the conflict in Europe, it is little wonder that the involvement of a small band of tribesmen on the other side of the world, committed by a pact made between their people and the Kaiser's great-great grandfather, King George III, in 1773 went largely unnoticed. Under the Peace Treaty of that year, the Caribs of St. Vincent were committed *"In time of danger to be aiding and assisting to his Majesty's subjects against their enemies."*

ARAWAKS.

The Caribs and their Arawak cousins were the indigenous peoples of neighbouring South America who took over the Caribbean region from the earlier Saladoid people. Their migration from the Orinoco region is well documented, as are their encounters with the first Europeans to visit the Caribbean, who christened this corner of the world after them. Enslavement in pursuit of gold soured what was at first a peaceful relationship, as did the introduction of unknown diseases between these unrelated peoples. By the time the Hanoverian Monarch, George III, inherited the British throne from his grandfather, the Caribs of St. Vincent, Dominica, and Guyana were in the last throes of their struggle to retain their homelands. However, their military prowess meant the highly-equipped British Army sent to the Caribbean to defend the colonies from the French and subdue the indigenous tribes was no match for the tribesmen of the Caribbean.

On the island of St. Vincent, it is believed that a shipwreck had led to the arrival of escaped Africans destined for slavery. They settled on the island and integrated with the original Yellow Caribs, forming a mixed race community known as the Garifuna or Black Caribs. These people were ultimately led by a man destined to become the National Hero of St. Vincent, Chatoyer, a Black Carib and the last of their chiefs. Like many West Indians, Chatoyer's story was a complex one, and one shared with his younger brother, du Valleé. The relationship with the colonialists, first in the guise of the French and then the British, was not always one of dispute. Indeed, like du Valleé, some Caribs were to adopt the same commercial practices as the Europeans. In the case of du Valleé, he was *"possessed of nine slaves and has a cotton plantation"*, being regarded at the time as *"the most enlightened of the Charaibes, and may be termed the fonder of civilisation among [the two brothers] them."* For du Valleé, at least, the bonds of mutual heritage between the Black Caribs

Chatoyer, the Chief of the Black Caribs in St. Vincent, with his five wives.

and Africans of St. Vincent proved weaker than the lure of commercial success. The rallying cry of his brother, Chatoyer, for support against the British was primarily to his own people, the Black and Yellow Caribs of the region, not to the enslaved Africans or their Creole descendants, although they too saw an opportunity for liberation and participated in the ill-fated war with the British in which their leader died.

After the defeat, many Caribs were transported to Central America as part of the on-going 'land grab' to which they were subjected for generations, leaving a small, weakened community on the island. By the outbreak of the First World War, St. Vincent had long been regarded as a centre of Carib life, although the tribesmen of Guyana far exceeded them in number, and the communities of Yellow Caribs in Guyana and Dominica maintained stronger links with the original culture of the Caribbean. As described by Raymond Breton, a French missionary who first encountered these people in the Seventeenth Century in Dominica, *"they are of good stature and well proportioned, strong, robust, ordinarily fleshy, and healthy…"* A lifestyle attuned to nature meant many exhibited a longevity and tendency not to age that was said to be remarkable, resulting in many centenarians found in their midst. This meant that at the outset of the war there might well have been those that had personally experienced the threat of Napoleon in the West Indies.

Carib tribal traditions and customs were prevalent at the onset of the First World War.

Caribs fishing with traditional bow and arrow.

These proud people bore the curse of Columbus who branded them cannibals. Whether this was a strategic move to justify their enslavement and attempts to convert them to Christianity is uncertain; however, it is a slight that has resulted in their poor treatment by other sections of Caribbean society ever since, and would have influenced their treatment at the time of the war. This was countered by the fact that they were renowned for their marksmanship. It was said *"not only do the Indians shoot straight, but they shoot so quickly that they can loose ten or a dozen arrows in the time it takes to load a gun."* Moreover, they were accurate, it being noted that they could hit half a crown at a hundred paces. The Caribs were hunters, and so this prowess was maintained, and like the tribesmen of Africa, the rite of passage for young men entailed competence in the practices of warriorhood. For a Carib warrior, surprise attack was an essential component in the art of war, a concept framed by their Chinese ancestors in the Fifth Century BC. A vehement respect for the dead and wounded also distinguished their brand of warfare from that practised in Europe at the time. This was pertinent, as the Caribs who rose and volunteered to fight for their King and Country during the Great War inadvertently did so in line with the terms of the 1773 Peace Treaty of St. Vincent. Their enlistment was recounted by the newspapers of the time that noted that, for some,

this would be their first experience of western clothing. Like their fellow West Indians, they were destined for the native labour corps whose tasks included digging trenches and latrines, shifting ammunition, and recovery of the dead and wounded. Never was a Carib arrow drawn and seldom was their extraordinary marksmanship put to the test. What was, was their heritage of patriotism that had commenced almost a hundred and fifty years before, when they were forced to recognise King George III as the *"rightful sovereign of their islands and dominion, and took an oath of fidelity to the British monarch promising absolute submission to his will."*

THE WEST INDIAN IN KHAKI.

During the past three years a great deal has been written of the splendid service rendered to the Empire by the gallant men from the Dominions. Apart from one or two perfunctory references I have read nothing of the loyal if necessarily limited service given by another class of men, the West Indian Regiment, with its handful of men from British Guiana. When the appeal for recruits came they poured in from cane fields and banana plantations, from docks and warehouses, and even from the distant Indian reservations in the hinterland. I saw these recruits in the making and became interested in them. A little band of the survivors of the one-time warlike Caribs and Arawaks walked from the reservation to the capital of the colony to offer their services. They had never been in a town before and could speak but one word of English. They acquired that from a missionary before they started, and it was "Fight."

It is impossible to say how the news of the outbreak of war had reached them. It was they who conveyed the information to the missionary, and he did not believe them. He received official news a week later. In some mysterious way these primitive men had secured the news before the only man who spoke English in the district, and he had a mail service at his disposal.

Confined to a reservation which no intruder might penetrate, the people's knowledge of the outside world was extremely limited. To them England represented something very nebulous. It was a place across the sea, and even the sea was a mystery. Stories of the "great waters" had been handed down to them from their ancestors, who originally hailed from the shores of the Caribbean, and had been driven inland by the white pioneers of three centuries ago. Three centuries is a long time, and the present-day aboriginals had come to look on the sea as a legendary thing which had at some time existed. Their lives had always been lived in the confines of fifty square miles of forest and savannah land. The only weapon of which they had any knowledge was the one they utilised to obtain their food—the bow and arrow of their forbears. Their weapons doubtless would not impress the members of the English Toxophilite Society, but on the other hand English devotees of archery would cut but poor figures if their food depended upon their skill in bringing down fast-flying birds and swiftly moving fish. Fishing with bows and arrows is to the aboriginals no more difficult than salmon-netting is to us.

The life of these people is strangely simple. From the day of their birth to the hour of their death existence is undisturbed by the worry of profit and loss. They do not know what money is, and are but slightly acquainted with the elements of barter. One wild duck may be reckoned as the equivalent value of two handfuls of cassava, from which the native bread is made. Each man has his plot of ground wherein he grows his cassava, his yams, eddoes, and ochroes; and if he fall ill and is unable to procure flesh or fish or fowl then he barters his ground provisions to obtain it. He lives a day at a time. He rises early and tends his plot in the morning. In the afternoon he goes in search of fish or food, and in the evening he says his prayers and retires to sleep, the sound sleep which comes to the untrammelled mind. His wife, or such women-folk as he may possess, cooks his food and washes his scanty raiment. She rears his children, keeps his hut clean, and on occasion may join him in the chase.

Few races could be more unfitted by temperament and environment for the turmoil of a great war. When I saw them mastering the difficulties of the English words of command, suffering the agonies of having their feet confined within boots, and with their skin, accustomed to be free to the air, tortured by the roughness of the army shirt I marvelled that these children of nature could submit at all to the rigour of military discipline. In less than a month they were translated from the most primitive conditions to the height of modern civilisation. Imagine the astonishment and

perplexity of a man who has never before seen a rifle in his life being initiated into the mysteries of the Lee-Enfield and Lewis guns. I have never seen anything more pleasing than the joy expressed in the face of one of these men one day on the rifle ranges. It was by no means his first appearance, and a man less intent on attaining efficiency would have thrown up the task in disgust. On this particular afternoon a squad of men destined to follow the flag to France were firing at plates at 200 yards—rapid. They were a polyglot collection. There were, so far as I remember, an aboriginal Indian, a Portuguese creole, two or three blacks, an East Indian who had come to the Demerara sugar estates from distant Madras, a half-caste or two, and a Chinese boy. With the exception of the first-named they had all lived in the principal town of the colony all their lives, so they did not interest me. But we were all interested in the aboriginal, and for short we called him John. His real name was too formidable for general usage. His first shot hit the bank below the target. The second just tipped the edge of the plate, and it shook. John clutched his rifle very tightly as the plate gave a topple and fell down. A very simple thing, but it signified a great deal. John realised the significance. He had found himself. His face wrinkled with smiles as, with smart, workmanlike action, he cleared the breech of his rifle and shot the bolt back home with a resounding click. As he once more tucked the butt into his broad shoulder he smiled again. Scarcely peeping down the sights, he fired, and his second plate fell. When his magazine was empty he had four plates to his credit.

John made progress from that day, and now he and his brothers are putting up the fight of their lives in France. They are taking their part in the greatest battle the world has ever known. I wish I could talk to John and find out what he thinks about it all, and still more would I like to hear his account to his own people when, if ever, he goes back to his native reservation. I hope he will go back, for he is a man among a race of men, already far too few in number, who are gradually becoming extinct.

A press cutting from the *Manchester Guardian* 1918.

Various Caribbean islands sustained populations of indigenous Caribs, as did sections of the Caribbean coast of South and Central America, which were also under British colonial rule and administered alongside the West Indies. Young men from these tribal societies also answered the call to arms, and experienced western clothing and culture often for the first time in their lives when they enlisted, as was poignantly captured by the British press at the time.

CREED

Christianity had been the dominant faith in the Caribbean since the arrival of Columbus in 1492, striking the death knell of the indigenous faiths of the Caribbean that had lasted a thousand years, which like those of the South Americans were spiritually attuned to nature. Various denominations of the Christian faith took opposing positions on the abolition of slavery, with the Anglican Church supporting the pro-slavery lobby. The Moravian, Pentecostal, Seventh Day Adventist and Quaker faiths not only opposed slavery, but were also among the first in the Americas to accept black congregations. Those with strong ties to Africa struggled to retain their culture and heritage under the brutal regime of slavery and were forced to devise discreet ways of practising the religions of that continent in a manner loosely based upon tradition, using resources close at hand. Modified during the passage of time, these original religions were camouflaged by European symbolism and rituals. On many islands, as in the southern states of America, Voodoo, known by some as Obeah, evolved as a religious dialect that originated in Africa but is unique to the New World, a creolised religion.

With wave after wave of migration came a wide range of religions new to the Americas that took root, commencing early on with religious refugees from the Spanish and Portuguese inquisitions that brought the first Jewish settlers to the shores of the Caribbean, thus forming the first Jewish settlement in the whole of the Americas.

50   The Mikve Israel-Emanuel Synagogue in Curaçao.

FRANK ALEXANDER DE PASS, V.C.

It was announced in a supplement to the *London Gazette* on February 19th, that His Majesty the King had been pleased to approve of the grant of a Victoria Cross to Lieut. Frank Alexander de Pass, late 34th Prince Albert Victor's Own Poona Horse, for conspicuous bravery and devotion to duty whilst serving with the Expeditionary Force.

It is deeply to be regretted that Lieutenant de Pass did not live to enjoy the honour— the highest in the gift of the King for military valour—conferred on him, which will, however, we may hope, help to soften the grief felt by his parents at the loss of their gallant son. Lieutenant de Pass was the second son of Mr. Eliot Arthur de Pass, West India Mer-

Lieut. Frank Alexander de Pass, V.C.

chant, and a valued member of the Executive of the West India Committee, and of Mrs. de Pass, who is a daughter of the late Mr. I. H. De Mercado, of Kingston, Jamaica. The reason for the award of the Victoria Cross is given in the *Gazette* in the following terms :—

" For conspicuous bravery near Festubert on the 24th November, in entering a German sap and destroying a traverse in the face of the enemy's bombs, and for subsequently rescuing, under heavy fire, a wounded man who was lying exposed in the open. Lieutenant de Pass lost his life on this day in a second attempt to capture the aforementioned sap, which had been reoccupied by the enemy."

Frank Alexander de Pass, a member of a long-standing, established Jamaican Family, who joined the Indian Army and was the first Jew to be awarded the Victoria Cross.

In 1651 Joao d'Ylan arrived in Curaçao with a dozen Jewish families from the Portuguese community of Amsterdam. Here they established the Congregation Mikve Israel-Emanuel, the oldest synagogue in continuous use in the western hemisphere. A second group followed in 1659, bringing with them a Torah scroll from Portugal, still in use today. In 1663 Sephardic Jews left the Caribbean and ventured to London where they founded the Holy Congregation Gate of Heaven synagogue, better known as the Bevis Marks synagogue, the oldest in the United Kingdom.

The plantation agriculture that had sustained the original settlers in the Seventeenth Century was not the best source of income for later generations, particularly as the soil on many islands had become exhausted from excessive sugar production. Caribbean Jews began to facilitate trade between Europe and the ill-equipped Spanish territories on the South American coast as a means of generating much needed income for the region. Their business connections with Europe's major cities enhanced by experience in international trade and maritime insurance meant the Caribbean Jews soon dominated the shipping, banking and insurance industries related to Caribbean commerce.

The Jewish community flourished, and by the Nineteenth Century Jews accounted for over half the white population of islands such as Curaçao. The two monumental synagogues that still stand in Willemstad are testaments to the strength of the community there, as are the various elegant mansions located in close proximity to the synagogue, a necessity as Jews may not walk more than two thousand cubits (3000 feet) on their Sabbath.

At the time of the First World War the 'would be' heroes of the Caribbean were sustained by a rich, diverse mix of religious beliefs that reflected the immense social and racial diversity of the region.

The vast diversity of the peoples of the Caribbean is reflected in the motto of the largest English-speaking island, Jamaica – *"Out of Many One People"*. The supporters of the country's coat of arms, a Carib couple, depict the indigenous people of the Caribbean. The Coat of Arms of Jamaica is said to have been personally designed by King Charles II, reflecting the great importance of the colony to the Crown.

During their training in Britain, the West Indian troops saw first-hand the poverty and disenfranchisement of the average Briton, and their poor state of health and standard of living. This caused many to question the justification of the subservience they had been conditioned to accept as the natural order of things within the Empire. This story was played out throughout the world, as the war dragged nation upon nation into its deadly vortex.

A considerable amount of effort was put into the enforcement of colonialism within the military and, although they were officially infantrymen, West Indians were constantly reduced to serving as common labourers, in many instances forced beneath the status of civilian labourers, a fate that also beset tens of thousands of Chinamen who manually dug the extensive trench system that scarred the face of Europe. The West Indians were given back-breaking, life-threatening tasks that included the movement of highly volatile fuel beside the frontlines of some of the bloodiest episodes of warfare the world had ever seen. As such, Passchendaele, Ypres, and the Somme rightfully reside among the battle honours of the British West Indies Regiment.

IMPERIAL FEDERATION. MAP OF THE
STATISTICAL INFORMATION FURNISHED BY CAPTAIN

Eventually the war spread well beyond the Western Front and Europe itself, entering the Middle East and Africa. At last non-whites were given the much sought after and prided place in action on the frontline. Moreover, the West Indians were armed with one of the most lethal weapons of all, the Vickers Machine Gun, capable of slaughtering dozens in one stroke. Notwithstanding their limited training and the technical flaws in a gun that was too heavy to manoeuvre with ease, and prone to overheating and misfiring, the West Indians excelled, quelling the risk posed by the once mighty Ottoman Empire.

In Africa their sister regiment, the West India Regiment, although recognised as having one of the most renowned reputations in the British Army for over a century, were demeaned by their deployment in secondary and labour roles. Men at the vanguard of West Indian military achievement, such as Samuel Hodge of the 4th West India Regiment, were long forgotten, as was the Regiment's prowess at the Battle of Orleans of 1814 when they were cited as the *"finest men in the British Army"*.

Care was taken to limit interracial social interaction, although this did not affect the camaraderie between West Indians of all classes, colour and creeds. The Caribbean Governors corresponded with individual servicemen, taking up their complaints and concerns with the relevant authorities in government.

Issues of racism arose frequently and were addressed as a necessity in maintaining West Indian commitment to both the conflict and the Empire. Although poor, the level of racial integration among the British forces was far greater than that tolerated within the American Army. Black American servicemen were so poorly respected by their own country that it fell upon the French to clothe black troops in French uniforms. In the presence of their fellow Americans, blacks of all ranks were obliged to defer to whites, even those of lesser ranks. Segregation of the servicemen reflected the segregation of American society at the time, a turbulent hierarchy that continued until the late 1960s. The experience of a Europe where overt racism was not so avidly practised was liberating for black Americans. Although Europe had instigated and nurtured the slave trade that had led to the displacement of millions of blacks from Africa to America, and ordained that they lose many of their human rights, at the time of the war, Europe showed more respect and compassion towards black Americans than their fellow countrymen. Consequently, after the conflict many black Americans returned to France where they gave birth to the Jazz Age whose cultural impact would be felt across the globe, challenging long established social divides.

For the West Indians, already steeped in European culture, as impersonated by the upper echelons of Creole society, the French had a poor reputation, choosing to retain slavery years after the British had abolished the practice. Unlike North America, blacks far outnumbered whites in the Caribbean, making the prospect of a change for the better a viable prospect there, unlike their neighbours on the continent. West Indians of every hue preferred to return home, particularly as racial tension and xenophobia grew in post war Europe, a place bankrupted by years of warfare that proved exorbitant in both financial and human currency.

A map of the British Empire in 1866

THE WEST INDIAN COMMITTEES

The West India Contingent Committee was established through the auspices of The West India Committee to address the interests of the thousands of Caribbean men and women keen to participate in the conflict. Whilst their desire to serve and support the colonial power of the time is greeted with scepticism and disdain by many today, it was real and forceful at the time, as evinced by the personal accounts of a great many West Indian war veterans. The lack of knowledge and appreciation of the region in Britain during the war meant the needs and aspirations of the thousands of West Indians that stepped forward to serve were best managed by institutions such as The West India Committee that had a foot in both camps – the British establishment and West Indian society. The charity was in the unique position of having an extensive working knowledge, respect and insight into the region, and placed the best interests of Caribbean people at the heart of its mission, as remains the case today. The West India Committee, and the various committees it spawned during the war, filled a gap in awareness and made up for the paucity of time and resources in war torn Britain to administer to the needs and aspirations of the people of the British West Indies.

Having challenged the War Office to permit West Indians to serve, the next battle for The West India Committee was how to safeguard their welfare as they did so. The West India Committee strived to ensure West Indian servicemen felt the comforts of home throughout the conflict wherever they served. This work interfaced with that of other charities of the time, such as the National Relief Fund. The West India Contingent Committee used The West India Committee's highly effective network of envoys in both the Caribbean and Britain to gather funds for this purpose, raising millions of pounds for Caribbean servicemen, enlisting its network of supporters and members that included leading Members of Parliament, members of the Royal family, and a myriad of Britain's most influential families. Membership of the Committees in the Caribbean was a multiracial affair, although, like those in Britain, structured by class.

"The path of Duty is the way to Glory"

With the Best Wishes
of the
WEST INDIAN CONTINGENT COMMITTEE
for
CHRISTMAS and the NEW YEAR
1916-1917

Gifts of tins of chocolate were distributed to West Indian troops throughout the war and were particularly popular.

The West Indian Contingent Committee strived to ensure West Indians felt the comforts of home on the frontline. For some, gestures of gratitude came in the form of personalised gifts like these cigarette cases exclusively distributed to all ranks of the British West Indies Regiment on New Year's Eve of 1916-17. One colonel wrote upon receiving the gift, *"I was more than touched by its being remembered in such a kindly fashion that I came from the West Indies."*

A GIFT CIGARETTE CASE.

Above is a reproduction on a reduced scale of one of the cigarette cases presented by the West Indian Contingent Committee to all ranks of the British West Indies Regiment.

Mahogany from Belize was used to make aeroplane propellers and last-rites crucifixes for use by Army chaplains.

Christmas puddings were among the many presents the Committee sent to the men wherever they were deployed, interfacing with charities such as the National Relief Fund run by the Prince of Wales. The Contingent Committee also used the West India Committee's chain of Caribbean based envoys to gather in funds and remit them to Britain.

The Caribbean was no stranger to providing comfort to the British military. Since the 1740s a tradition had arisen within the Navy of providing sailors with a daily ration of beer to boost morale amongst men that may have been on active service for years at a time. After the Napoleonic Wars, the 'daily tot' of rum replaced the beer, being more readily available in the region as a by-product of sugar production. Admiral Edward Vernon, who was known as 'Old Grog' because of his tendency to wear a cloak of Grosgrain, a corded fabric still used in formal uniforms today, made the rum tot compulsory, in so doing, it was christened 'grog'. The islands of Jamaica, Trinidad and Tobago and the British Virgin Islands were the main source of the naval rum ration. Later, to combat scurvy, lemon or lime juice from Montserrat and Dominica were added to the ration, earning the British the nickname- 'Limies'.

Parliament made various valiant attempts to revise what was a heady cocktail that invariably included rum as strong as 95% proof! Not only did it cause drunkenness and alcoholism, but it was also quietly administering lead poisoning, as rum was distilled and stored in unsealed lead vessels causing the deadly metal to leach into the alcohol. Eventually the rum was stored in safer, ornate wood and brass barrels, known as rum tubs, bearing the motto, ' The Queen, God Bless Her'. On 31st July 1970 - 'Black Tot Day', the centuries old custom came to an end, an event mourned by the Royal Navy to this day.

Despite the demise of the rations, the naval order to 'Splice the Mainbrace' continues in use, although now meaning 'an extra tot of rum for good service' but today only the Monarch may give the order. The practice of a rum ration was adopted throughout the British Empire, with the Royal New Zealand Navy being the last to end the ritual in 1990.

Based on centuries of supplying the Admiralty, a high demand for rum was anticipated in the Caribbean as a result of the war. The West India Committee Circular of 11th August 1914, a matter of days after Britain declared war on Germany, stated *"As far as we can see the price of rum is likely to rise inasmuch as with sugar standing at a high price there will be less inducement to make that spirit.... but... the requirements of the Admiralty are bound to be heavy while the Navy is mobilised."* In fact sugar production plummeted as exports to Europe were prohibited; however, demand for rum rose as the ration was extended to the Army. The West India Committee Circular of 9th February 1915 published an article entitled *'In praise of Rum'*, that attempted to justify the new Army ration.

IN PRAISE OF WEST INDIAN RUM.

A well-known Journalist's Views.

The use of rum in the dietary of our troops at the front has led to much public attention having been drawn to this form of alcohol. The *Evening News* of the 28th of January had a particularly interesting and illuminating article on the subject from the pen of Mr. Arthur Machen. As to the use of rum in the trenches, he says :—

"We are at war, and now and again our soldiers tell us stories of the terrors of the trenches, and of the hideous discomforts of their life therein. They write of snow and rain and freezing slush, and of icy water breast high ; and their only word of comfort is that they are nobly fed, and that their ration of rum enables them and sustains them. I should be sorry for that sergeant who should come round at the appointed hour with a ration of that once-bepraised barley water, in place of the expected rum. The best he could hope for would be a swift death. For the fact is that soldiers, weary and cold, wet and worn, can take nothing better than this generous and pure spirit."

Among the words of an eminent doctor to Mr. Machen are these :—

" You must remember that rum stimulates not only by its alcohol, but by its ethers and aldehydes. These exercise a general diffusive stimulation which makes the tired man feel less tired. And note this : if a man thinks he feels less tired, then he is less tired. . . . In my opinion the cold, wet, tired man is very much benefited by a small dose of alcoholic stimulant ; and the more moderate his previous use of it the greater the benefit will be. This stimulant is preferably administered warm, and rum is an admirable form in which to take it."

" People who have come back from the trenches have acquired a taste for rum," Mr. Machen continues, quoting the representative of a well-known firm of wine merchants, and he goes on to speak of old and curious Jamaica rums that were to be obtained by the learned in this matter. " There is, it seems, a rum of 1851, which delayed in the wood for fifty years, purging away its grosser and more peccant parts. A rare drink this, but who is to have it ? Ghostly admirals, I would say ; Commodore Trunnion of ' Peregrine Pickle,' the captain of Richard Midleton's 'Ghost Ship,' Morgan the Buccaneer, good men and bad men who have done wondrous things upon the seas ; such a noble drink is sure too good for mere mortality."

" They told me," he further says, " singular things concerning rum in Seething Lane, by the Tower, where there is an association which concerns itself particularly with West Indian products."

" Demerara rum, these gentlemen contended, is inferior to Jamaica rum, because in the former place sugar is the main object, rum a by-product, while in Jamaica the reverse is the case. And they spoke delicately and reverently of the ethers that give good rum its fragrance and its merit, and now for the first time I heard the root of the matter concerning that pineapple rum wherein the red-nosed man, Stiggins, did so grievously exceed. This pineapple flavour, it seems, pertains to the best rum by nature; it is the flavour of 'butyric ether.' I told how the publicans were wont formerly to hang pineapples in nets in their rum puncheons.

" ' Yes ; but that was merely to enhance the flavour.'

" And I was told secrets of the fermentation ; how these subtle ethers will only pass over in a tropical climate—you could not make good rum in England of imported molasses—how one plantation excels another in its peculiar ferment, even as in Burgundy *clos* excels *clos* in the nobility of its juice."

He tells the tale of the Liverpool tavern keeper :

" He looked through his little window on his bar, and said :

" ' There go the brandy people ; they are good for twelve years. There are the whisky people ; nine or ten years will settle them. And there are the rum people ; I don't know what will stop them.' "

Mr. Machen concludes his article with a recommendation which should be taken to heart by all.

" But if anyone, not a warrior, not a sailor, untossed by savage seas, unvexed by shells would relish rum, let him take a bottle, and add to it an equal measure of green tea that has not been brewed more than five minutes. Add also the juice of six lemons and of three oranges, add golden and amber rings of lemon peel and orange peel, and let the sugar—some twenty lumps—have been rubbed on the rind of the lemons.

" Lætaberis, you—and your friends—will be glad, as Apuleius declares, introducing the Twelve Books of his Metamorphoses, commonly called the Golden Ass."

It is not, however, generally known that our soldiers in the trenches get but small quantities of rum. Every other day each man in the firing line is given three tablespoonfuls, amounting to 4½ oz., or a little more than two wineglassesful per week.

The islands ensured rum flowed to the frontline and the Navy, continuing another tradition of exporting to the rum warehouses of West India Quay, the foundation of London's Docklands built by members of the West India Committee and opened in 1802. Today exports of rum account for a significant percentage of the Caribbean's economy, remaining one of the few products unique to the region, together with stalwarts such as Angostura Bitters, made from a secret recipe, which is also found in many a drinks' cabinet throughout the world.

WE are glad to know from personal inquiry, says the *Wine and Spirit Trade Record*, that, contrary to the general opinion, the Government is sending to the troops a really good quality of rum, which ought to be a source of great comfort to our brave soldiers, many of them knee-deep in half-frozen slush. The work of packing and despatching the spirit from the West India Docks proceeds rapidly, two gallon jars being packed in each case. Confirming what we stated last month, a writer who has spoken with many soldiers returning from the front, says :—

" Certain pettifogging hagglers and teetotal fanatics, in Parliament and out, are horrified at the fact that rum is supplied to men in the trenches. It may interest those people to know what the soldiers themselves say about it. I was told with pathetic earnestness by many of these men, maimed and battered from the field, that, standing waist-deep in water, they felt it a God-send when they got a drop of rum. 'You can feel the warmth and glow of it going through your veins,' said one man. And another told me, 'Oh, it is a comfort. It seems to put new life into you when you are soaked through and chilled to the marrow.' And he might have added, when you are likely to be killed by a shell at any moment. Yet there are actually members of Parliament and members of that pious and moral body, the United Kingdom Alliance, who have approached Lord Kitchener and raised the question in Parliament in their zeal to get the soldier's rum stopped. I should like to send these cold-blooded gentry into the battle themselves, to stand in cold water, and face cold bayonets on cold stomachs."

Wine and Spirit trade record taken from the West India Committee Circular 1st December 1914.

Angostura Bitters (Dr. J. G. B. Siegert and Sons), Ltd.

The accounts for the year ended September 30th last show a net trading profit of £17,343 4s. 3d. (as compared with £20,872 19s. 11d. for the preceding year). After applying to Advertising, Legal Expenses and Trade Marks Registration the sum of £3,411 6s. 8d. (as against £5,083 13s. 3d.), and after payment of London Expenses, there remains a net profit of £12,067 13s. (as against £13,621 5s. 9d.). Of this amount the Directors have placed the sum of £1,206 15s. 3d. to Reserve (as compared with £1,583 2s. 6d. to Reserve, and £1,500 to Special Reserve for contingencies). The amount available for distribution is therefore £10,860 17s. 9d. (as against £10,538 3s. 3d.), which, with the addition of the sum of £1,521 13s. 7d. brought forward from last year (as against £2,033 10s. 4d.) makes a total of £12,382 11s. 4d. (as against £12,571 13s. 7d.). An interim dividend on the Preference and Ordinary Shares to the 31st March last at the rate of 3 per cent. having already been distributed, the Board recommend the payment of a final dividend for six months to 30th September last on both Preference and Ordinary Shares at the rate of 3½ per cent. for the half-year (making a dividend for the year of 6½ per cent. per annum), leaving a balance of £1,332 11s. 4d. to be carried forward. In their report the Directors state that the business of the company has, so far, suffered less in England and the Colonies than might have been anticipated from the war, but, generally speaking, the state of war has seriously interfered with the Company's business during the last two months of the year under review. Sales to Austria and Germany have entirely ceased, and the consumption of Angostura Bitters in other parts of the Continent has been greatly reduced. The Board announce with great regret the death of their colleague, Sir Hubert E. H. Jerningham, K.C.M.G., and have appointed Mr. R. H. McCarthy, C.M.G., to fill the vacancy so caused.

Taken from West India Committee Circular 29th December 1914.

A small sample of the vast varieties of rum, a product unique to the Caribbean.

The West India Contingent Committee kept a watching brief on the experiences of West Indians during the war years, and was regularly advised directly by the Governors and island assemblies of the conditions civilians and serving West Indians experienced. Where necessary, as was frequently the case, the West Indian Contingent Committee lobbied Parliament for improved pay and conditions for the troops, securing equal pay on more than one occasion. Use of the West India Committee's extensive records and photographic collection was also encouraged, resulting in the two iconic Jamaican stamps of the Caribbean's Great War being made up of photographs from the Committee's collection.

A Ladies' Committee, which was largely composed of the wives of Committee members, many of whom, like Lady Davson, great-great granddaughter of William Wilberforce, had direct links with the Caribbean. The Ladies' Committee was presided over by Her Highness Princess Mary Louise of Schleswig-Holstein as Patron, thereby ensuring a high profile for the Committee's efforts in Britain when so many were struggling for attention and support. The Princess was a granddaughter of Queen Victoria and, although a first cousin of the German Kaiser, Wilhelm II, worked tirelessly for the British war effort. In July 1917, at the height of the conflict, whilst still patron of the Ladies' Committee, on the orders of her other first cousin King George V, the Princess discontinued the use of her German titles and simply became known as Her Highness Princess Mary Louise. At a time when women in Britain enjoyed few personal human rights, the allocation of tasks to the ladies would be regarded as sexist by today's standards. Knitting circles, one of which was said to have been visited by Queen Mary at the West India Committee's rooms, and matters of personal welfare were the mainstay of their work. The outcome far exceeded expectations. The involvement of upper class ladies in Britain brought with it influence which secured the support of individuals, companies and institutions that may not otherwise have engaged with West Indian troops, such as Harrods which placed its premises at Number 5, Trevor Square at the disposal of the Ladies' Committee. Similarly these ladies opened their homes and estates to wounded West Indians recovering in Britain.

On the other side of the Atlantic, the ladies of the Caribbean established their own committees from the very outset of the war. These committees played a vital role in the recruitment campaign, encouraging young West Indian men to join the newly formed British West Indies Regiment. Their members came from all walks of life, reflecting the extensive diversity of the region. As in Britain, the upper classes took leading positions, motivated by a general desire to ensure the Caribbean was not regarded as a colonial backwater, but a place that could equal their counterpart, Britain. Such was the impact of the regional Ladies' Committees that some islands lobbied for them to become a permanent element of their governments. Their Flag Days were legendary, garnering not only much needed funds for the Allied war effort, but also securing thousands of enlistments.

Her Highness Princess Mary Louise.

THE WEST INDIAN CONTINGENT COMMITTEE.

EXECUTIVE.

Chairman.
SIR EVERARD IM THURN, K.C.M.G., C.B.

Deputy Chairman.
SIR FREDERIC HODGSON, K.C.M.G., V.D.

Hon. Treasurers.
COLONEL SIR EDWARD WARD, Bart., K.C.B., K.C.V.O.
SIR SYDNEY OLIVIER, K.C.M.G.
ROBERT RUTHERFORD, Esq.

THE EARL OF HAREWOOD, K.C.V.O.	SIR ROBERT LLEWELYN, K.C.M.G.
LORD GLENCONNER.	SIR JAMES HAYES-SADLER, K.C.M.G.
SIR HENRY BLAKE, G.C.M.G.	C. B. HAMILTON, Esq., C.M.G.
SIR GEORGE R. LE HUNTE, G.C.M.G.	EDWARD R. DAVSON, Esq.
SIR CHARLES LUCAS, K.C.B., K.C.M.G.	WILLIAM GILLESPIE, Esq.
SIR FRANCIS FLEMING, K.C.M.G.	W. A. M. GOODE, Esq.
SIR WILLIAM GREY-WILSON, K.C.M.G.	J. RIPPON, Esq.
SIR OWEN PHILIPPS, K.C.M.G., M.P.	G. MOODY STUART, Esq.

Hon. Secretary.
ALGERNON E. ASPINALL, Esq.

LADIES' COMMITTEE.

Patron.
HER HIGHNESS PRINCESS MARY LOUISE OF SCHLESWIG-HOLSTEIN.

President.
THE COUNTESS OF STAMFORD.

THE HON. MRS. HENRY EDWARDES.	LADY SENDALL.
LADY LE HUNTE.	MRS. ASPINALL.
LADY IM THURN.	MRS. BONYUN.
LADY CAMERON.	MRS. BROMLEY.
LADY DAVSON.	MRS. GORDON GORDON.
LADY FLEMING.	MRS. HARLEY MOSELEY.
LADY GREY-WILSON.	MRS. JAMES RICHMOND.
LADY HAYES-SADLER.	MRS. RIPPON.
LADY HODGSON.	MRS. RUTHERFORD.
LADY LLEWELYN.	MRS. MOODY STUART.
LADY OLIVIER.	MRS. WADE.
LADY PHILIPPS.	

Hon. Secretary—Miss MARY MOSELEY.

Bankers.
THE UNION OF LONDON AND SMITHS BANK.

Offices.
THE WEST INDIA COMMITTEE ROOMS, 15, SEETHING LANE, LONDON, E.C.

A list of members of the West India Contingent Committee Executive and The Ladies' Committee prior to 1917 when their patron, Princess Mary Louise, was obliged by her first cousin, King George V, to renounce her German titles upon the creation of the House of Windsor.

Gifts for the Contingent.

The West Indian Contingent Committee have to acknowledge with thanks the following gifts received during the past fortnight :—

Bed jackets (50), helmets (36), gloves (120 prs.), mittens (12 prs.), from Lady Phillips.

Mittens (10 prs.) and gloves (9 prs.) from Mrs. James Richmond.

Mufflers (2), mittens (2 prs.), and socks (1 pr.) from Mrs. Beckett.

Belts (3), mittens (4 prs.) from Mrs. Sheldon.

Scarves (2), helmet (1), and socks (1 pr.) from Mrs. Algernon Aspinall.

Shirts (5), scarves (5), helmet (1), socks (1 pr.), stockings (1 pr.), putties (3 prs.), from 2nd Lieut. W. B. Wolseley.

Mittens (3 prs), scarves (2) from Miss Goffe.

Mittens (6 prs.), for British Guiana men, from Miss Lynch Thomas.

Mittens (6 prs.), scarf (1), for Jamaica men, from Miss A. J. Davy.

Warm gloves from Mrs. Lindley Nunn (3 prs.); Miss Porterfield (2 prs.); E. Phillips (1 pr.); Mrs. Norton Taylor (2 prs., for Jamaica men); Mrs. Arthur Johnson (8 prs.); Miss James (4 prs.); Miss Tremearne (1 pr.); Mrs. Gordon Turner (6 prs., for Demerara men); Miss L. Jeffrey (1 pr.); the Hon. Mrs. Henry Edwardes (8 prs.); Lady Hayes Sadler (20 prs.).

Mittens, from Mrs. T. William Wilkinson (14 prs.), Miss Gardner (1 pr.).

Scarves (15) and sundry comforts from Mr. G. H. Bailey.

Scarves (4), socks (15 prs.), mittens (13 prs.), helmet and magazines from Mrs. Rutherford.

Scarves (2), mittens (1 pr.), from Mrs. Cunningham Craig.

Made bandages (12), rolled bandages (12), slings (6), eye bandages (12), slippers (2 prs.), mittens (9 prs.), scarves (17), socks (12 prs.) from Lady Llewelyn.

Khaki handkerchiefs (4 doz.), for Barbados men, from Miss Braithwaite.

Shirt (1), socks (1 pr.) from Miss Thomson.

Scarf (1), mittens (5 prs.), socks (4 prs.) from Miss K. Gray.

Mufflers (18), mittens (12 prs.), gloves (25 prs.), from Mrs. Seymour Kane.

Mittens (12 prs.) from Mrs. Nourse.

Scarf (1), mittens (1 pr.), socks (1 pr.) from Mrs. Harley Moseley.

Mufflers (2), from the Hon. Mrs. Henry Edwardes.

Scarves (5) and mittens (6 prs.), from Mrs. Moody Stuart.

Scarves (6), socks (2 prs.), mittens (6 prs.), from Miss Smith.

Gloves (2 prs.), socks (1 pr.), from Mrs. W. Hart.

Ladies took pride in having their personal accomplishments publicised:

Mufflers for the Troops.

To the Editor of The West India Committee Circular.

Sir,—I have been requested by the authorities at the War Office to collect 250,000 mufflers as quickly as possible for the use of our troops at the front. I shall therefore be most grateful for contributions either in money or kind towards the fulfilment of this object. The mufflers should be two yards long by 12 inches wide, with no fringes (but any length would be accepted), and the colour of the wool should be khaki or grey.

Parcels containing mufflers, if sent by post, should be addressed to me at the Manor House, Waltham Cross, Herts; but if sent by rail should be forwarded to Enfield Station (G.N.R.).

I am continuing to keep open my fund for the supply of socks and shirts, contributions to which should be sent to the depot at 54, Beauchamp Place, S.W. I would venture to request contributors to either scheme to be so kind as to mark their goods "Carriage Paid," as in many instances railway charges have had to be paid twice over. Might I add that I have now 90 women working for me, both at Messrs. Harrods' and also in a room kindly lent me by Messrs Tudor? These women would otherwise be out of work owing to the war, and I am naturally anxious to obtain sufficient funds to enable me to keep them employed throughout the winter.

Yours faithfully,
Eleonora French.

The work of the Ladies' Committee was in great demand.

The West Indian Ladies' Committees fast became a formidable war machine in the Caribbean for which no task seemed impossible. When asked to produce a quarter of a million knitted garments for the troops, they not only satisfied the order, but also did so notwithstanding the region running out of wool.

Whether knitting socks for West India troops stationed at the Somme, hosting the wounded in their country homes, or devising new fundraising campaigns, women on both sides of the Atlantic rose to the occasion, no doubt spurred on by the suffragette movement of the time, which challenged the subservient position of women in British society. Freed slaves transported to Sierra Leone were the first women in the British Empire to be given the vote. In the UK this was finally granted in 1918, after years of struggle, whilst the women of the Caribbean had to wait until the 1960s to be granted the same democratic freedom by some of the first black governments in the region.

Popular songs encouraged ladies to knit as did this aptly named ditty "Every Girl is Knitting for Some Mother's Son in France".

It should be possible to give in an early issue of the CIRCULAR some further particulars about the West Indian Flag-day, which is being organised throughout the West Indies on behalf of the West Indian Contingent Fund. A complete list of the ladies who are so kindly giving their help has not yet been received, but from the information already received it is clear that the matter is being taken up with enthusiasm. Most of the flags and badges have reached the West Indies safely, though we regret to state that those shipped to Jamaica have gone to "Davy Jones' Locker."

A B.W.I. 1D. BADGE.

The picture of one of the silk flags, which was published in the last CIRCULAR, is now supplemented by a reproduction of one of the cardboard badges.

As already stated, it is not proposed to observe the Flag-day officially on this side of the water, but a goodly supply of flags has been reserved for disposal among friends at home, it having occurred to the organisers that many folk connected with the West Indies would like to purchase flags and badges as souvenirs. In this connection readers are reminded that the Hon. Secretary of the West Indian Contingent Committee (15 Seething Lane, E.C.) would be glad to hear from any who may be willing to help in disposing of these flags. The note to this effect published in last CIRCULAR has already brought in several applications, one lady sending £10 for flags, which augurs well for the success of the appeal.

A SILK B.W.I. FLAG.

The West India Committee helped to sell flags on both sides of the Atlantic.

The Antiguan Ladies' Committee

The first recruitment meeting held in Kingston, Jamaica where the Ladies' Committees were strident.

A bustling flag day in Kingston, Jamaica, raising much needed funding for the war effort.

COLLECTORS IN ANTIGUA.

A GROUP

SELLERS IN BRITISH GUIANA.

SOME WEST INDI

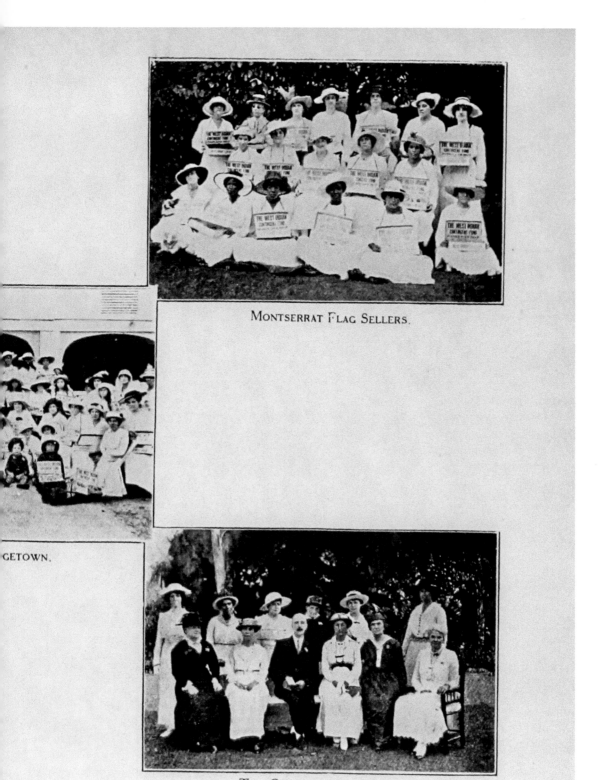

MONTSERRAT FLAG SELLERS.

GETOWN.

THE COMMITTEE IN ANTIGUA.

LAG DAY GROUPS.

One of Britain's most effective war machines - the Ladies' Committees of the Caribbean.

ENEMIES IN THE CARIBBEAN

The Caribbean had long been the preferred theatre of war for European conflict, causing islands to change hands dozens of times, depositing a mosaic of cultural imprints that made each distinctive and unique. Not since the Battle of Waterloo, a century prior to the Caribbean's entry into the conflict, had Europe embraced its disputes within its own boundaries on such a scale. The sheer intensity and magnitude of carnage and destruction in the early years of the First World War shocked and disorientated

TWO PRIZES IN CASTRIES HARBOUR, ST. LUCIA.

Two German ships captured in St. Lucia. Featured in the West India Committee Circular of 8th September 1914.

the high commands of the Great Powers, leaving little initial thought of the fate of their respective empires and the millions of their subjects scattered across the globe. As far as Britain was concerned, the Caribbean, sheltered by its continental neighbour, America, faced a relatively minor threat from Germany and her allies. It was, however, deeply affected by the naval conflict that raged in the Atlantic which cut the Caribbean off from Europe, one of its most important markets, starving it of much needed income and supplies.

Imports.			
	Total.	From Germany.	From Austria.
	£	£	£
Barbados	1,465,431	17,044	450
British Guiana ...	1,703,355	15,134	646
British Honduras ...	366,049*	8,217	115
Jamaica	3,050,479	56,541	44
Trinidad	2,594,143†	32,721	—
Leeward Islands ...	113,483	2,451	—
Grenada	279,874	605	70
St. Lucia	214,769	2,764	—
St. Vincent	129,142	877	19
Total	9,916,725	156,354	1,344

* Exclusive of goods in transit £362,453.
† Exclusive of goods in transit £2,088,182.

Exports.			
	Total.	To Germany.	To Austria.
	£	£	£
Barbados	1,085,569	1,136	—
British Guiana ...	1,798,596	2,669	—
British Honduras ...	232,555*	—	—
Jamaica	2,709,283	105,791	21,759
Trinidad	2,384,395†	97,680	—
Leeward Islands ...	563,342	8	—
Grenada	285,590	—	—
St. Lucia	108,514	2,006	—
St. Vincent	111,684	—	—
Total	9,279,528	209,290	21,759

* Exclusive of goods in transit £362,453.
† Exclusive of goods in transit £2,088,182.

German and Austrian imports and exports during the war.

The Caribbean was rich in oil and coal, and as such, during the age of steam, was an attractive refuelling destination. The West India Committee reported in its circular of 8th September 1914 *"The belief that several German warships were in the Caribbean was causing apprehension in some quarters, but the defence forces and police were preparing to give the enemy a warm reception in the event of any raid being attempted and a visit of HMS Bristol to St. Lucia had had a reassuring effect."* In 1915 two German ships were captured off the coast of St. Lucia. Their crews were marched down the streets of the island by the Home Guard, made up of local policemen, to a detention camp where they remained for the duration of the conflict. The impact of enemy shipping in the Atlantic and embargoes placed on trade with Germany and Austria blocked their exports to the Caribbean that ranged from foodstuffs such as beer, wine, butter, margarine, china, earthenware to luxury goods that included porcelain, glass, perfumery, textiles, clothing and millinery. The extent of this trade was considerable, with thousands of Caribbean men and women avid fans of German millinery in the run up to the war.

The Caribbean had also exported its wares to Germany and had experienced an element of tourism from this part of Europe. Caribbean tourism continued through the war years and The West India Committee, as one of the leading promoters of tourism for the region, continued to advertise the destination, advocating a Caribbean holiday as a means of avoiding the war.

Many German families had settled in the Caribbean during the Nineteenth Century and were successful merchants there. Islands such as Jamaica had distinctive German communities that were concentrated in various towns and villages that they called their own. Suspicion of collaboration and the odd case of subversion led to the edict that all Germans should be detained as a matter of national safety. This included German Creoles, despite being born in the British West Indies and therefore British subjects in their own right.

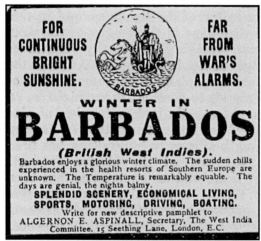

MR. LOUIS WESSELS, the head of an important firm at Kingston, Jamaica, has been ordered to leave the island. He is partner in a New York house which is said to have supplied stores to the *Karlsruhe*.

A clipping from the West India Committee Circular 3rd November 1914. Mr Louis Wessels was asked to leave the island for supplying Germany.

FOR CONTINUOUS BRIGHT SUNSHINE.

FAR FROM WAR'S ALARMS.

WINTER IN
BARBADOS
(British West Indies).

Barbados enjoys a glorious winter climate. The sudden chills experienced in the health resorts of Southern Europe are unknown. The Temperature is remarkably equable. The days are genial, the nights balmy.
SPLENDID SCENERY, ECONOMICAL LIVING, SPORTS, MOTORING, DRIVING, BOATING.
Write for new descriptive pamphlet to
ALGERNON E. ASPINALL, Secretary, The West India Committee, 15 Seething Lane, London, E.C.

An advert for holidaying in Barbados from the West India Committee Circular 1914.

German Prisoners being escorted to Detention Camp, St Lucia.

Officers of the German Warship *Spreewald* on the way to detention at Morne Fortune, St. Lucia, under the watchful eye of the Home Guard.

THE NAVY

BY DAVID WELLS

West Indian involvement in the naval war was not as extensive as in other areas of conflict but nevertheless there are numerous examples of West Indians serving in dangerous conditions in both the Royal Navy and the Merchant Marine. Although the threat was always limited, naval warfare would prove to be the greatest danger to the West Indies themselves and there were concerns over the safety of the islands' boats in the face of possible aggression from German vessels. This led to higher shipping prices, which negatively affected the economy of the region. The Panama Canal opened in 1915, making the region strategically important as there was the potential for the German Pacific Fleet to sail through the canal to access the Atlantic. However, this threat was limited to the earlier years of the war and was believed to be over by 1916.

Many West Indians were merchant seamen, technically civilians but directly in the line of fire from German ships in a manner experienced by no other civilians during the First World War. It is difficult to say exactly how many West Indians were in the Merchant Marine because 'British' was used to describe all imperial subjects. It is estimated that around 10% of British merchant seamen were drawn from colonies and protectorates in the West Indies, Africa, South East Asia and Arabia. A further 20% were drawn from India. Many West Indian sailors formed large transient populations who lived temporarily in many of the world's larger ports; in Britain this included places such as Liverpool, Cardiff and London. The role of the Merchant Marine was vitally important as Britain was heavily dependent upon imports from its colonies and other countries. Such was Britain's economic might in 1914 that, together with its dominions, it owned 43% of the world's merchant vessels. The raw materials and food brought to Britain were vital to both the war effort and to life on the British Home Front. This, however, made merchant ships a prime target for the German Navy, particularly U-boats.

Merchant seamen found themselves enduring heavy casualties, with over 90% of them subjected to submarine attacks. In total, 14,287 merchant seamen lost their lives during the First World War. This figure was in fact largely due to the use of submarines, not only through the sinking of ships but also through failing to rescue survivors. Whilst a civilian sailor might expect to be rescued from the sea, the nature of submarine operations and the cramped nature of life on-board a submarine meant that this was not possible. Thus, by the

The badge of the British Merchant Navy.

end of the war, the Merchant Marine had lost thousands of sailors, many of them known to be from the Caribbean, in addition to 6,924 Allied ships and around 13 million tons of assorted cargo. The hard work and sacrifice of the Merchant Marine led King George V to change the name of the service by decree to that of the Merchant Navy in 1928.

At the time of the conflict, *His Majesty's Dock Yard Bermuda* was the Royal Navy's main base in the Western Atlantic. It not only served as a facility for resupplying and coaling ships but also as a Royal Naval Wireless Telegraphy station with land at Daniel's Head being used for the aerials. Many local Bermudans, and men from other areas of the Caribbean, became apprentices at the Dockyard, where they learnt the requisite skills to help service the ships.

The Dockyard and its ships were employed in protecting Allied Merchant shipping across the Atlantic, thus ensuring important West Indian goods, such as sugar, reached Britain. Convoys were assembled at Bermuda before being escorted by armed vessels across the Atlantic to Europe, in order to protect them from attack by German U-Boats. However, this convoy system was not fully implemented until May 1917, due in part to initial resistance from the First Sea Lord of the Admiralty, Admiral Jellicoe, who had, among other issues, concerns about the delays that would be incurred by the not inconsiderable time it would take to assemble convoys and by the potentially slower speeds at which they would then travel. It would, however, prove to be the sensible option as losses were heavily reduced from the 881,027 tons of shipping sunk by U-boats in April 1917. Ships from HMD Bermuda were also employed against the German East Asiatic Squadron.

The German East Asiatic Squadron, under the command of Vice-Admiral Maximilian von Spee, was mainly a threat in the Pacific. However, before their defeat at the Falklands, many ships such as *HMS Princess Royal* were sent to the Caribbean to prevent the Squadron utilising the Panama Canal to make their way into West Indian waters, where they could seriously disrupt British shipping on their way back to Germany.

Rear Admiral Christopher Cradock commanded the 4th Cruiser Squadron at the outbreak of the war. He had the responsibility for protecting British shipping in the West Indies against German threats, although he died at the Battle of Coronel in an engagement with the German East Asiatic Squadron on 1st November 1914. There were only two German light cruisers in the West Indies, the *SMS Dresden* and the *SMS Karlsruhe*, under the command of Fregattenkapitän Erich Köhler, but locating these vessels was not easy in the days before radar and regular aerial reconnaissance, so the fact that Cradock and those under his command were able to keep British shipping secure in the early days of the war is noteworthy. The task was particularly difficult given the small islands of the region, which could be used as hidden bases by German vessels, especially the 700 islands of the Bahamas. *SMS Karlsruhe* was a particular threat. At the beginning of August 1914, having sighted the German ship, Admiral Cradock gave chase, signalling the *Berwick* and *Bristol* for assistance. The *Bristol* fired, but was out of range and, using her superior speed, the German cruiser escaped and was able to evade further detection. The *Karlsruhe* particularly threatened the shipping route between Barbados and Trinidad and this resulted in defences being constructed for Bridgetown, the capital of Barbados.

At least 26 cruisers and armed merchant cruisers took part in the search for the *Karlsruhe* at different times. During the hunt, *HMS Berwick* captured three foreign steamers, the *Spreewald*, *Thor* and *Lorenzo*. These were brought to the harbour of Castries, St. Lucia and their crews interned. The steamers contained ammunition and other supplies that were believed to be meant for the German cruisers. Such was the concern over the cruisers that Mr Louis Wessels, who was a partner in a New York firm that was said to have supplied the *Karlsruhe*, was asked to leave Jamaica, despite being the head of an important firm in Kingston.

The *Karlsruhe* captured 16 British targets in total, as well as a Dutch ship that was carrying British cargo. The last of these ships was the liner *Vandyck*, which was captured on 26th October 1914, carrying 200 passengers in addition to a large amount of stores. The *Karlsruhe* was responsible for the loss of over 76,000 tons of cargo, with a value well in excess of £1 million in the money of the day, which would be approximately £43,060,000 today. The *Karlsruhe* was destroyed by an on-board explosion, believed to be an ammunition magazine accident, on 4th November 1914, with the loss of 262 men including her Captain, but this was not discovered by the Allies until March 1915, meaning that tensions in Caribbean waters remained high in the intervening period. Although wreckage from the *Karlsruhe* had been washed ashore during that period, many dismissed these finds as a German trick.

After the Battle of the Falklands, much of the potential threat to the Caribbean dissipated. The *Dresden* participated in the battle but was able to escape the British Fleet due to its superior speed. The *Glasgow*, *Kent* and *Orama* later sank it on 14th March 1915, off the Island of Juan Fernandez. However, the naval war continued in other parts of the globe, as did attacks on Merchant Marine shipping. West Indians serving on both Royal Navy and mercantile vessels distinguished themselves and often sacrificed their lives in the conflict. There are many tales of individual courage.

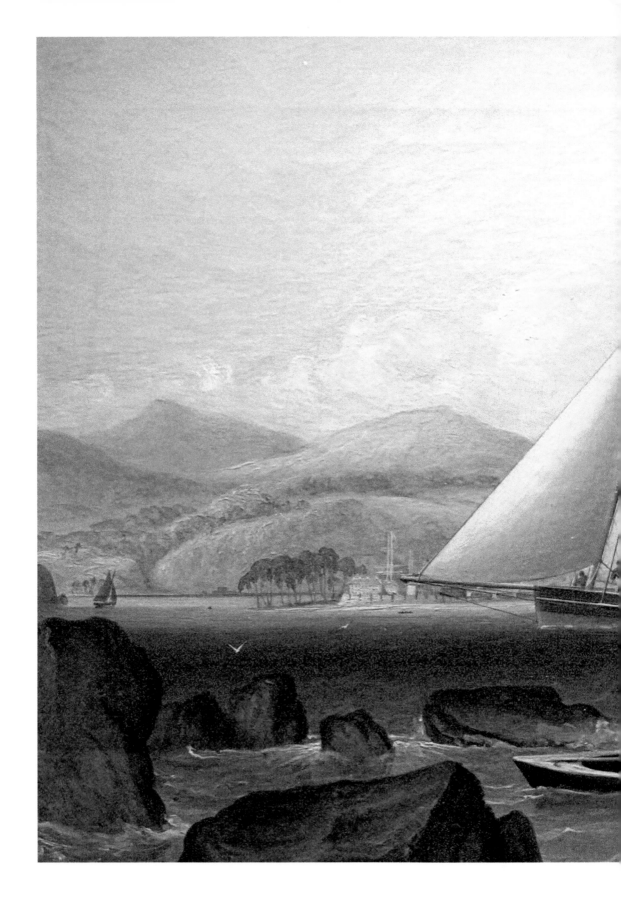

Bermuda had been valued by the Royal Navy as a port long before the First World War. A 1831 painting by John Lynn of a three-masted Bermuda sloop of the Royal Navy, entering a West Indies port.

One particularly interesting West Indian sailor was Edward Leicester Atkinson, born in 1881 in St. Vincent. He was noted by those who served with him for such qualities as his devotion to duty, courage, reliability, cheerfulness and optimism. Having studied medicine in St. Thomas' Hospital, Lambeth, he joined the Royal Navy in 1908 and was a part of Captain Scott's Antarctic expedition. As surgeon and the last surviving officer, he led the search party that discovered the bodies of his doomed colleagues and retrieved the diaries, drawings and letters that told the fate of Scott and his men. He also wrote the epitaph for Captain Oates.

Having been made Staff Surgeon in 1913, during the war Atkinson served with the Royal Navy at Gallipoli in 1915 and then with the Royal Marine Howitzer Brigade in France between 1916 and 1918. He was wounded twice and was mentioned in dispatches on multiple occasions, being granted the Distinguished Service Order in 1918. On 16th September 1918, his vessel, the monitor *HMS Glatton* exploded in Dover Harbour owing to an accidental fire in one of its ammunition magazines. Atkinson risked his life to rescue five seamen, despite having sustained severe wounds from the explosion, before escaping

Edward Leicester Atkinson in 1911.

the ship. Vice-Admiral Keyes was forced to order the torpedoing of the *Glatton* so as to prevent further explosions, which could have caused severe damage not only to the rest of ships at Dover but also the town itself. Atkinson was awarded the Albert Medal for Lifesaving for his actions. He was also promoted to Surgeon Commander the same year. He retired from the Navy in 1928 and died the following year as Ship's Surgeon of the *SS City of Sparta*.

The first Bermudan to die during the war is believed to be William Smith, who served as a Royal Navy cook on the *HMS Aboukir*. Early in the morning of Tuesday, 22nd September 1914, *HMS Aboukir* was on patrol with *HMS Cressy* and *HMS Hogue* in the North Sea when a German U-boat, *U-9*, fired a torpedo at the *Aboukir*, which sank with the loss of 527 men, Smith amongst them. The *Cressy* and *Hogue* were also struck, leading to the loss of 1,459 men within the space of 90 minutes. This incident established the power of the submarine as part of naval warfare. William Smith's name is recorded with others on the *HMS Aboukir* memorial at Southsea near Portsmouth.

Lieutenant-Commander Harrington Edwards was a Creole who won the Distinguished Service Order for special service on a submarine in September 1915. He died the following year, his submarine not returning to port after leaving Harwich on patrol in March. Commander Robin Llewellyn who was born in Spanish Town, Jamaica achieved his rank at the age of 30 but went down with the *HMS Queen Mary* in the infamous Battle of Jutland.

The dangers that the Mercantile Marine faced are demonstrated by the fate of the *SS Belgian Prince*, aboard which were five sailors of Caribbean origin: Solomon Brown (a Fireman and Trimmer), born in the West Indies, three Trinidadians, Nicholas Christian, Jo Mifaries and Charles Skerritt and Charles de Sousa from Nevis, who was Chief Steward.

On 31st July 1917, during a voyage from Liverpool to Newport News, Virginia, a torpedo struck the *Belgian Prince* fired from German *U-Boat 55*, under the command of Oberleutnant zur See Wilhelm Werner. This disabled the engines and also made it impossible to send any distress signals. The crew abandoned ship in three lifeboats, whilst *U-55* continued to shell the *Belgian Prince* in order to disable its radio, not knowing that it was already destroyed. The entire 42 man crew of the merchant vessel was ordered to disembark from their lifeboats by Werner and to stand on the hull of the U-boat. The Master, Harry Hassan, was taken below and was never heard from again.

Under orders from Werner, the U-boat crew took most of the lifebelts from the survivors and then scuttled the lifeboats, save for a small boat which five of the German crew used to board the damaged *Belgian Prince*. Once they had signalled that they had done so, the U-boat crew re-entered the submarine and closed the hatch, leaving the remaining 41 men on the outer hull. After sailing for two miles, the U-boat then submerged. There were only three survivors. This was not the first time that Werner had ordered this action; he had done the same to the crews of the *Torrington* and the *Toro* in the April of that year.

Unfortunately, after the war, a large number of seamen from the Caribbean and the West Indies that had joined either the Royal Navy or the Merchant Marine found themselves unemployed and unable to get new work as shipping companies in Britain were unwilling to hire non-white sailors. The National Sailors and Firemen's Union and the National Union of Ships' Stewards, Cooks, Butchers and Bakers both had policies of opposing the employment of African, Asian and Caribbean seaman if white crews were available, despite the fact that many of those seeking work were union members. However, during the war tentative support had been offered to black sailors, who were more readily accepted as British than Asiatic sailors and who were also seen as less likely to undercut wages than the latter. Despite this, after the war, West Indians often faced discrimination along with other ethnic minorities and this led to the race riots of 1919 in various port cities such as London, Cardiff, Glasgow, Liverpool and South Shields. So many sailors from ethnic minorities were unemployed that the Government set up Repatriation Committees to enable those who wished to return to their countries of origin to do so. Many West Indians took up this offer, but many chose to stay and the communities formed by those sailors continue to exist to the present day.

The names of the crew of the *Belgian Prince* on the memorial at Tower Hill, London.

71

THE WEST INDIA REGIMENT

The West India Regiment, sister regiment of the British West Indies Regiment, was founded in 1795 and formed part of the British Army. This marked a step change in colonial recruitment, targeting local men and Africans as opposed to the more conventional strategy of transporting troops from Britain to the region.

The French Revolution of 1789-99 brought turmoil to the Caribbean, much as the English Civil War had caused social and political rifts in Barbados during the previous century between those supporting the monarchy, the Cavaliers, and those favouring a republic, the Roundheads. Within this chaos slaves saw an opportunity to fight, not for their colonial masters, but for their personal freedom. As the Caribbean was the most affluent region in the world at the time and Britain was at war with the French Republic, troops were sent to the region in their thousands to protect British interests. The military suffered heavy losses there. During five years of conflict over 40,000 were killed, with another 40,000 incapacitated, not by the enemy, but by deadly tropical diseases such as yellow fever and malaria. European soldiers were not suited to the tropical climate, and were further impeded by their heavy-duty uniforms, designed for colder conditions. Moreover, food rations did not contain fresh fruit nor vegetables and the daily rum ration caused many to die from alcoholism and lead poisoning. To make up for the persistently heavy losses, increased by an uprising of the Carib people in 1795, the British Army followed the example of French Royalists and recruited soldiers from the black populations

A West India Regiment bandsman whose uniform is still in use today by Caribbean defence forces.

of the islands, creating the original eight West India Regiments. This was not only more economical than transporting troops from elsewhere in the Empire, but also provided a more effective, acclimatised, and culturally aware force.

OUR WEST INDIAN "TURCOS."
An inspection of the West India Regiment at Up Park Camp, Jamaica.

The West India Regiment was stationed at the Up Park Camp, Jamaica - still in use today by the Jamaican Defence Force.

However, there were many immediate difficulties to be faced. Plantation owners refused to lose the best of their work force to the Army, just as adamantly as freed blacks refused to surrender their newfound freedom to a life of military authority.

A cap badge of the West India Regiment.

As a result, the British Army became the single biggest slave owner in British history, purchasing African slaves to staff the regiments until 1807. After the abolition of the slave trade, the Royal Navy began to police the African coastline to ensure foreign competitors could no longer access slave labour and undercut British planters, who were soon to be denied this source of cheap labour for the erstwhile lucrative business of sugar production. Instead, many unfortunate Africans 'rescued' from the clutches of the infamous trade by the Royal Navy found themselves escorted to the safe haven of the West Indies where they were promptly enlisted into the regiments. This was a move viewed by some as a form of slavery in itself, a reasonable interpretation as military service for black soldiers could last for a lifetime or until dismissal, which usually only occurred when a man was no longer physically fit enough to serve.

The high percentage of Africans in the early West India Regiments meant translators were needed to facilitate communication between the officers and their men. The situation was exacerbated by the fact that senior officers were largely absentee Europeans, a situation that was commonplace during an era when military commissions were treated as a commodity that could be both purchased and traded. Absence from service by the higher ranks was rife as the Caribbean was regarded as an unattractive and unhealthy posting to be avoided at all costs. In some instances, these officers never saw their men, let alone action, and it therefore fell to lower ranking officers to lead the Regiment, many of whom, as a matter of practicality, were local blacks.

Black soldiers were equal in the eyes of the Army. Their uniforms, rations, and pay were the same as their white colleagues, yet they were not free. The right to treat them as such was not governed by the Army, but by the legislation of the island on which they were stationed. Whereas a white soldier caught committing an offence was punished in accordance with military law, the fate of black soldiers was dictated by slave legislation that invariably meant a harsher form of punishment befell them. The abolition of slavery emancipated black soldiers in the regiments and caused the Army to look elsewhere for its troops. An influx of free Africans to the region after emancipation, in search of work, continued to fill the ranks of the West India Regiments, as did the slaves 'liberated' by the Royal Navy. This was essential as the Napoleonic Wars raged on, and many battles were staged in the Caribbean.

The West India Regiments, heavily staffed with Africans, were routinely used to put down slave rebellions, a strategy that went some way to reducing antagonism towards the islands' plantation owners. Instead, resentment was deflected towards the Regiment. Black soldiers proved unwilling to jeopardise their prized military status by any feelings of racial kinship with black slaves, having been indoctrinated into considering themselves their superiors. Accepting the 'King's Shilling' was a recognised symbol of enlistment, committing the men to the Monarch himself. In later years, this term was re-appropriated for the post-emancipation era of Queen Victoria's reign when the men of the West India Regiment collectively identified themselves as the 'Queen's Gentlemen'. Their relationship with this monarch was reciprocated when the Queen personally designed their uniform, based upon that of the French Zouaves, a uniform still worn today by bandsmen of the defence forces of the region - successors of the West India Regiments.

Battle of New Orleans by painter Edward Percy Moran in 1910.

The West India Regiment had attained a reputation as a formidable force within the British Army. One of its finest hours was the Battle of Orleans, when an invincible Armada of sixty great ships set sail from Negril Bay, Jamaica on 26th November 1814 for Louisiana. Captain Gleig, a British officer, in his history of the campaign cited the 1st and 2nd West India Regiments as comprising over 700 men each. Contributing to one of the most important battles in American history, they were regarded as the *"choicest troops then on Earth"* and were described by General Eyre Coote as being *"some of the best soldiers we have [in the British Army]!"* The Regiments went on to win further accolades in other theatres of war. A mere five months after Orleans, troops from the Regiment were to find themselves at Waterloo with the important task of maintaining the escape route for the Allied forces at Halle, serving under Dutch command. In the event, this option was never taken due to Wellington's success in a battle he was to call *"the nearest run thing you ever saw in your life"*. After the battle, the West Indians were also charged with the duty of participating in the destruction of Napoleon's Old Guard - Napoleon's most formidable force that famously chose death over surrender. Waterloo eclipsed Napoleon's star, which was never to rise again. As they did not participate directly in the events of the battle on 18th June 1815, the role of the West Indians, much as that of the Turks who fought for Napoleon, was largely forgotten, with recognition finally being bestowed through the kind offices of the 9th Duke of Wellington at the bicentenary of the Battle of Waterloo in 2015. The end of the Napoleonic Era brought a period of peace in the Caribbean, and the redistribution of property rights between the islands. British islanders, such as the Anguillans, who were awarded titles to land on French St. Martin, referred to these awards as their "Waterloo Money".

After the Napoleonic Wars were brought to an end, there was little need for such a large standing army in the Caribbean and most of the West India Regiments were disbanded, despite being feted as some of the bravest and most disciplined bodies of men Britain had ever sent into battle. There was little desire amongst the troops to return to Africa, and although many islands refused them the right to stay, Trinidad and Belize welcomed them. By 1819 only the 1st and 2nd Regiment remained in active service. It was at this time that the Sierra Leone Company requested their service, as tropical diseases that the West Indians were known to have resisted had decimated the Royal Africa Corps. The two regiments alternated, with one serving in Africa whilst the other remained in the Caribbean.

Troops from the West India Regiments were offered their freedom, and granted land in Sierra Leone where the town of Waterloo was founded for them in 1819. Here Jamaican patois mixed with the local African tongue, French and Portuguese to form a dialect, still prevalent today, known as Kriol, a name reminiscent of the term Creole meaning a person born in the West Indies. For the next century the West India Regiment protected British interests in West Africa, aided by the Royal Navy. They fought admirably in numerous conflicts and achieved particular renown in the Ashanti and Boer Wars. It was during this period that Samuel Hodge of the 4th Regiment, from Tortola in the British Virgin Islands, became the first black man to be awarded a Victoria Cross for gallantry at the Battle of Tubabakolong in Gambia, at which a badly wounded Hodge saved the life of his commanding officer, Colonel D'Arcy.

When the First World War commenced, the West India Regiments were given little opportunity to fight, despite having the longest combat record in Africa out of the entire British Army. Even though the High Command was more than satisfied to have a force of black troops fighting their black enemies, with black troops serving in West Africa from the outset of the war, there was a reluctance to pitch black troops against white German troops in Africa, despite being in opposing forces. As a result, official attitudes towards the West India Regiments changed and they were prevented from performing anything other than a supporting role for less experienced white troops. A small detachment of signallers from the 1st Regiment was used in the Cameroons Campaign, serving for periods as long as 15 months at a time.

Meanwhile, the 2nd West India Regiment sailed to the east coast of Africa, to be deployed along with other non-white troops such as the Indian Army and the King's Africa Rifles, where very little progress had been made against the formidable German commander, Colonel Lettow-Vorbeck. In February of the following year, 515 men of the 2nd Regiment arrived under the command of the South African General Smuts capturing Kilwa Kivinje, a strategic harbour town. Once the British forces arrived to secure the position, the 2nd Regiment advanced a further 80 miles to the coast to take the Lindi. The remainder of their service in Africa was less active and in 1918 they were transferred to Lydda in Palestine to guard munitions and stores during demobilisation.

The limited participation of the West India Regiment in the conflict meant the British West Indies Regiment played the lead role in the Caribbean's war effort, whilst the older, more experienced West India Regiment saw little action in comparison. After the war, locally raised forces replaced the West India Regiments' traditional role in protecting Britain's African possessions. In 1920 the 1st and 2nd Regiments were combined into one, and in 1927 the West India Regiment was finally disbanded after one hundred and twenty five years of loyal and distinguished service. This was primarily for financial reasons and because, by that time, the Caribbean had long been a peaceful region.

The West India Regiment was revived in 1959, a year after the founding of the Federation of the British West Indies. This new defence force was headquartered in Jamaica, inheriting the cap badge, Regimental March, and the regimental silver from the original regiments. By 1960 a second battalion was raised in Trinidad and Tobago, composed of men from the entire region recruited in direct proportion to the population of each island. The 1st Battalion was deployed domestically. In 1962 they were to oversee the referendum that disbanded the Federation and, in turn, the Regiment itself. The men of the former West India Regiments then became the infantry units of both Jamaica and Trinidad and Tobago pending the re-establishment of local defence forces.

Queen Victoria's Uniform: The ceremonial uniform of the West India Regiment was designed according to Queen Victoria's instructions. It is based upon the iconic French Zouave uniform and continues to be used by bandsmen of the defence forces of the Caribbean.

THE BRITISH WEST INDIES REGIMENT

Columbus' Ship:
The ship in the centre is the *Santa Maria*, which was captained by Christopher Columbus, the European who discovered the Caribbean in 1492. The ship was likely chosen to represent both the region generally and the voyage that the men of the Regiment had to make across the Atlantic to fight in the war.

Tudor Crown:
The Tudor Crown was chosen because the English settled in the Caribbean during the Tudor dynasty (1485 - 1603).

A Wreath of Laurel:
This is common in heraldic symbols. In ancient Greece and Rome the laurel leaf (left hand side) represented victory.

A Wreath of Palm:
The palm wreath (right hand side) symbolises the Caribbean.

THE BADGE OF THE BRITISH WEST INDIES REGIMENT.

The King has graciously sanctioned the inclusion of the Imperial Crown in the badge of the British West Indies Regiment. The design of the badge has now been approved by the Army Council, to whom it was submitted by the West Indian Contingent Committee. The Committee is presenting to the Officers, Non-Commissioned Officers and Men of the British West Indies Regiment cap badges according to this design.

The British West Indies Regiment's badge was designed and prepared by the West India Committee.

From 1914 the Caribbean had rallied to the aid of the Mother Country. The well respected and highly experienced West India Regiment was placed on a standby footing and local defence forces stepped up their training and exercises in readiness for the hoped for deployment in European theatres of war - but the call never came.

At first Britain, like all of the Great Powers, had underestimated the nature of the conflict and its consequences. Within less than six months of the first shot being fired, the very heart of Europe was laid to waste. Modern technology meant the High Commands of each participant could not rely solely upon their experience, but were obliged to ensure their strategies were capable of evolving at the same rate as innovations in warfare.

The sons and daughters of Europe's upper classes were the first to lead the charge into a war that they fully expected would be over by Christmas 1914. Sadly it was not to be, and few were prepared for that eventuality. One of the few was Kitchener, the leader of the British Army. He had anticipated an arduous fight that would take years to complete. Despite his anticipation of the need for men, Kitchener's experience as a colonial soldier had shaped his opinion of colonial troops, and he was against their use in this war. Britain's military infrastructure was only designed to accommodate the needs of one of Europe's smallest armies and had little scope to accommodate colonial servicemen. Moreover, the country's strength had long been its navy and it was here its resources had been concentrated for centuries.

Heavy losses on the Western Front placed an enormous strain on Kitchener's edict – not to pitch non-whites against Europeans in combat, an attitude that reflected the core values of colonialism that placed one nation in a position of superiority over others. Kitchener, a complex character that often clashed with his peers during his meteoric rise through the ranks of both British society and the military, was an Irishman faithful to the Crown.

EMPIRE PATRIOTS.

GALLANT DEEDS OF FIGHTERS FROM THE WEST INDIES.

Little has been said in the war news of the British West Indies Regiments, but when the history of the Empire's sacrifices has been written down a foremost place will surely be given to the deeds of the gallant fighters from these remote islands.

At the outbreak of the war the islanders clamoured to be allowed to fight, but the authorities held them back to defend, if necessary, the islands.

"When the danger was over leading merchants in Jamaica took up the matter, and the first contingent was definitely formed and accepted for service by the Army Council," said Mr. Algernon E. Aspinall, of the West Indian Contingent Committee, to a DAILY GRAPHIC representative yesterday.

MEN FROM EVERY COLONY.

Recruiting proceeded with enthusiasm, and the first contingent arrived here in the early autumn of 1915. On October 26th, 1915, the King approved the formation of the West Indies Regiment. The men came from every single West Indies Colony—Bahamas, Barbados, British Guiana, British Honduras, Jamaica, the Turk Islands, the Leeward Islands, the Windward Islands, Trinidad, and Tobago—described by Defoe as the home of Robinson Crusoe.

Taking their relative importance these Colonies have provided as strong a unit as any of the Dominions, and they defray cost, pensions, etc.

—THE BRITISH WEST INDIES CONTINGENT.

West India Troops in heavy military 'great coats', protection from Britain's foreign climate.

SOLDIERS OF THE KING.

Home from the trenches, the Jamaican, a private in the Staffordshire Regiment, inspected the Lifeguardsman in Whitehall yesterda

le continued his walk along Whitehall with one of his white comrades.

At the time the British West Indies Regiment was formed, West Indians that had travelled to Britain and India independently were also serving in other regiments alongside English, Scots and Indians.

As such, he was all too aware of the benefits of a strict social order. From his base in the War Office, he fought against the introduction of troops from regions such as the West Indies, notwithstanding support for colonial troops from both the King and the Colonial Office. However, in 1915 King George V, in his capacity as King Emperor of the British Empire, finally won the day, intervening in this on-going dispute between the War and Colonial Offices. Issuing a personal statement to the colonies, the King granted permission for colonial men to fight on behalf of their King and Country. These words marked a victory for the Colonial Office and for the men of the Caribbean as on 15th October 1915 the British West Indies Regiment came into existence, placing patriotism firmly above colonialism. As a sign of his personal endorsement, the King gave his permission for the Tudor Crown to be incorporated into their regimental insignia, which was designed by members of the West India Committee, depicting the heritage of this enthusiastic band of brothers.

New recruits at play before the realities of war take hold.

Both the King and the Queen showed great personal interest in the West Indian volunteers. In 1917 the King publically demonstrated his devotion to these subjects by inviting representatives from Britain's colonies and dominions to attend the State Opening of Parliament, forming the Imperial Procession in which the King and Queen lay at the heart. They were invited to attend a reception at Buckingham Palace where the King and Queen further acquainted themselves with men that represented an Empire that accounted for a third of the world's population, a family of nations that was to evolve into today's Commonwealth, comprising 53 countries from the vast to the minute.

ONE OF THE LION'S "CUBS."

A recruit in Trafalgar Square, London. The first Trafalgar Square in the British Empire is in Bridgetown, Barbados, a country as familiar with Admiral Horatio Nelson's exploits as Britain. The colony was well known to Nelson, who served there and married into a creole family.

Despite recognising the huge scale of the war, unlike many others in the High Command, Kitchener failed to provide sufficient ammunition, resulting in him being stripped of responsibility for munitions and strategy. This reduction in his authority and his untimely death in 1916 eventually paved the way for the eager West Indians to play what they anticipated as being a more meaningful role in the conflict.

Statuesque troops from the Bahamas. Beside the boy scout in the centre, a soldier stands seven feet tall, living up to their sobriquet, "Huge and Mighty Men of Valour".

The ...
West India Committee Circular.

Vol. XXX.   TUESDAY, SEPTEMBER 21st, 1915.   Subscription £1 1s. per ann. post free.
Single Copies 1s. Published Fortnightly.   **No. 443**

TABLE OF CONTENTS.

The West India Committee Rooms,

Telephone :
  6642 CENTRAL.   15, SERTHING LANE.
                LONDON, E.C.,
Telegrams :
  CARIB, LONDON.   *September 20th, 1915.*

OUR KNOWLEDGE OF EMPIRE.

THE men of the British Guiana detachment of the West Indian Expeditionary Force are, from all accounts, winning golden opinions for themselves. From the inhabitants of Seaford they have received a very cordial welcome, and soldiers and civilians at that little seaside town are vieing with each other to make the men feel at home in their new surroundings. The visit of so many troops from overseas will help to awaken a new spirit in this country, and it must be admitted that in spite of the great progress made in recent years, the people of England are still lamentably ignorant about our Empire. In the schools, the history of Europe is drubbed into the heads of the rising generation to the exclusion of that of our Imperial possessions, with the result that a lamentable ignorance prevails with regard to the latter. The geography of Empire, too, is hopelessly neglected, the chief offenders in this respect being our great Public Schools. It is not surprising, then, to learn that so little is known of the British West Indies at the Sussex town where our men are now quartered, that the Vicar, in desperation, has appealed for a lecturer to tell the inhabitants something about our oldest group of colonies. The need for this will be apparent when we mention that one correspondent has already identified British Guiana with New Guinea, while another has expressed his agreeable surprise on learning that the men from the West Indies speak such good English ! One of the troubles hitherto has been that the average textbook of the Empire has been written far above the man in the street. Most writers on Imperial topics, being saturated with their subject, presuppose a knowledge of it on the part of the layman which the latter has not got, and bewilder-

ment results. We have now before us, however, a small volume entitled, "The British Empire," by SIR CHARLES LUCAS,* who does not fall into the common mistake made by so many experts. The book contains six lectures dedicated to the members of the Working Men's Club, which is doing a splendid work. SIR CHARLES LUCAS possesses a unique knowledge of the British Empire, and in this book he tells his readers in a simple and lucid style the story of the making of England and of her far-reaching possessions oversea. In some spirited introductory remarks the author refers to the lack of the appreciation in this country of the realities of the Empire before the outbreak of war. It was steadily growing; but it was only half knowledge or less. Among a large section of Englishmen there was a suspicion of Empire, both the word and the thing, as implying jingoism, vainglory, and hypocrisy ; hence arose the baleful term of Little Englander, of which we hope we have now heard the last. " Coupled with this, there was a feeling among some, at any rate, of the working men of England that the Empire was of no use to them, and that they had no use for the Empire." We warrant that this feeling was not shared by the members of the essentially loyal and patriotic Working Men's Club. The copious references to the West Indies in the index are an earnest that SIR CHARLES LUCAS keeps a warm corner in his heart for our oldest group of Colonies, whose destinies he controlled to a great extent when he was head of the West Indian Department of the Colonial Office. He leaves little or nothing untold in describing the colonisation of Greater Britain, touching in that connection on such matters as constitution, immigration and religion, etc. In East Indian immigration he is evidently a firm believer, for he says that "In the coming time India may be looked on as a kind of Mother Colony to the tropical dependencies of the Empire." With regard to the Constitutions of the Colonies, he reminds us that the "Barbadians are for all practical purposes a small self-governing community with unbroken tradition of English liberty and English constitutional rights," a statement which will be balm to the inhabitants of our ever-British colony, who so much resented the misdescription of their status in the Colonial Office Regulations, which have now, thanks in large measure to the representations of the West India Committee, been amended. We hope that this book will be taken up as a text-book in the schools in this country, for it strikes us as being an eminently clear and practical exposition of our Colonial History.

*The British Empire. Six lectures. By Sir Charles P. Lucas, K.C.B., K.C.M.G. Macmillan & Co.

All in all, West Indians were well received by communities in Britain.

TRAINING IN BRITAIN

Whilst rudimentary training was provided in the Caribbean, and many had received training as members of the local defence forces, formal training for the British Army was conducted in Britain at a series of rapidly constructed training camps along the south coast. This reduced the cost of transporting the novice servicemen away from the ports that would be their points of departure once trained. Men of the newly-formed British West Indies Regiment were sent to Withnoe near Plymouth and Seaford in Sussex, where they undertook training for frontline action. Their experiences there were formative, as their first introduction to the lives of the average Briton was a far cry from the impression perpetuated by the colonial system. The British Army, as the Royal Navy's poor relation and a fraction of the size of its enemies' armies, was under immense strain from the outset. As a result most British troops experienced bad conditions in their UK based training. Not only were the training camps poorly constructed, but also the standards of accommodation, equipment and medical facilities were equally poor. Despite a good reception by local communities, who were invariably fascinated by people whose culture, race and very existence were unknown to all but a few, the troops found life in Britain hard and disappointing. In Seaford a well-meaning local vicar took it upon himself to redress his congregation's ignorance of the Empire and its people by giving a lecture on the subject. He openly complained about the lack of education among the British about such important matters. The concept of global citizenship had yet to be invented, notwithstanding Britain's pivotal presence at the epicentre of a third of the world's population.

Despite efforts to make the Caribbean troops feel 'at home' and their inclusion in the community by initiatives such as extending membership of the local working men's club to them, the troops did not find the climate as welcoming, and large numbers of Caribbean men succumbed to colds, flu, bronchitis and pneumonia. Many lost their lives in these conditions long before their active service had commenced. This was largely due to a failure to anticipate the effects of the British climate, poor accommodation and inadequate medical facilities on men from the tropics. The loss of so many demoralised their comrades and reduced the flow of volunteers from the islands. The effects of poor conditions in the training camps were significant. Whilst 178 men were killed in action, or died of wounds, and another 697 were wounded in action, a staggering 1,071 died of disease in Britain during training, according to the West India Contingent Committee minutes of 29th May 1919. Approximately one third of troops in the entire world war died as a result of disease or infection, whilst the West Indians lost two thirds of its contingent in this manner.

The Lord Mayor of London swearing in recruits from Trinidad and Barbados at the Lord Mayor's Show of 1916.

FIGHTING FIT

The West Indian troops were impressive, not only because they were regarded by the masses as exotic, but because of their fine physical condition. Unlike their British counterparts, these men had been raised on what we now recognise as a healthy, balanced diet of fresh foods. Despite the diseases that continuously beset the Caribbean, they proved physically superior to many British troops, particularly those from the lower classes where poor diet and inadequate housing had taken its toll on their health.

Colonial contingents such as those from the West Indies were feted and highly publicised as an intrinsic part of the recruitment drive. In 1916 the Lord Mayor of London embraced this strategy, inviting Trinidadian and Barbadian troops to participate in the Lord Mayor's Show.

Happy Darkies at the Front: No Bad Teeth in that Lot!

"Witness" Exclusive War Photos

THE BLACK MAN DOES NOT SEEM TO BE TROUBLED BY THE TEETH PROBLEM AS A BAR TO ENLIST-MENT, JUDGING BY THE SETS OF IVORIES DISPLAYED ABOVE! THE FACES, IT WILL BE SEEN, BEAR A REMARKABLE RESEMBLANCE TO THE AFRICAN TYPE.

The picture is of some of our West Indian troops, taken in camp in England. They have since gone to the front. They are splendid soldiers; and all speak English fluently. They have taken with them to Europe the manners and customs of the plantations, and their merry dispositions made them great favourites with the neighbourhood while in camp. The picture shows a game of cards in progress, one 'cute darkey being lucky enough to hold three aces.

The dramatic landscape of the Lord Mayor's Show and the welcome shown to the West Indian volunteers fuelled pride, with one recruit, a Private Peter Lambert, remarking in the press, *"I was proud to be cheered by the people of London"*. His account demonstrates how black West Indians were received, often with a far more rapturous welcome than their white comrades, a situation that was to give a false hope of acceptance of black British troops throughout the war. At the time of their arrival in 1915, the War Office was in the throes of a mass enlistment drive that required considerable effort in the face of the mass slaughter being meted out on the Western Front. Reluctance by the War Office to embrace West Indian troops set them on the path of using their patriotic enthusiasm to participate to shame local men into enlisting.

LORD MAYOR'S WEST INDIES GUESTS.

The Lord Mayor entertained to tea at the Mansion House yesterday about 100 members of the Trinidad and Barbados contingent who arrived on Monday in this country to join his Majesty's forces. The men were sworn in on the previous day by Sir Charles Wakefield, and now appeared in khaki. Both the Lord Mayor and the Lady Mayoress served tea to their guests, and Sir Charles congratulated the men on having donned khaki. Most of the men had joined the Royal Fusiliers.

THE LORD MAYOR'S SHOW AS SEEN BY

PRIVATE PETER LAMBERT (of the West Indian Contingent).

" I have never seen anything before like the Lord Mayor's Show. When they told us we were to take part in it I asked, ' What is the Lord Mayor?' They told me he was the Governor of London, so I said I always thought King George governed London and England. Then I was told that London had more than one governor, which isn't surprising, for London is a wonderful place and must want a lot of looking after. I've never been in such a big town since I left Kingston (Jamaica).

" I was proud to be cheered by the people of London, for I've come a long way to fight for them. When I was a boy my father used to tell me about England—he had been there —and about General Gordon. I never thought I should be a soldier, like General Gordon.

" The people in the streets cheered us black boys more than the white boys. ' That's because you're black,' said someone to me. But we are English really; it's only the climate we've lived in that makes us black."

ARGYLL & SUTHERLAND
HIGHLANDERS
(PRINCESS LOUISE'S)

WHY ARE'NT YOU ONE OF THEM ?
GO AND ASK FOR PARTICULARS FROM
YOUR POST OFFICE or
THE NEAREST DRILL HALL or
THE NEAREST RECRUITING OFFICE

During the first two months of recruitment in Britain, over half a million men volunteered, plummeting to less than 100,000 by the time the British West Indies Regiment was formed. The Military Service Bill of January 1916 became law in March of that year, ensuring that every single man and childless married man between the ages of 18 and 41, except those attested as being occupied in an exempt profession under the Derby System, was deemed to have enlisted. However, rejection rates for various communities remained high on grounds of poor health, especially in Britain's industrial heartlands such as Glasgow, where the situation was particularly marked. Throughout this recruitment campaign, West Indians steadily volunteered, as was the case throughout the entirety of the war, rendering adoption of compulsory conscription unnecessary in the Caribbean.

The invitation by the Lord Mayor, and the flurry of press attention they attracted in Britain raised the expectations of West Indians who were feted for their superior physique and health as "Huge and Mighty Men of Valour". Yet reservations about race continued to be harboured by the War Office and on occasion, in order to side step potential racism, the men were passed off as men that " had worked in the sun".

The Lord Mayor of London inspects an early contingent from Trinidad during the Lord Mayor's Show of 1916.

ALL IN THE DAY'S WORK.

Soldiers from the West Indies armed with mops and pails for a camp clean up.

LEAD TO CITY LADS.

Men from West Indies Enlist While Home Slackers Look On.

TRINIDAD SENDS HER SONS.

Sixty-nine men from Trinidad and twenty-three from Barbados were sworn in for Army service at the Mansion House yesterday.

The men from Trinidad are known as the Merchants' Company, and those from Barbados as the Citizens' Company, their expenses up to the time of enlistment being paid by the merchants and citizens of the two islands.

The contingent paraded outside the Mansion House at a quarter to twelve. The Trinidad men, most of whom were natives, wore their usual yellow canvas suits with B.P. hats. The men from Barbados were clad in dark blue civilian suits and wore Alpine hats.

After being drawn up in double file before the Walbrook entrance to the Mansion House the men were inspected by the Lord Mayor, who delivered a short and stimulating address.

"Sturdy sons from far-away Trinidad and Barbados," he said, "it is a great privilege for me to welcome you here to the City of London.

"You men have left your wives, your homes and your business to come over 1,000 miles to fight for your King and country.

"I see here men of the City of London who have not yet come into the Mansion House and joined up in this great fight. But to-day, when they look at you men who have made this great sacrifice, no further appeal will be necessary.

"May God bless you! He will bless you, because you have done the right and noble thing."

The men were then marched into the Mansion House, where the members of the Trinidad contingent were attested by the Lord Mayor. It is understood that the great majority of them have elected to join the 4th City of London Fusiliers, of which regiment the Lord Mayor is honorary colonel.

Like the Lord Mayor, the War Office made much of the patriotism of colonial troops and used their arrival as a means of shaming Britons into service.

TRENCHES AT WITHNOE CAMP

WEST INDIES HEAR THE CALL.

INTERESTING VISITORS TO THE MANSION HOUSE.

Additional interest is lent to the recruiting rally at the Mansion House to-day by the presence of contingents from the West Indies—sixty-nine men from Trinidad and twenty-three from Barbados. The Trinidad men were dressed in khaki, with "B.-P." hats, while the others were in navy blue, with Alpine hats.

The Lord Mayor addressed them in very cordial terms, and declared that Englishmen who had not yet come forward could not fail to be struck by the sight before them.

Subsequently the men marched into the Mansion House, where the Trinidad contingent was attested by the Lord Mayor. I was not necessary to attest the Barbadc contingent.

The men, who arrived in London la night, will immediately join various re ments, but before doing so are the guests the Y.M.C.A. at Tottenham Court-road

THE BRITISH WEST INDIES REGIMENT.

The Officer Commanding, Colonel A. E. Barchard; the Adjutant, Lieut. A. P. J. Hibbert, and some men of the Regiment at Seaford Camp, Sussex.

(Photographs by courtesy of the London News Agency Photo Co., Ltd.)

THE HALIFAX INCIDENT

Enlistment occurred throughout the British West Indies, and volunteers were sent to major ports of embarkation on larger islands where British Naval ships converted for use as troop carriers collected them. Jamaica, Barbados and Trinidad were ports of call for these ships, whose mission was to take the novice servicemen to Britain for formal training. Basic equipment was sent by Britain and issued to them in the region. However, like their European counterparts, uniforms and equipment were seldom standard issue, not least of all because the War Office had underestimated the extent and impact of the conflict. In many cases the islands used the resources they had to hand, roughly basing their designs on an interpretation of British military uniforms that had, by now, moved away from the flamboyant to the practical with the introduction of camouflage and khaki. Where necessary, the soldiers themselves supplemented the uniforms when British supplies ran low. These provisions sufficed until the men arrived at the training camps and received more standardised equipment. This initiative revealed naivety among both the regional administrators and the War Office in that the uniforms were mainly lightweight and only suitable for use in the tropics. This meant the safety of the troops during the long voyage to Britain depended heavily upon clement weather conditions.

On 6th March 1916, the *SS Verdala* set sail from Kingston, Jamaica for England with 1,000 newly-enlisted West Indian servicemen on board. The issue of a stamp, using an image from the West India Committee collection, commemorated the arrival of the first contingent of men on the *SS Verdala* in 1915. Such journeys were fraught with the risk of attack by enemy shipping in the Atlantic, and the troopships were provided with armed escorts to provide safe passage. However, on one occasion, due to the risk of attack by German U-boats, the *SS Verdala* was forced to divert to Halifax, Nova Scotia, one of Britain's most northern colonies. The ship encountered a terrible blizzard en route and the heating system on-board failed, exposing the inadequately clad soldiers to sub-zero temperatures for the first time in their lives. Many suffered frostbite, losing limbs and fingers, and five men died of hypothermia. The ship was forced to return to Jamaica with the injured recruits, having buried the dead. The plight of the men shocked and alarmed Caribbean people. Although the War Office placed an embargo on reporting the incident in the press, the West India Committee reported the 'Halifax Incident' in its Circular, expressing the anger that rightly ensued as a result of the negligence. The Admiralty expressed regret but, along with the Army, sought to play down the situation in the hope of maintaining morale and enlistment in the Caribbean.

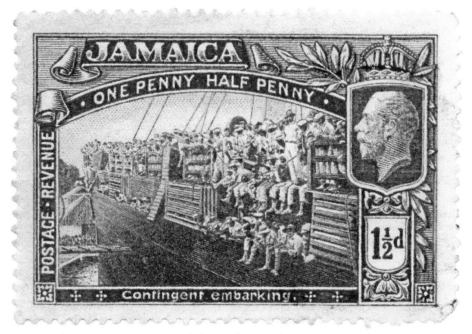

A Jamaican stamp issued during the war depicting the *SS Verdala*.

Two hundred men were sent back to Jamaica for rehabilitation, with no compensation or welfare support. *The Gleaner*, Jamaica's leading newspaper, publicised the ordeal on the front page of its 6th April 1915 edition, stating that *"We can't guess who it was that sent a thousand men from a hot tropical climate to a country of Arctic cold. Rest assured this country's indignation has been fully conveyed by the Colonial Office"*.

A West India Committee photograph.

A commemorative stamp displaying the return of the contingent in 1919.

SAILING OF THE FIRST CONTINGENT

The West India Committee photographs were used in commemorative stamps of the time.

"GLEANER" WANTS
"Gleaner" Wants Ads.
Work for You
While You Sleep.

The Daily Gleaner.

SIXTEEN PAGES.   (Established 1834)   SIXTEEN PAGES.   PRICE ONE PENNY.

LXXXII NO. 80.   KINGSTON, JAMAICA, WEDNESDAY, APRIL 5, 1916.

MYERS

Fred L. Myers & Son,

SOME MEN OF OUR 3RD WAR CONTINGENT ARE FROST-BITTEN AT HALIFAX: A POWDER PLANT BLOWS UP IN KENT WITH HEAVY LOSS OF LIFE!

ZEPPELIN RAIDS.

Over One Hundred Persons were Killed and Wounded by Bombs Dropped by German Airships on Eastern English Coast.

FRENCH AND GERMANS CLAIM GAINS IN WEST.

Turkish Forts at Points on the Smyrna Coast Have been Destroyed by a British Warship According to Report Reaching London

AEROPLANES ACTIVE OVER WESTERN FRONT.

(BY DIRECT WEST INDIA CABLE CO.)

Paris, April 3—The War Office yesterday afternoon published the following communiqué:—

"Between the Rivers Somme and Oise, our artillery was this morning particularly active in the regions of Parvillers, Foucaucourt and Lassigny. In the latter region several German trenches were shattered by our destructive fire.

"West of the Meuse the Germans launched several powerful attacks on the corner of the Avocourt Wood. All their attacks were repulsed.

"East of the Meuse the artillery action has been quite spirited throughout the day in the region of Douaumont and in the vicinity of Vaux. After a preparatory bombardment, the Germans directed four simultaneous attacks against our positions between Fort Douaumont and the Village of Vaux. Southeast of Fort Douaumont, they penetrated Caillette Wood. Our counter attack, which was delivered immediately afterwards, drove them back to the northern part of the wood. South of Vaux our lines run along the immediate outskirts of the village.

"In the Woevre district, there has been intermittent artillery activity in the vicinity of Bois le Pretre.

"In the Vosges the fire of our batteries last night caused an explosion in an enemy munitions depot west of Muenster.

"Last night one of our aerial bombing squadrons dropped 26 shells on the railway station at Dun, and also on enemy bivouacs established on the outskirts of the village of Nantillois. On the same night our aeroplanes dropped twenty-two shells on the villages of Azannes and Brinailles on the Meuse, causing numerous fires. Today our aviators brought down three enemy machines on the Verdun front, and compelled two others to land precipitately in the same region.

"This morning the Belgian artillery bombarded the German position at Merckem. In the sector east of Ramscapelle, in the direction of Dixmude, there has been a violent artillery action."

BRITISH WAR STATEMENT.

London, April 3—Last night's official announcement from General Headquarters follows:—

"Grenade fighting continues at St. Eloi, where we have taken several prisoners. Two hostile aeroplanes were driven to earth behind the German lines. One of our machines has been missing for twenty-four hours."

THE NEWS SENT OUT FROM BERLIN.

Berlin, April 3—Officially—Teutonic troops have cleared one thousand yards of French trenches north-east of Haucourt, in addition to the positions taken on March 30th.

"On the eastern bank of the River Meuse, our troops, after due preparation, took possession of the enemy defences and flanking works north-west and west of the village of Vaux. The enemy's counter-attacks failed. We captured 11 officers, 720 men and five machine guns.

"The aviators on both sides have been displaying great activity. There have been numerous aerial battles, all of which have terminated in our favour. In addition, several enemy aeroplanes have been brought down beyond our lines, and an English biplane brought up earth near Hollebek, the occupants of which were captured."

ZEPPELIN RAIDS ON ENGLAND.

London, April 3 — The Official Press Bureau announces that the total number of casualties reported in the Zeppelin raid on the night of March 31st-April 1st, reaches 43 killed and 66 injured. Nearly two hundred incendiary bombs were dropped. A Baptist Chapel, three dwelling houses and two cottages were demolished. A Town Hall, four private houses, 13 cottages and a tram car shed were partially wrecked. No military damage resulted. A number of our aeroplanes attacked the raiders. An enemy machine was reported damaged, and our land batteries brought down the Zeppelin L. 15, at the mouth of the Thames, at 9 a.m. on Saturday. The crew of the Zeppelin was captured by a scouting trawler.

THE BLOCKADE AT WORK IN NORTH SEA.

BRITISH PATROL SHIP HOLDING UP SUSPICIOUS SHIP AT NIGHT. A good idea of how the British blockade is maintained can be obtained from the above picture. Here we see one of Britain's watchers approaching a suspicious neutral.

DISASTROUS EXPLOSION

Powder Factory Blows Up in Kent, England, Yesterday Morning, with the Result that Two Hundred Workmen Lose Their Lives: Buildings for Miles Around were Shaken.

THE CAUSE OF THE TERRIBLE CATASTROPHE NOT YET ASCERTAINED

Special Cable to the Gleaner

(By W. I. & P. Telegraph Co.)
(From the Gleaner's Special Correspondent)

London, April 4—A disastrous explosion took place in a powder factory in Kent, this morning, resulting in the loss of no less than 200 lives, principally in the factory.

The explosion was of a tremendous nature, shaking buildings for miles around. Up to the present the cause of the disaster is not known.

LATEST U-BOAT MAY COMMAND CONTINGENT.

FROST BITTEN.

Transport with Third Contingent Runs Into a Canadian Blizzard at Halifax, Volunteers Suffer Severely.

106 MEN REMOVED FROM SHIP TO HOSPITAL.

Three of the Soldiers will Lose One or Both Feet, but it is Expected that all The others will be Able to Go to War.

NON-SUFFERERS GO TO WARMER CLIMATE

The mail from Arctic arriving here on Monday brought letters and possibly from some of the men who left Jamaica in the last battalion of our Contingent. Unhappily the news that came this time from our recruits was not of a pleasant nature. Exaggerated accounts of the misfortunes of the voyage began at once to be circulated, and some information which reached this office was of a distinctly alarmist nature. Wishing to obtain the authentic story of what happened to the men who left for England, a representative of the Gleaner called yesterday at His Excellency the Governor at King's House, and asked if he would give the public some information as to what had happened to the men who left Jamaica during last month.

Where the Transport Went.

It may be stated here that no one in Jamaica knew whither the transport was bound when she left our shores in the second week of March. Some persons said she was going down to England, and would be conveyed from Jamaica thither, others asserted that she was bound for Bermuda; one or two hazarded the guess that her destination was Halifax, though they could not know for certain. These were right. The ship herself, as before, sailed under sealed orders, every precaution being taken to prevent her movements from coming to the ears of the enemy. These precautions were for the good of the men on board and for the safety of the transport. Unfortunately those who made the arrangements in England never considered that those to be conveyed from Jamaica to Halifax, at a extremely cold time of the year, were men who had lived all their lives in a tropical colony and were therefore as may pray to cold.

The Governor was much concerned and deeply sympathetic. Only yesterday morning he had received letters from Halifax, and from there he took the facts contained in the statement from him which follows. He said:—

The Governor's Statement.

"I have received from Halifax some statements of what happened during the voyage of the last transport. The ship was not heated and the weather was very cold. The men were supplied with warm woollen clothing which no doubt was only suited for the English climate at this time of the year, but on approaching Halifax a blizzard came on and the cold was intense. Naturally the men, going from a tropical climate to a region of arctic coldness, suffered severely. One hundred and six were frost-bitten. These were at once removed to a hospital in Halifax, where they were promptly attended to by competent medical men, and where, I am very pleased to say, they are being treated with every kindness by the Canadian people. No advices state that three of these will lose one or both feet, while between thirty and forty others may lose a toe. The latter amputation will not interfere with the efficiency of the men as soldiers, and if they are still keen upon going to the front they will be sent on to England as soon as they are completely recovered.

"Those in sound men who are not sent on to England will be brought back to Jamaica and properly looked after. I think myself that most of these who will lose a toe or the loss of a toe will still decide to go to the front. The transport, of course, after landing the one hundred and six frostbitten men, immediately left for a warmer country, where the men are also. Those, they will be conveyed to England.

"It is very unfortunate that this thing should have occurred, but I do not think it will have any effect upon recruiting. The men who have suffered have suffered in the cause of their country quite as much as those who are damaged in action. Of course, they would much have preferred receiving their injuries in action, but as I have said, I believe that those who can go on to England after they recover will certainly do so. They also took well that they were taking risks, and they were not afraid of them.

(Continued on Page 14.)

121/Overseas/1939.

No.A.173/E/1

From,
    H.E.Lieut-General Sir G.M.Bullock,K.C.B.
      Commander-in-Chief, Bermuda.

23170

Rec̄ᵒ
Reġᵈ 17 MAY 16

To,
    The Secretary,
      War Office, London, S.W.

                      Headquarters, Bermuda.

                        17th April, 1916.

Sir,

        In accordance with the request contained in your telegram No.4853 (Q.M.G.2.) dated 12th instant, I have the honour to forward herewith the reports of the Officer Commanding the Troops and the Medical Officer as to the accommodation and cause of sickness on board the transport "Verdala". It is reported to me that on approaching the colder climate of Halifax the men used their blankets to cover up their heads and shoulders and so left their feet exposed. This is a very usual custom among the coloured people of the West Indies and I am of opinion that it was a contributory cause of many cases of frost-bite.

        It will be observed that most of the information contained in the two reports was embodied in my despatch dated 30th March, 1916, which enclosed a detailed account of the voyage submitted by Major G.V.Hart, West India Regiment, Commanding Troops, H.M.T. "Verdala".

                I have the honour to be,

                    Sir,

                      Your obedient Servant,

                      (Signed).   G.M.Bullock,

                              Lieut-General,

              Commander-in-Chief, Bermuda.

An extract from a report made by the Commander-in-Chief, Bermuda to the War Office, London on 17th April 1916, containing a possible explanation for the nature and magnitude of the casualties in the Halifax incident.

THE ROYAL FLYING CORPS

Warfare had entered the sky over a century before the Great War had commenced when the French introduced the use of hot air balloons for reconnaissance. It remains debatable whether Napoleon's decision to disband his Balloon Corps before Waterloo cost him that war.

The success of the Wright brothers in designing and building the world's first successful aeroplane changed the dynamic of the First World War. Like Napoleon's balloonists, the Royal Flying Corps were initially deployed in a reconnaissance role, swiftly moving to air to ground combat and then air to air combat, as the nations strove to out-rank each other's use of cutting-edge technology. Meanwhile,

The Wright brothers' first flight.

Germany's mammoth Zeppelins had been audaciously used to bomb London with some success. Notwithstanding a perpetual delay in the reporting of the war in Europe, the Caribbean was attuned to the technological needs of the Mother Country and raised vast sums to send nine aeroplanes to help the war effort.

Sergeant William Robinson Clarke

Many of these planes were named after the islands that had donated them. At the commencement of the conflict Sea Island cotton was one of the major products of the region. The demand for Sea Island cotton grew rapidly as the conflict took to the air, the lightweight material being used to cover the wings of the biplanes, and to manufacture the frameworks of the balloons and blimps used to patrol the Home Front. Barbados was particularly productive in supplying much needed material for the newly fledged Royal Flying Air Corps.

There are few accounts of West Indians participating in the aerial conflict. The best documented is that of Sergeant William Robinson Clarke, who is recorded as having served as a British observer and pilot. He was a RE8 pilot, and ended his war when wounded in action over Ypres in 1917. Clarke had joined the Royal Flying Corps, a service where the average life expectancy of servicemen was measured in weeks or months, not years, as the fatality rate was amongst the highest in the conflict. Yet men still wanted to join and many transferred from the army, including the British West Indies Regiment, to the Royal Flying Corps later to become the Royal Air Force, when that service was founded on 1st April 1918 by the union of the Royal Flying Corps and the Royal Naval Air Service. One prospective pilot was Norman Manley, the future Prime Minister of Jamaica, who was eventually deterred by the great expense of attending flying school.

Claude Vincent, born in Trinidad and educated at Queen's Royal College, originally joined the army and then transferred to the Royal Flying Corps in early 1918. He stayed in the military after the war and became one of the most successful of all Caribbean airmen, serving with distinction in the Third Afghan War and the Second World War. He ended his career as Air Vice-Marshal in the 1950s, having been awarded the Distinguished Flying Cross and the Air Force Cross, and having been made a Companion of the Order of the Bath and a Commander of the Order of the British Empire. He died on 8th August 1967 at the age of 71.

John Mills of Jamaica joined the Royal Flying Corps in July 1917, having originally joined the 5th Battalion of the British West Indies Regiment. He was the first man to fly to Mesopotamia and back from Egypt. He unfortunately died in an air accident in June 1919, whilst millions of servicemen were waiting for demobilisation.

Lieutenant John A.E.R. Daley, whilst serving with the 4th British West Indies Regiment, was acting as an observer when the pilot was killed. Without having flown before, he climbed into the pilot's seat and successfully landed the plane. He later transferred to the Royal Flying Corps. He died following an accident in July 1918 when, owing to engine trouble and bad light, he landed too fast, resulting in his plane overturning. He was awarded the Distinguished Flying Cross, the second to be won by a West Indian, for destroying five enemy aeroplanes and two kite balloons *"displaying marked skill and daring in these several actions, and also in attacking troops close to the ground."* The Army Chaplain later said, *"He has done splendid work both as an observer and pilot, and his death will mean a great loss to the Flying Corps. He was brave almost to recklessness, and I know he set other pilots a fine example."*

One of the most tragic stories of the Caribbean's Great War is that of Frank Watson Baille, who was born at Savanna-la-Mar, Jamaica. He joined the RAF in October 1917, receiving his commission a few months later. Like so many airmen of the time, he died in an aeroplane accident at Hounslow on 15th September 1918, less than a month before his 18th Birthday.

H.M. BIPLANE "DOMINICA"—THE GIFT OF THE ISLAND OF THAT NAME.

At the outbreak of war, the United States had a robust and vibrant Caribbean diaspora of which Eugene Jacques Bullard was a member. Born in Columbus, Georgia, Bullard was the child of a mixed-race Native American of Haitian origin and his African-American wife. Known as the Black Swallow of Death, like Clarke he entered the air force through an indirect route, serving in the French Air Service where he was a gunner. During the war he attained celebrity status and returned to a more liberal France after the war, where he received fifteen awards and was made a Chevalier of the Légion d'Honneur, a fact barely recognised in his country, America, until his death in 1961. The experience of black Americans was distinct from that of black West Indians. The legal regime of segregation that prevailed in America led the authorities to place these men on the periphery of the American Military. They were effectively treated as outcasts to such an extent that it fell upon the French to clothe black American servicemen in French uniforms.

Eugene Bullard, The Black Swallow of Death.

Unlike the Caribbean, America practised statutory segregation, preventing social integration, whilst the West Indians largely regarded integration as the norm, although less likely among its upper classes. Not only did black Americans experience poor treatment from their authorities, but also from their fellow Americans. There is little evidence of this being the experience amongst the multi-racial West Indian contingent. For black Americans the respect shown to them by many Europeans was liberating, and unlike West Indian soldiers who were keen to return home at the end of the conflict, many black Americans returned to Europe, and Paris in particular, spawning the Jazz Age of the 1920s and 1930s that would impact upon the world at large, literally placing black Americans on the world stage.

Bullard in French uniform with his pet monkey beside an early aeroplane.

Toussaint L'Overture, a slave who became Emperor of Haiti.

At the time, unlike North America, blacks comprised the majority of the population in the Caribbean, and, as such, the prospect of a change for the better was more attainable for them. Moreover, the experience of black West Indians and black Americans differed considerably. For West Indians the French were a nation that was tardy in abolishing slavery, a nation that had imprisoned and murdered Toussaint L'Overture, the erstwhile Emperor of Haiti, the first black state in the Americas, and one in which a liberated British slave could have been re-enslaved had they strayed into French territory. At the time of the conflict in Europe both black West Indians and black Americans - indeed, all colonial and allied troops - were feted as much needed support for an otherwise flagging European war effort. Nonetheless, by the end of the conflict, West Indians chose the mantra of political freedom and racial harmony at home over the syncopation of Jazz in Europe and promptly returned to the Caribbean in the pursuit of it.

The fact that black Americans were in the minority in the United States meant they would have to wait another half a century before attaining the civil rights that West Indians went on to secure for themselves after the war, many of which had been enjoyed since emancipation. This colossal social advancement for the black man was finally adopted in the United States over thirty years after it had occurred in the British West Indies.

Josephine Baker, an African American. One of the legendary stars of the Jazz Age who played upon the stereotypes of African natives in the media at the time.

Dr Martin Luther King, America's leading human rights campaigner for African Americans during the 1950s and 1960s. The youngest man to receive the Noble Peace Prize, awarded in 1964, four years before his assassination by a white supremacist.

93

A DIFFERENT EXPERIENCE OF WAR
BY DAVID WELLS

Anyone who has studied the First World War at school in Britain will have formed an image of the conflict, picturing the British Tommy fighting in appalling conditions in the muddy trenches of the Western Front. The First World War is popularly referred to as the first instance of total war. At the very least, it was the first war in British history to so deeply affect the people on the Home Front. Everyone knew someone who died during the war and most families lost at least one member. This personal link with the war has created that particular image that continues to be emotive to the present day, as shown by such representations as R.C. Sherriff's *Journey's End* and the humorous, but ultimately no less poignant, *Blackadder Goes Forth*. Yet this powerful image has tended to result in other theatres of the war, with the passage of time, being forgotten by the wider public, with a few notable exceptions such as the Gallipoli campaign. Not only are these other theatres neglected but also the role played by other peoples in the British War effort, namely those from the Colonies of the British Empire.

The contributions to the Allied War Effort of the men of the British West Indies Regiment fall firmly into these latter categories. Although they played a small part in the grand scheme of the war, it was no less vital than other regiments. Their experience of war was, however, for the most part noticeably different from that experienced by the stereotypical British Tommy. In many respects, the British West Indies Regiment presents the ideal opportunity to examine those parts of the war that do not correspond with the popular image, because it was composed of non-Europeans and the battalions that comprised the Regiment either fought in the Middle East, where a very different style of warfare was practised compared to that in Europe, or fulfilled the often undervalued role of Labour Battalions on the Western Front. By the nature and location of their service the difficulties and sacrifices made by these men have been overlooked for almost a century. Although in many ways their experiences during the war were very similar to their British counterparts, at the same time there was a marked contrast owing to the discrimination they faced for not only being colonials but also for belonging to a different race.

Of particular interest will be the experience of those battalions that fought as part of the Egyptian Expeditionary Force in the Palestinian campaign, far removed from the static trenches of France and Belgium. Even so, for those battalions that did serve in the European Campaign, their experiences differed considerably from those of the 'Tommy in the trenches'.

Mex Camp near Alexandria, Egypt.

These West Indian servicemen pose with camels that would have been a new sight to West Indians serving in the Middle East, although camels had been introduced to Antigua and Barbados without success by early settlers during the Seventeenth Century.

The Middle East Campaign

Sir Edmund Allenby.

The Middle Eastern Front produced a very different style of warfare from that of the Western Front in Europe. The British forces in Egypt were originally known as the Mediterranean Expeditionary Force and the Force in Egypt, but were amalgamated into the Egyptian Expeditionary Force on 19th March 1916 and consisted of British, Australian, New Zealand, Indian, West Indian and Egyptian Troops. The Egyptian Expeditionary Force was originally led by General Sir Archibald Murray and subsequently, from 1917, by General Sir Edmund Allenby. Their primary foe was the Ottoman Empire, which was referred to in popular contemporary parlance as 'Johnny Turk', with whom the British Empire had enjoyed an uneasy, yet largely peaceful, relationship within the region until the declaration of hostilities on 5th November 1914.

There were fewer troops in the Middle Eastern theatre than on the Western Front to the point that neither the Allies nor the Ottomans had sufficient numbers to man large-scale static defences. Static defence was therefore, of necessity, limited to key points. Thus, there were areas not covered by intense machine gun and artillery fire in which troops could manoeuvre; hence, the use of mounted cavalry (both horse and camel) and the deployment of cyclists in this theatre. Companies and other detachments frequently operated some distance from the main body of their battalion or regiment. Indeed, it was the good performance of cavalry in this region that would help preserve its use by the British Army, despite the trend towards mechanisation.

Members of the British West Indies Regiment with bicycles in the Middle East.

Map of the Ottoman Empire in 1914.

The other fundamental differences between the two theatres of war were the lines of communication and transport. The lines of communication and supply were much shorter in Europe than in the Middle Eastern theatre. Thus, given the dearth of mechanical transport, particularly in the early years, the armies in the Middle East found it difficult to concentrate large quantities of men, material and munitions and were therefore less capable of mounting the intense, sustained artillery barrages which became the norm on the Western Front.

Supplies were transported by camel.

There were, however, some similarities between the fronts: the combinations of trenches and barbed wire were used in both, as was the tactic of using artillery to break through the wire so as to allow access to enemy positions. However, it is safe to say they were not such an obstacle for the more manoeuvrable troops in the Middle East as they were on the static Western Front. The communications problems faced in the Middle East required innovative strategies. Germany had, as part of its basic battle plans, envisaged the strategic use of railways to serve the front. Moreover, the basic rail and road infrastructures on both sides on the Western Front were more developed than those in the Middle East. The lack of a developed road network meant that those railways that did exist in the Middle Eastern theatre were therefore very important. Soldiers of the 1st Battalion of the British West Indies Regiment were given assignments relating to trains, e.g. the construction of defences to protect the railway at Sheikh Zowaide or the building of a Decauville railway (a type of railway that was easy to construct, deconstruct and transport to wherever a railway may have been needed) under the guidance of the Royal Engineers.

The environment in the Middle East prevented trains being so widely used as they were in Europe, due to the impossibility of laying tracks on sand. The sand also caused other transport problems. As the writer of the 1st Battalion's War Diary reported in July 1917, the methods of transport provided to the Battalion were useless on the heavy sands of the Sinai desert. As the soft desert sand could severely impede both the movement of light vehicles and infantry, a 'road' of rabbit-netting could be laid out across the sand to assist with movement. Yet this was not an all-purpose panacea for the problem, as heavier loads could not be supported. Although other battalions and regiments were provided with camels to assist with carrying supplies and baggage, unfortunately this was not the case with the 1st Battalion, which meant that most of their supplies and baggage had to be transported by rail during their early period in Egypt, including the reserve ammunition. This meant that each man only had 120 rounds of ammunition, with no means of replenishment if they came under attack as they marched to their destination and were separated from the ammunition sent by train. The water tanks and the field kitchens also had to be carried by train, the former being especially important in the extreme heat. The 1st Battalion diaries indicate that, whilst on a march in the first half of 1917, they were able to access plentiful wells and pipelines along their routes (presumably because their routes had been reconnoitred to ensure such supplies). This was not, however, always the case and in mid-1917, through a period of intense training and marching, troops were placed on a maximum allowance of one gallon of water a day for all of a soldier's needs, such as drinking, washing and cooking. This was in temperatures of up to 112 degrees Fahrenheit/44 Celsius. Eventually though, many of the transportation problems were rectified and Lieutenant Colonel Wood Hill would claim that no unit in Palestine had better transport than the British West Indies Regiment. At one point, one of the battalions had 120 horses and mules and 36 camels attached to it. After six weeks in the Jordan valley in 1918, followed by a week of heavy marching and fighting in the hills of Moab, the regimental transport returned to Jerusalem all fit and well; this was attributed to the fondness that the men had for their animals and the great care that they showed them, as many of the men had learnt to handle animals, such as mules, from a young age on the plantations of the West Indies.

The different environment also resulted in a different set of problems for soldiers to face. Whilst troops on the Western Front had to deal with the problems caused by the cold and wet climate in Europe, such as trench foot, as well as the insanitary conditions imposed by trench warfare, in the Middle East soldiers had to face the intense day time heat, cold nights and the difficulties with the water supply. This meant that troops ran the risk of developing heat-related issues during the day, such as sunstroke, and problems relating to the cold at night; in addition, without sufficient water, they would suffer from dehydration. Whilst these difficulties were ever-present in the Middle Eastern Campaign, they could be exacerbated if troops had to take part in extended operations and thus have to move at speed via a march in the intense heat, with no opportunity to rest or refill their water bottles. Whilst soldiers on the Western Front could also catch a variety of debilitating illnesses, troops in the Middle East suffered from some particularly virulent diseases, such as Spanish influenza, malaria and sand fly fever. Disease would prove to be the biggest killer of the soldiers of the British West Indies Regiment, an experience that was not unique during the war. They also had to deal with the fauna of the region such as scorpions, lizards, snakes and large numbers of insects. In one short period, between December 1917 and January 1918, the issues they faced were more akin to those of the Western Front. At the end of 1917 the 1st Battalion took part in the pursuit of enemy troops into the mountains of Judea, following the successful British assault on the Gaza-Beersheba line. The climate rapidly changed and they went from experiencing great heat to cold and rain up in the mountains. They had nothing to counter these inhospitable climatic conditions save the summer clothing and single blanket they had carried in the Gaza-Beersheba operations; as speed was essential to the operation, they had no time to equip themselves with their winter clothing, greatcoats, extra blankets and bivouac sheets. These remained at the railhead and could not be conveyed to them owing to a lack of transport. The heavy rains also did significant damage to the roads, preventing transport by this means and the men had to deal with ankle-deep mud. Over 92 men were admitted to hospital with bronchial infections. Despite this, it was noted that the men carried out their duties with great diligence and cheerfulness.

The following January was little better, with the plains of Judea, where they were now positioned, described as being transformed into a mire of mud and water by heavy rains. During a march from Gharbiyeh to Esud, they had to proceed by a narrow track, which the heavy rains had almost obliterated and covered with water and mud; this made marching an entirely heavy, arduous task with many of the men sinking over their waists into mud and water. In another incident, the 1st Battalion's transport vehicle became stuck in mud and could not finish its journey, resulting in the Battalion having to spend a very unpleasant night with no shelter from the heavy rains. Several men contracted pneumonia during this month, with 7 dying as a result of exposure to the elements. They would face similar problems during the operations in the Jordan Valley, with a lack of blankets and coats on the march to Es Salt, and many officers and men had to be evacuated to hospital, suffering from the effects of exposure and also from an outbreak of malaria.

The British West Indies Regiment in service in the Middle East.

The Africa Campaign

Africa was also quickly drawn into the conflict with the German colony of Togoland, modern day Togo and the Volta region of Ghana in Western Africa, invaded by a force of British and French troops soon after the beginning of the war. It fell quickly and the Germans surrendered on 26th August 1914. There was also fighting in the Cameroons, another German West African colony. The West India Regiment, which had been in existence since the end of the Eighteenth Century, was involved in the conflict in this region. However, it was on the other side of the continent that British West Indies Regiment soldiers were deployed.

Paul Emil von Lettow-Vorbeck, the commander of the German Forces in East Africa, is a notable figure in that he was the only German officer permitted a victory parade upon his return to Germany after the war. He adopted a strategy of guerrilla warfare, with the aim of controlling Allied territory and thus drawing Allied resources away for the Western Front in Europe. This strategy was highly successful and the German forces were able to inflict significant casualties on British forces, whilst only receiving a sixth of the casualties they had inflicted in return.

Africa at the onset of the war, completely colonised by the European Powers Britain, Germany, France, Italy and Portugal

South African General Jan Smuts was in overall command of the Allied forces in East Africa, until he left to join the Imperial War Cabinet in 1917. This force was eventually numerically superior, including 13,000 South African and Rhodesian (modern Zimbabwean) men and over 7,000 troops from other colonies. The latter figure included the West India Regiment and a small detachment of the British West Indies Regiment. Although the fighting was difficult, Smuts' force was able to hold off the Germans and contain them. However, arguably Lettow-Vorbeck achieved his aims by keeping a large number of Allied troops occupied, whilst also maintaining his own troops as an effective fighting force. He kept fighting until after the Armistice, having only learned of it on 13th November 1918, two days after it was signed. Unlike the rest of the German forces he had not surrendered during the conflict, a fact respected by the Allies.

General Jan Smuts.

Warfare in Africa was problematic, with poor transport links making the movement of troops and supplies difficult. There were few railways and roads, and a scarcity of motor vehicles to utilise. Even pack animals were of limited use, especially in East Africa where they were subject to the lethal diseases spread by the tsetse fly. Thus, armies were reliant on human carriers to move supplies but these men had often been forced into service and, consequently, desertion rates were high, exacerbating the problem. Owing to a lack of supplies, both German and Allied forces lived off the land, plundering settlements to acquire what they needed. Disease was also rife, being the largest cause of death for troops in Africa; malaria was rampant, although dysentery was the bigger killer.

Paul von Lettow-Vorbeck during his victory parade, the only such parade by a German permitted by the victorious Allied forces.

Labour Battalions

The role of Labour Battalions in all theatres of the First World War is often overlooked, yet they performed a vital function that enabled the front-line troops, to whom, then as now, more 'glamour' is attached, to fight.

The function of a Labour Battalion was straightforward; it performed a variety of tasks that allowed the business of war to continue. For example, a Labour Battalion could be involved in the loading and unloading of supplies from a ship or train, constructing military defences and railways, manning headquarters or other installations, retrieving or burying the dead or carrying shells during battle for the artillery. The Labour Battalions were regarded as inferior by civilians and their fellow soldiers, with one view being that their role was easier than those on the front line, an impression that led to resentment amongst some fighting troops. This perceived lower status of Labour Battalions meant that it was unusual for someone to volunteer for service in one. Most men who volunteered for military service did so with the aim of being assigned to a combat unit. Indeed, Lieutenant Colonel Wood Hill, who was in command of the 1st Battalion British West Indies Regiment, commented, during a conference in Cairo in November 1916, that the use of the 3rd and 4th Battalions of the British West Indies Regiment for labour purposes in France was doing *"untold harm"* to recruitment back in the West Indies. Men would not want to join up if they knew that they were just going to be used for labour purposes rather than fighting the enemy. Thus, Labour Battalions were often assembled from those men who were unfit in some way for front-line service, either medically or by reason of age.

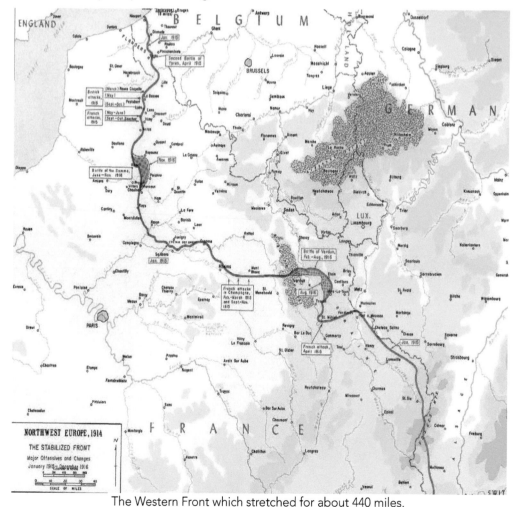

The Western Front which stretched for about 440 miles.

The widely-held view that the Labour Battalions were in some way inferior, or that they had a relatively comfortable war compared to the front-line units, does not in most cases hold true. They often had to perform psychologically and physically challenging tasks in very difficult situations; situations that were just as dangerous as those faced by the front-line soldier. For example, defences and other installations often had to be built under heavy enemy shell-fire. They also came under fire whilst serving as shell carriers for the artillery in battle. Some of their work was carried out in very exposed positions, particularly dangerous for those

A British West Indies Regiment stacking shells on Gordon Road, Ypres.

men who were unarmed and therefore not able to defend themselves. Nor were they safe from the other dangers on the Western Front i.e. disease and the elements. Indeed the British West Indies Regiment Battalions suffered terribly from the cold, in part due to a lack of adequate heating in their quarters. This was a problem exacerbated by the exceptionally cold winter of 1916-17 when water turned to ice in the hutments of the 3rd and 4th Battalions, despite the presence of two fires in each. They also had to contend with rats, lice and fleas like the rest of their comrades in arms on the Western Front.

The work that Labour Battalions performed was vital to the logistic supply of what was the first fully industrialised war. Building railway lines allowed for the rapid movement of men and supplies to the fronts, whilst building defences allowed the combat troops to engage the enemy in as safe a manner as possible and freed the latter to fight.

As stated, Labour Battalions were often drawn from those men who were in some way unsuitable for front-line service, such as those men who were too old or otherwise unfit. Hence British regiments frequently had Labour Battalions as part of their structure. Occasionally, Conscientious Objectors were used and sent to these battalions, although there was difficulty in utilising men who objected to anything to do with the war; to an extent, different roles were given to them, including that of stretcher bearers. The British Army also frequently used foreign nationals to provide labour and, in addition to the Battalions of the British West India Regiment who served on the Western Front, there were even larger numbers of South Africans and Chinese, along with smaller numbers from India and Egypt and some German POWs. The British Army also employed local people in the areas in which they were operating. Unfortunately, very few records of Labour Battalions were kept at the time; this lack of information is further exacerbated by many War Office records being lost during the bombing of London during the Second World War, thereby making it difficult to determine exactly what their individual roles and deployments were. Thus, they have often been neglected by historians. However, it is undeniable that their supporting role was vital to the war effort.

The Army Council during the war estimated that 3 non-combatant troops were required to keep 1 combatant fighting. The estimate provided by the soldiers themselves, and later military thinking, was closer to 14 to 1. By the time of the Armistice, there were almost 125,000 men serving in the Labour Battalions on the Western Front, of whom approximately 8,000 were from the British West Indies Regiment (although this is not a certain figure), accompanied by 96,000 Chinese, 20,000 South Africans and small contingents from Egypt and India.

THE BRITISH WEST INDIES REGIMENT'S OPERATIONS IN THE FIELD

BY DAVID WELLS

Battalion	Area of Deployment
1st Battalion	Egypt and Palestine
2nd Battalion	Egypt and Palestine
3rd Battalion	France and Flanders
4th Battalion	France and Flanders
5th Battalion (Reserve)	Egypt
6th Battalion	France and Flanders
7th Battalion	France and Flanders
8th Battalion	France and Flanders and Italy
9th Battalion	France and Flanders and Italy
10th Battalion	France and Italy
11th Battalion	France and Italy
12th Battalion	France and Italy
Drafts from 1st, 2nd and 3rd Battalions	East Africa

The British West Indies Regiment had a wide and varied role in opposing the enemy owing to the manner in which its Battalions were divided between the Middle East, the Western Front and, to a lesser extent, East Africa. In all theatres of war, they made significant contributions, demonstrating some outstanding examples of bravery under enemy fire, thus proving that the War Office's original concerns about the ability of the Regiment were largely unfounded.

In the Middle East, where the actions of the 1st Battalion are particularly well-recorded, the Regiment took part in some tough front-line fighting, contributing to the capture of Jerusalem by the Allied forces and were praised by General Sir Edmund Allenby, Commander-in-Chief of the Egyptian Expeditionary Force, for their distinguished service. Although their role differed significantly from their comrades in the Middle East, the British West Indies Regiment Labour Battalions on the Western Front also won praise for their efforts on some of the most famous battlegrounds of the war, such as Ypres and Passchendaele. The soldiers stationed in East Africa, separated from their comrades in the West India Regiment, were also commended for their vital work in keeping lines of communication open. In short, the Regiment distinguished itself during operations in the field.

Egypt and Palestine

The Allied forces in the Middle East faced the Turkish Ottoman Empire, whose army was supported by German officers. For over a century, the empire that the Turkish had built was considered 'the sick man of Europe', an empire on the path towards dissolution with a stagnant economy and outdated political structure. In 1916 the men of the British West Indies Regiment arrived in Egypt, then controlled by Britain, to join the fight against the Ottomans.

As has been previously noted, warfare on the Middle Eastern Front was in marked contrast to that on the static Western Front, featuring greater manoeuvrability of units and thus leading to a different style of warfare. In Palestine, the Battalions of the British West Indies Regiment had the opportunity to serve in front-line battles and add to the reputation that they had already earned in Egypt for smartness and soldierly bearing. The Regiment found itself advancing across the Sinai desert, past Gaza and Beersheba, up through Judea, Galilee and Samaria before finally reaching Northern Syria, at which juncture the Ottomans left the war. Stationed in the Middle East were the 1st, 2nd and 5th Battalions. The 3rd and 4th Battalions had also originally been transported to Egypt but were later deployed to France to serve as Labour Battalions, a destiny shared by all the later Battalions. The 5th served as a reserve Battalion, whose job was to train new men arriving in the Middle East and then send them as drafts to the two other Battalions to increase or replenish their numbers.

The 5th Battalion of the British West Indies Regiment in Egypt.

Despite being in Egypt since 1916, the 1st Battalion's first experience of combat came on 7th April 1917 when an enemy aircraft flew over their encampment at El Burj at 09:30 hours. The Regiment and the No.1 armoured train's anti-aircraft machine guns opened fire but apparently did not hit the enemy. Whilst obviously an inconclusive engagement, it is notable as it was the first instance of the Battalion having fired upon the enemy. Several other instances with similarly inconclusive results occurred over the next month and a half, as the enemy carried out bombing raids on nearby positions. Before the Battalions were truly accepted as combat units, their time was spent in training, guard and patrol duties, as well as in building engineering works. These tasks would have also occupied them in the long gaps between their periods of active combat.

The 1st Battalion's first true test came later that year on the nights of 20th and 21st July at Umbrella Hill. The Machine Gun Section, attached to the 162nd Machine Gun Company, took part in a raid on this Turkish position; this was undertaken by the Bedford Regiment, commanded by Lieutenant Colonel Brighten. The enemy post was made entirely of sand and consisted of a front line fire trench, which followed the crest of the hills, with a trench near the foot of the rear slopes, in which dugouts were burrowed. To the north and south of the trenches lay barbed wire entanglements that were four feet high and between three and four yards broad. This wire was to be breached by artillery fire, with the aim of preparing three gaps in front of the Turkish front trench by 18.00 hours on 20th July in order to allow the raiding party access.

The aim of this raid was twofold: firstly, to destroy enemy manpower by either killing enemy troops or capturing prisoners, and secondly, to destroy or capture enemy materials such as ammunition and other supplies. The role of the 1st Battalion's Machine Gun Section, along with the rest of the Machine Gun Company, was to form a box barrage; this was a barrage of fire from three sides, with the aim of preventing enemy reinforcements from advancing and, additionally, to cover a friendly force around the area that was to be raided. In preparation, the 1st Battalion had to undertake much hard work such as building suitable machine gun emplacements and moving suitable supplies of ammunition and gun stores; this was done under cover of darkness. During the night, the Machine Gun Section fired from 21:05 to 21:50 hours at an approximate rate of 50 rounds per minute. During this period they came under heavy enemy fire, being shelled with high explosives and shrapnel rounds. Fortunately, however, they suffered no casualties and, having completed their task, were withdrawn at around 02:00 hours on the morning of the 21st. The raiding party encountered little opposition when they entered the Turkish trenches and were able to carry out their objectives, save in the extreme right corner of the position. One Turkish officer and 110 other ranks were counted dead, with 17 taken prisoner. The raiding party was also able to bring back a machine gun, a trench mortar and a number of rifles.

Men of the British West Indies Regiment armed with a Vickers machine gun.

The Battalion's first proper engagement had been very successful and its conduct had not gone unnoticed. The officer that commanded the 162nd Machine Gun Company reported that *"The men worked exceedingly well, displaying the qualifications necessary for a machine gun section viz: - a keen interest in their work; cheerfulness and energy, coolness under shell fire, and an intelligent application of what was required of them. In addition, although they were only issued with Vickers Guns (a type of machine gun) a few days before the raid, their immediate action [i.e. dealing with stoppages of the guns] was excellent and they were able to keep their guns in action in a severe test."*

They were able to repeat this success a little less than a week later on the night of 27th and 28th when another raid was carried out, albeit on a smaller scale. This time heavier Turkish resistance was encountered and the raiding party had to resort to bayonet fighting in the enemy trenches.

Again, the Machine Gun Section's conduct resulted in enthusiastic commendations. Major General Hare, who commanded the 54th Division, reported that both the Brigadier and the Machine Gun Company with whom they had been working were *"full of their praises. They were under heavy shell fire and behaved splendidly."* General Allenby sent a telegram to the Governor of Jamaica, Sir William Manning, on 8th August informing him of the *"gallant conduct"* of the Machine Gun Section and commented that they had contributed *"in no small measure to the success of the operations"*. One member of the Machine Gun Section, Lance Corporal Alexander of British Guiana (No. 18), even received the Military Medal; a decoration first introduced the year before and awarded for bravery under fire. On the night of the first raid, he was operating a machine gun in a front-line position and managed to keep firing for 45 minutes despite being subjected to heavy shelling and having his own gun hit by enemy fire. During the second raid, he managed to keep firing for 30 minutes even though the flash blind and the screw were knocked down. All in all, the raids were a resounding success for the 1st Battalion, even though their action had been limited to just the Machine Gun Section. A larger-scale test would come later in the year at Two Tree Farm and Atawineh Redoubt.

Towards the end of 1917 the 1st Battalion took part in a more extensive operation, planned by General Allenby, on a Turkish defensive position known as the Gaza-Beersheba line. The objective of this attack was to cause the Turkish defences to collapse and thus allow Allenby the opportunity to capture Jerusalem. Symbolically, this was hugely significant, given the city's religious and historical importance.

As part of the preparations for this grand assault, the 1st Battalion moved into the trench network at a place called Dumbell Hill on 25th September. By 29th October, all the preparations for the attack were complete. The 1st Battalion of the British West Indies Regiment, which was attached to the 20th Indian Infantry Brigade, was assigned to a body known as Composite Force, comprising Headquarters' signal section, the Imperial Service Cavalry, the 2nd Queen Victoria's Own Sappers and Miners, the Detachment Français de Palestine, a Bersaglieri Battalion of the Italian Contingent and the Tenth Field Company.

SOME OFFICERS OF THE BRITISH WEST INDIES REGIMENT.

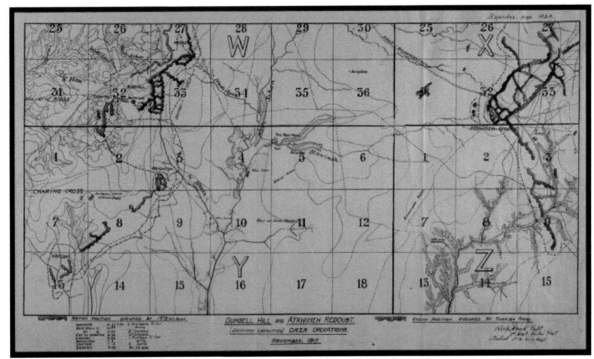

1st Battalion's War Diary Map of Dumbell Hill Locality.

The Battalion's role was to fill the gap between the XXth and XXIst Army Corps, specifically the line between Dumbell Hill and Um Riul. Whilst their job was to advance the line closer to a Turkish position known as Atawineh Redoubt, which was held by the 3rd Battalion of the Turkish 58th Regiment, the aim was to induce the defenders to believe that an attack was imminent and thus pin them down to hold their position, presumably so that they would not then be able to intervene against the main forces of the XXth and XXIst. This objective had been achieved by 1st November but until 8th November the enemy heavily shelled the line at Dumbell Hill. By nightfall on 6th, it was clear that the wider Allied attack on the line was a success, with Gaza being evacuated by the Turks. However, the Ottoman army still held the Atawineh Redoubt and thus a squadron of Imperial Service Cavalry, led by Lieutenant Kelly, was sent along with two platoons of the 1st Battalion to take up position at Two Tree Farm in between Dumbell Hill and the Redoubt. From there they were to proceed to the Redoubt for a reconnaissance in force of the position. Upon reaching the farm, the two platoons were left to hold the position whilst the cavalry proceeded up the Wadi Atawineh. When they reached the head of the Wadi, they dismounted and proceeded in skirmishing order towards the Redoubt. At 11:30, when they were within six hundred yards of their target, they came under heavy shell, rifle and machine-gun fire and were thus forced to retreat towards the farm. In this attack a bursting shell killed Lieutenant Kelly. At 12:00, whilst the cavalry were arriving back, Two Tree Farm was being visited by Lieutenant Colonel Wood Hill, commander of the 1st Battalion, and his adjutant Captain Fink. At this juncture there was apparently confusion, as the orders given to Kelly had not been passed to his subordinates. Presumably on Wood Hill's orders, Captain Fink assumed command of the mission, whilst Wood Hill went to report to Brigade Headquarters. A stretcher party was dispatched to retrieve Kelly's body and the cavalry were ordered to withdraw back to the British line whilst the two platoons of the 1st Battalion provided cover. At this point the farm came under heavy shellfire and the Wadi Sihan, the only route of exit from Two Tree Farm, was subjected to a heavy barrage. Taking up successive positions down the Wadi, the platoons withdrew through the barrage fire and reached Well Farm, which was already held by another platoon of the 1st Battalion.

Later, at 23:00, two platoons commanded by Second Lieutenants Garrett and Clarke and the Signal Section under Second Lieutenant Masters, under the overall command of Captain Fink, returned to Two Tree Farm. They then proceeded up towards Atawineh Redoubt in order to determine if the position was still held by the enemy and then, if possible, planned to cut through the barbed wire defences and enter the Redoubt. The advanced works were found abandoned, but then there was a slight loss of direction that resulted in a patrol reaching the Gaza-Beersheba road with no sign of either barbed wire or the enemy. As it was getting light by this time, the patrol returned to Two Tree Farm and reported to headquarters. Under the cover of the morning mist, a second patrol commanded by Second Lieutenant Garrett reached the Redoubt to find it abandoned with large amounts of supplies left.

The action surrounding Two Tree Farm, although not as successful as originally envisaged, was still an important test for the Regiment and demonstrated their skill and bravery, with all ranks noted to have proved resilient under trying circumstances. To demonstrate this, several men were decorated for their actions. Firstly, Captain Fink was given the Military Cross for his *"high qualities of skill and leadership"* in his actions of taking command, re-organising the troops and then successfully withdrawing the whole party under heavy fire without sustaining a single loss. Three other ranks were awarded the Military Medal for their actions at Two Tree Farm. The first award went to Lance Corporal Johns of Jamaica (No.2331), who had laid a telephone wire from Dumbell Hill to Two Tree Farm and had established a telephone station there. He remained with the troops covering the cavalry's withdrawal and held his post, in a particularly exposed position under heavy fire, thus maintaining telephone communications with Headquarters throughout. Secondly, Private Hyndman of Trinidad (No.368) demonstrated a fine example of courage and devotion to duty and his comrades by repeatedly volunteering to run messages from Captain Fink to the advance troops during the withdrawal from Two Tree Farm, despite the heavy shellfire. Finally, Private Pullar of Jamaica (No.2434), who was engaged as a scout in No Man's Land on the night of 7th to 8th of November, was recognised for his bravery. When the main patrol to Atawineh Redoubt had failed to reach its objective, he volunteered to reconnoitre and brought back valuable information about the enemy's movements. Following these operations and the subsequent fall of Jerusalem, Lieutenant Colonel Wood Hill was temporarily detached from the 1st Battalion to serve as the Provisional Commandant of Jerusalem, which indicated that he was held in good regard by Command.

General Allenby entering Jerusalem.

During these operations, the 2nd Battalion did not engage in any front-line combat but they too had a role to play. The four companies were divided, with C and D companies acting as Corps Troops for Headquarters XXI Corps, and A and B attached to the Desert Mounted Corps. Although they engaged in no actual fighting, they were constantly under artillery and aircraft fire, and also guarded and escorted prisoners as well as holding outpost and reserve posts. The commanders of both Corps expressed their thanks for their actions and Captain/Adjutant Thomas was awarded the Military Cross for gallantry. Captain Cox and Lieutenant Rutty were mentioned in dispatches. However, the 2nd Battalion would have an opportunity to prove their mettle in battle the following year when both the 1st and 2nd Battalions would find themselves serving in the Jordan Valley.

MEDICAL INSPECTION, SINAI DESERT   KIT INSPECTION

Early in July 1918, following a period of intense training, the 1st and 2nd Battalions were ordered to join the 232nd Infantry Brigade of the 75th Division. However, this had to be cancelled owing to an outbreak of Spanish influenza. Instead, when August came they were assigned to join the Desert Mounted Corps in the Jordan Valley and be attached to the A.N.Z.A.C. Mounted Division. The force defending the Jordan Valley was known as Chaytor's Force, after its overall commander Major General E.W.C. Chaytor.

Major General Sir Edward Chaytor

It was composed of Chaytor's own A.N.Z.A.C. Mounted Division, the 20th Indian Infantry Brigade, the two British West Indies Regiment Battalions, the 38th and 39th Battalions of the Royal Fusiliers and four Batteries of the Royal Artillery. Their purpose was to engage the enemy, draw their attention and, if possible, make them think that their force was larger than it truly was. Upon their arrival in the Valley, they spent September in preparation for operations. An unnamed correspondent in the 1st Battalion wrote to the West India Committee Circular saying that *"This valley is not a health resort and the conditions of life are trying. The heat is intense and malignant malaria is prevalent."* It was discovered from captured and deserting enemy soldiers that, holding the Turkish line in front of the 1st Battalion, was the enemy's 1st, 2nd and 3rd Battalions of 58th Regiment whom they had previously engaged at Atawineh Redoubt. The men were lightly equipped so that they could move about with ease, and with speed should it be required. All reserve water was to be carried by separate transport.

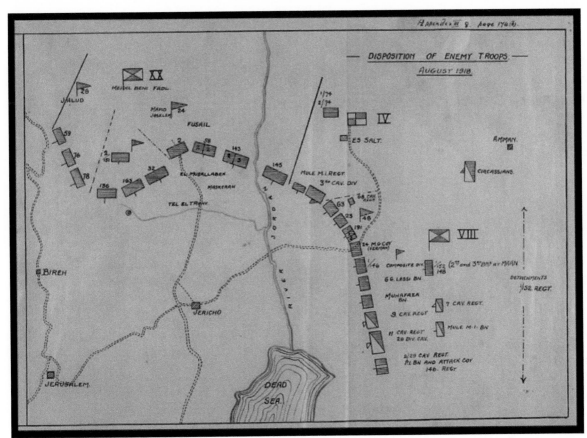

A map from the War Diary of the 1st Battalion showing the 'Disposition of Enemy troops, August 1918'.

On the night of 18th and 19th September the 2nd Battalion performed its first action in combat. Stationed at a post on the Wadi Abeid, they were ordered to advance towards Bakr and Chalk Ridges, with the aims of clearing all the intervening foothills of enemy posts, of discovering their foe's strength and of preventing them from working around the right flank of the XXth Corps. This would straighten the British Line and also prevent the enemy attacking the right flank of the 53rd Division. At 04:30, three companies, B, C and D, under the commands of Captains Cox, Roper and Orrett, began their advance across 600 yards of open country with great steadiness in the face of heavy enemy fire. The correspondent in the 1st Battalion commented that *"The moment the men appeared over the crest, they came under heavy artillery fire and the behaviour of the men was simply splendid, in fact, could not have been better"*. Frank Cundall reports that an Artillery Major, whose name has been lost to history, presumably upon seeing the West Indians advance over open ground through a hail of shrapnel, commented in a tone of blank astonishment: *"My God! Are they Angels or damn fools? Don't they see shells, don't they hear shells, don't they know what shells are?"* The action was completely successful and the 2nd reached their objective on the right bank of the Wadi Bakr, taking cover from enemy fire under no more than that afforded by the rocky slope, having demonstrated that they could well match their comrades in the 1st for bravery; 40 men were wounded and 9 were killed. By the morning of 20th September, two platoons of the 2nd's B Company held Bakr and Chalk Ridges.

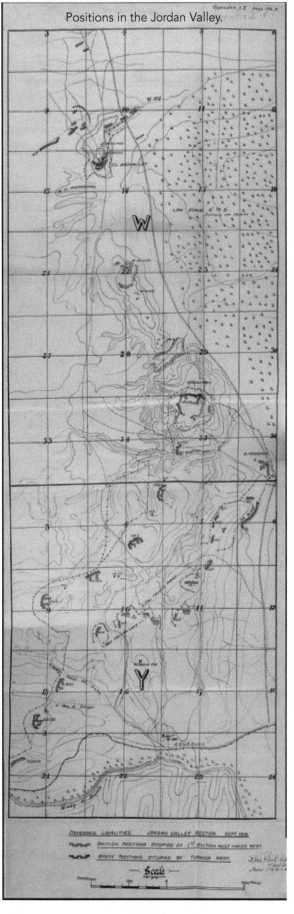

That same day at 06:00, two platoons of the 1st's B Company, under Captain Cavenaugh, occupied Grant Ridge and Baghallat, with both positions having been reported previously abandoned by the enemy. An hour after this, Captain Craig and A Company moved out to reinforce them, but no sooner than they had left the British defensive wire, they came under heavy fire. They made it to the new position after moving through a barrage with slight casualties. However, B Company, who had been intended to withdraw when A Company arrived, owing to this heavy fire, had to wait until nightfall before they could move. The enemy barrage also made it difficult to supply water and ammunition to British positions furthest from the line.

At 16:00 on 21st the 1st Battalion were given orders to concentrate at Fusail at midnight to meet up with the New Zealand Mounted Brigade. They had to leave their positions at Meskerah, Mussellabeh, Grant Ridge and Baghallat, which were all manned by D company that was to be left behind. Upon their arrival, they received orders to proceed to Jisr-El-Damieh where they would be required to take part in an action the next morning. This necessitated a long, arduous and, above all, rapid march. Thus, the 1st and 2nd line transports and the brigade train were left at Fusail, as were the men's blankets and kit. The march would have to be carried out across the enemy's front, east of the River Jordan and the road that they would be using was under enemy observation, thus making it imperative that they travelled under cover of darkness. They managed to arrive at 05:00 following a 15 ½ miles march, with each man only having the water contained within his own bottle and no water supplies available on arrival. Following an hour's rest, C Company under Major Harragin moved into action on the right of the Auckland Mounted Rifles, who were held up opposite the Damieh Bridgehead. At 10:50 they managed to break through the enemy defence with a bayonet charge and occupied the heights overlooking the bridge itself. From this position, small parties pushed down towards the river itself, bayoneting the gunners and bombers of the bombing post left by the enemy, and were then able to secure the crossing. Four of the Battalion's Lewis guns were brought to bear, killing parties of the enemy that attempted to cross and also preventing the remainder from escaping, thus allowing them to be captured.

An extract from the War Diary of the First Battalion.

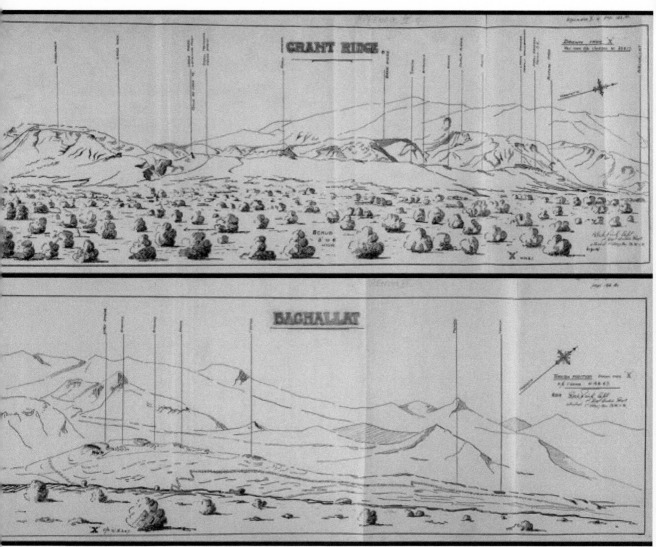

Maps from the War Diary of the 1st Battalion.

The action of capturing a key bridgehead over the Jordan was a great success with only one 'other rank' being wounded. This was attributed to taking the enemy by surprise and the action being carried out so swiftly that the Turks had no time to reorganise. As a result, enemy fire became very wild and inaccurate. Over 100 Turkish prisoners were captured, including 8 officers, as well as 3 machine guns, an auto-rifle and a number of horses and pack mules. It was estimated that about 200 Turkish troops were buried at the bridgehead. Following this, the 1st Battalion held the bridge position whilst the Auckland Mounted Rifles proceeded to chase the retreating enemy troops.

Whilst the 1st were engaged at Damieh Bridge, the 2nd Battalion found themselves having to counter an enemy force of between 400 and 500 men. This force had crossed the Jordan at Mafid Josele Bridge and proceeded to counter-attack in the direction of Fusail, thus threatening the right flank of the New Zealand Mounted Brigade and the 1st Battalion, with the aim of cutting the British lines of communications 8 miles to the rear of the line.

Fortunately, the 2nd was able to intercept this incursion, with Lieutenant Colonel Poë leading out A, B and C Companies to meet the enemy force within 1000 yards of the Roman road to Fusail. B and C Companies moved in, with A Company in reserve. B and C Companies came under heavy machine-gun and artillery fire but, upon being reinforced by A Company, they were able to push forward and succeeded in driving the enemy back to the wadis covering Mafid Josele Bridge. The Turks were able to hold the 2nd Battalion until dusk, when they were repelled back across the Jordan by 18:15. The 2nd Battalion were able to capture 40 of the enemy and prevent them from destroying the bridge. Unfortunately, this action was not as casualty free as the 1st's, with the 2nd Battalion War Diary noting 5 wounded and 1 captured, though fortunately the latter was recaptured the next day.

MESS AT BEERSHEBA

SHELLAH

DAMIEH BRIDGE

CHURCH PARADE, SHEIK ZOWAIED

Following these actions, the 1st Battalion found themselves on a hard march to Es Salt in the mountains and then proceeded to Amman, where they were deployed in guarding valuable rolling stock and dumps of captured guns and other enemy materials. This was to be the Regiment's last participation in an action in the Middle Eastern Campaign. In the meantime, the 2nd Battalion guarded the Damieh Bridgehead and then returned to Jerusalem. An armistice was signed on Thursday 31st October 1918 between the Allies and Turkey; the campaign in the Middle East was over.

Again, the Regiment won several awards for their actions in the Jordan Valley. Captain Craig, from British Guiana, of the 1st Battalion won the Military Cross for taking his company through the artillery barrage on their way to reinforce B Company, in a *"most efficient"* manner. The fact that casualties were so few in number, although his company was under shellfire day and night, was attributed to his leadership. Major Harragin of Trinidad also won the Military Cross for his leadership at Damieh Bridgehead, having shown *"great judgement"*.

Several soldiers were also recipients of the Distinguished Conduct Medal. Lance Corporal Richard Turpin of Trinidad (No.503) ran a signal wire some two and a half miles between Mussellabeh and Baghallat on 20th under heavy fire. He also went out twice by himself to repair the wire, again under heavy fire. When he returned to HQ that afternoon, he volunteered to go out and do so again in similar circumstances. Private Hezekiah Scott from Jamaica (No.6357) volunteered to take a message from Baghallat to Grant Ridge on 20th. He crossed 700 yards of open ground under heavy fire and delivered the message. On his return journey, he stopped to deliver aid to Sergeant Chan who had unfortunately already died, the only fatality the 1st Battalion suffered in the Jordan Valley operations. Sergeant Julien of Grenada (No.1454), at Damieh Bridge, in the absence of his officer, commanded his platoon with the utmost efficiency during the attack on the bridgehead, showing "high powers" of command and leadership. His platoon took the attack with "great dash" and after the successful assault he organised his platoon and led them with impressive gallantry into the broken ground overlooking the river, which was still occupied by the enemy, and was able to capture a number of prisoners and machine guns.

There are many examples of individual valour. Amongst those soldiers of the 1st Battalion who won the Military Medal was Private Dick from Trinidad (No.594), one of a party of Lewis gunners at Damieh who were working forward of the line. Noticing an enemy machine gun within close range, he rushed forward alone under heavy fire, bayonetting two of the enemy gun team and capturing the gun. Private Marques from Trinidad (No.9192) singlehandedly worked around an enemy bombing post's flank and destroyed it using explosives, killing six of the enemy, wounding two and taking two prisoners. Lance Corporal Leekham of Trinidad (No.661) was in charge of four Lewis Guns at Damieh, showing great resource and handling his guns with great efficiency. He greatly assisted the company in the attack by taking up a forward position on the flank and bringing heavy fire to bear on the enemy. After the success of the attack, he took his guns forward, of his own accord, to the high ground overlooking the bridge and brought heavy fire to bear on the bridge, thus preventing the enemy escaping.

Although their citations for bravery are not recorded in such detail as their 1st Battalion counterparts, the 2nd Battalion also won several awards: Lieutenant Colonel Poë, the Distinguished Service Order; Captain Thomas, the Distinguished Service Order and bar to his Military Cross; Surgeon Captain Curphey and Capt. Cox both won the Military Cross; Regimental Sergeant Major Clements (No.8001) and Regimental Quartermaster Sergeant Inman (No.5707), the Distinguished Conduct Medal; Sergeant Halliburton of Jamaica (No.1955) won his Military Medal for his actions in repelling the enemy incursion across the Jordan; Lance Corporal Sampson (No.2063) and Private Spence (No.2401), both from Jamaica, received the Military Medal for their role in the advance to Bakr and Chalk Ridges.

Sergeants of the British West Indies Regiment in Palestine.

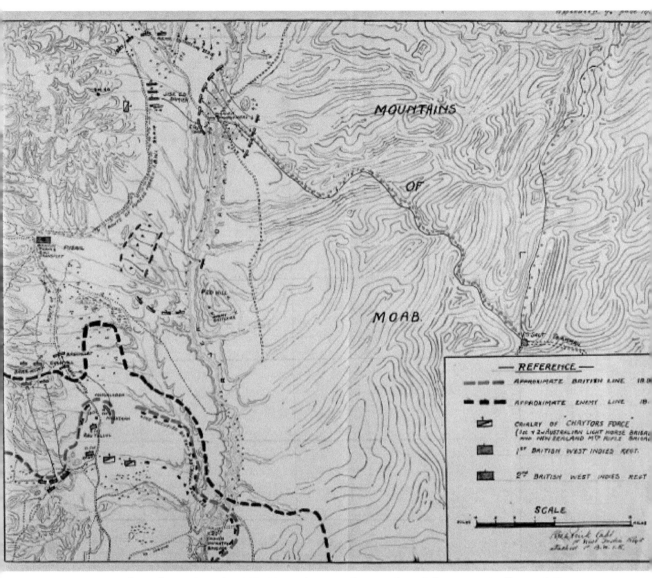

A Map from the 1st Battalion War Diary showing the position of the troops in Chaytor's Force.

Major General Chaytor was very impressed by the work of the Regiment and sent telegrams to the Battalions saying that there were no troops outside his own division whom he would rather have with him and that they had won the "highest opinions" of all those who had served with them in the Jordan Valley. He repeated this sentiment when he inspected the 1st and 2nd on 22nd November by saying that his own division liked fighting alongside the Regiment and could not wish for better; all reports of them had been favourable. With that he thanked them, told them that the war was over and wished them a safe return to their own country.

East Africa

The Regiment also had a presence in East Africa during the war. The aim of the campaign was to eliminate the threat of the German colony of Tanganyika, today known as Tanzania.

A draft of 500 men was sent to the region, comprising 2 officers and 300 other ranks from the 1st Battalion, three officers and 100 other ranks from the 2nd Battalion and the same from the 3rd. They arrived from Egypt in August 1916 at Kilikandi in order to aid the British force that was being outmanoeuvred by the enemy Askari. Their role whilst there was minimal, mainly consisting of guard duties, although this in itself did play a part in the strategy for the overall capture of Dar-Es-Salaam. Owing to their small numbers, the fact that they would not be able to receive reinforcements, and that their effective strength had been reduced by the harsh effects of the climate, they were not included in a division for a later advance against the enemy. Despite this, in 1917 a detachment of the draft was sent to capture an enemy supply base at Maduba, a successful operation that resulted in Captain Cressell, the detachment commander, being awarded the Military Cross for his role in the action. Later in the year, a small party of 6 men, led by Corporal Tomlinson, found an enemy ammunition dump located south of the Rufugi River and then made a march of over 300 miles to re-join the main body of the draft. For this feat they were mentioned in dispatches. When

A German Askari soldier

inspected in June 1918 by Lieutenant General van Deventer, who was Commander-in-Chief of the force in East Africa, he commented that they had done all that was asked of them and that they had coped well with the difficult environmental conditions in which they found themselves.

A colonial map of East Africa.

The Western Front

In contrast to the well-documented exploits of the 1st and 2nd Battalions, it is much more difficult to produce an ordered account of the exploits of those British West Indies Regiment Battalions that served in a labour capacity on the Western Front. Technically speaking, the units were never officially designated Labour Battalions and remained as Infantry Battalions; some were armed accordingly, yet in their function they clearly served as the former. Corporal William Dale of the 10th described his armaments as a Lee Enfield rifle with a bayonet and shoulder strap, a dagger and a buttoned holster with a Wembley revolver. The Battalions were primarily involved in manning ammunition dumps, loading and unloading supplies and ammunition at railheads, and moving shells at batteries. These positions were, of course, particularly dangerous for the men because they were constantly at risk of enemy attack, as the Germans wished to destroy reserves of ammunition, break up the railways to hinder or halt Allied supply lines and destroy Allied artillery. As such, most of their work was carried out under heavy fire and they endured heavy casualties. Sir Etienne Dupuch O.B.E., later the editor of the *Nassau Tribune* and a member of the Bahamian House of Assembly, wrote about his First World War experiences at Passchendaele Ridge: *"We were taken there to expedite the delivery of shells to the heavy artillery. Our location was a real danger spot. We lost a lot of men there. The Germans laid down a barrage that covered a wide area."*

Passchendaele, infamous for the mud and scale of the casualties which exceeded 325,000 for the Allies and 260,000 for the German army.

Men of the West India Regiment who will soon help to swell the British ranks at the front. Inset: Three of these doughty fighters cleaning their rifles. There is no part of the Empire that has not sent soldiers to the Homeland in her time of need.

The British West Indies Regiment's efforts in the face of such carnage contributed to the Allied action at some of the Western Front's most iconic battlefields, including the Somme, Ypres, Vimy Ridge, Passchendaele, Arras and Messines. They were also engaged in a variety of other tasks: they dug cable trenches, worked on railways and gun emplacements, moved supplies and those who were armed were assigned to guard duty. All these tasks provided vital support for the front line.

Given the low esteem in which most Labour Battalions were held, it might have been expected that those Battalions of the British West Indies Regiment assigned to this support role would be unhappy with their task, yet this does not necessarily appear to have been the case. When the Commanding Officers of the 3rd and 4th Battalions, Lieutenant Colonels Barchard and Hurt, heard about the conference in Cairo, which resolved that the Regiment would be best used in warmer climates and in a more active role, they wrote a letter to the War Office which rejected the idea that the officers and men of the Battalions were unhappy moving shells and stated that they did not wish to go to Egypt. It is also clear that the men took a certain pride in their work, hence the *"King George Steam Engine"* moniker that they adopted. This name may have also helped them to distance themselves in some way from other Labour Battalions. Yet this positive attitude appears not to have been shared by all the men. On 23rd January 1917, the men of the 3rd, who were working on coaling the *SS Megantic* at Marseille docks, apparently were a source of some trouble, which resulted in several of them being arrested by the Provost Marshal. This discontent with coaling appears to have continued throughout the month. The reasons for this trouble are unknown. It may be that carrying shells and ammunition may have been more in line with the expectations of volunteers who wished to strike at the enemy, whilst coaling ships may not have had the same appeal.

The 3rd and 4th Battalions were the first contingents to arrive in France at the beginning of September 1916, having come from Egypt. Upon their arrival they were deployed at the Somme, where they were primarily used for moving ammunition. It was partially due to the success of these Battalions in fulfilling their orders that the creation of later Battalions was requested. The 6th Battalion was the first to be sent directly to France in April 1917 and, following a spell of training at Arras, they proceeded to the Ypres Salient. They handled ammunition at dumps, railheads and the batteries in this area during the taking of Puckem Ridge, Poelcappelle and Passchendaele. The 7th Battalion would soon follow, landing at Brest in June 1917. A month later, the 8th arrived and the 9th arrived in August 1917.

The 10th Battalion arrived in France at Le Havre in October 1917 and from there proceeded to St Omer where they were divided into two. A and D Companies went to the Ypres Salient to act as shell carriers for the artillery. It is also attested by Corporal William Dale that they spent time guarding land recaptured from the Germans whilst the Allied Forces advanced. B and C companies were attached to the Royal Flying Corps stations near St. Omer until the beginning of January 1918. In January they left for the Taranto base, where they were to spend the rest of the war. The 11th Battalion was sent to work at Taranto as soon as they arrived in Europe.

Ruins at Ypres.

Many of the Battalions wintered at the Taranto base in Italy during 1917-18, where they engaged in construction work, loaded and unloaded ships and trains and loaded lighters with stores and ammunition for the British Forces in the East. This decision to move them to a warmer area was probably due to the difficulties that the Regiment had faced in the previous winter. The 8th and 10th Battalions spent their time at Taranto from May 1918 to the Armistice working on the quays, a role that was of particular importance as it was through Taranto that all ammunition, clothing and food reached the British Forces in Salonika, Mesopotamia and Egypt. This was primarily due to the presence of enemy submarines near Gibraltar, which prevented it from being an effective supply base.

Whilst the support role of the British West Indies Regiment on the Western Front did not share the 'glamour' of their comrades' actions in the Middle East, they too had their own share of anecdotes and awards to take home. Only a selection of their exploits is recorded here.

Second Lieutenant Dunlop of the 4th Battalion won the Regiment's first Military Cross of the war for his actions on 7th November 1917 for extinguishing a burning ammunition dump. As mentioned previously, Second Lieutenant J.A.E.R. Daley of the 4th Battalion successfully landed an aeroplane without having flown before. Captain Robertson of the 4th was awarded a Military Cross for his actions at the railhead on which the Battalion was working whilst supporting the Canadians during the operations at Vimy Ridge; he rescued wounded men and saved ammunition.

On 2nd July 1918 enemy aircraft bombed La Bezeque Farm ammunition dump and it was only saved through the actions of Sergeant Miller (No.500), Sergeant McDonald (No.4136), Corporal Evans (No.5781) and Lance Corporal Cummings (No.14997) of the 3rd. In October 1917 the 4th Battalion won around eight Military Medals, thanks to the efforts of Sergeant Holland (No.3970), Company Quartermaster Sergeant Goater (No.19259), Private French (No.4368), Private Barton (No.4736), Private Davis (No.5777), Private De Pass (No.5766), Private Williams (No.8292) and Private Ferguson (No.6260). On one occasion, two of these men jumped on a cordite dump that was on fire and in the process of exploding. They pulled off the tarpaulin covering and helped to separate the burning ammunition and extinguish it. Several boxes exploded whilst they were

The War Illustrated, 7th October, 1916.

New Colonial Warriors

on the stack and one man's clothing was badly burned. Private Walker (No.7936) of the 7th Battalion won the Military Medal on 1st September 1917 for remaining behind on the top of a lit ammunition dump when all others had left; he rescued live rounds, with already ignited charges, from the centre of the dump and removed the adjoining boxes which had not exploded, despite having caught fire.

On 7th November 1917 an incendiary bomb was dropped on the Harengo ammunition dump near Boshinge. Private Thomas (No.10686) of the 7th Battalion noticed that the resultant fire was near to the boxes containing gas shells and high explosive shells and alerted the other men. He then proceeded to run to the dump to extinguish the flames and was quickly joined by Corporal Walker (No.10799), Lance Corporals Archer (No.9621) and Boyce (No.9741) and Private Smith (No.10619). Despite the heavy bombing of the area, they were successful in quelling the fire. For this Corporal Walker had a bar added to the Military Medal he had received previously; the others received the award for the first time.

Men of the British West Indies Regiment on the Albert-Amiens Road.

There are contradictory reports regarding the performance of the British West Indies Regiment on the Western Front. The 4th were well regarded by the officers in charge of the ammunition dumps at Puckevillers; apparently the West Indian soldiers *"worked exceedingly well"* and gave *"every satisfaction"*. Colonel Balfour, who was in charge of the 15th Labour Group, was very pleased with the manner in which they had unloaded ships at the Quai de France when they were stationed at Rouen. Sir William Manning, following a visit to the British West Indies Regiment Battalions in France, made a speech in December 1917 to the Jamaican Legislative Council in which he recalled that an officer of the High Command had said to him, *"I understand that there is some probability that the men may be moved from this area; if that is so, I do not know how I should get on without them"*. In one instance, 60 men of the 6th Battalion unloaded a staggering 375 tons of ammunition in less than two hours. Reverend Ramson, the Padre of the 6th Battalion, later recalled how everyone who came into contact with the British West Indies Regiment was always full of admiration for them and that officers of other Labour Companies, upon encountering his Regiment, always spoke very favourably of *"those fine fellows from the West Indies"*. On 28th October

1918, the 7th Battalion received a communique from 4th Army Command which thanked them for their hard work and commented on their zeal, energy and industriousness, as well as their continually upbeat attitude and endurance of hardship. Field Marshal Haig himself wrote to the West India Committee to comment that, *"In spite of casualties, the men have always shown themselves willing and cheerful workers, and the assistance they have rendered has been much appreciated by the units to which they have been attached and for whom they have been working"*. Despite all of these very favourable reports, however, there were others that cast doubt on their effectiveness. During the 3rd and 4th Battalions' stay at Marseilles in early 1917, the British West Indies Regiment work rate was allegedly inferior to their counterparts in the Bermuda Royal Garrison Artillery, moving only 1.12 tons of coal per man per working day as opposed to 4.92 tons. A 1918 report on the British West Indies Regiment in France described them as *"of considerable value in handling ammunition in warm weather, but practically useless in wet and cold weather. On the whole, however, this labour was not a success"*.

Portrait of Haig at General Headquarters, France, by Sir William Orpen, an official war artist, May 1917.

A question remains as to whether the British West Indies Regiment ever took a more active role on the Western Front. Despite no clear military evidence that they were ever used in combat, George Blackman of the 4th Battalion later reported an incident in which he fought in the trenches alongside white soldiers.

Field Marshal Haig's Comments in the West India Committee Circular, 10th January 1918.

However, no official record of usage in combat exists. As the War Office records of the Regiment were destroyed during the Blitz there is little supporting evidence remaining.

The excellent performance of the 1st and 2nd Battalions in Egypt and Palestine demonstrated that the War Office's claim that they were not suited to a combat role was fundamentally wrong. Those troops who were stationed in East Africa were too few in number to really distinguish themselves and mainly served as guards, but did take part in action on rare occasions. The work done by the Labour Battalions on the Western Front, while not sharing the perceived glamour of front line units, was still vital to the war effort and they performed hard, physical work in conditions no less dangerous than that of their comrades in the Middle East. Whilst there appears to have been some who resented this role, most seem to have embraced it; though some expressed concerns about their work, on the whole they seem to have been held in high esteem. It is evident that the soldiers of the British West Indies Regiment performed well across all theatres of war in very dangerous and climatically inhospitable conditions, notably under shell fire, whether in support roles or in direct action.

The King's Christmas Message 1918

We are no longer fighting. God has blessed your efforts. The Queen and I offer you our heartfelt good wishes for a happy Christmas and many brighter years to come. To the disabled, sick and wounded we send a special greeting, praying that with the returning health you may be comforted and cheered by the vision of those good days of peace for which you have sacrificed so much.

King George V's Christmas Message to the British Empire.

WEST INDIAN HEROES

The decorations awarded to the men of the Caribbean were won in the service of various regiments in the British and Indian Armies. This was the case for Alexander De Pass, a member of a distinguished Jamaican family, who was awarded the Victoria Cross posthumously for his service in the 34th Prince Albert Victor's Own Poona Horse for conspicuous bravery and devotion to duty whilst serving in the Indian Army as part of the Expeditionary Force in 1914. Like so many impatient young West Indians, Du Pass made his own way into the army rather than wait for the formation of a new contingent from the region. As there are no comprehensive, consolidating records of men such as De Pass who took this route into the military, it remains impossible to identify all who served and learn of their experiences and achievements. This exercise is further hindered by the huge diversity in the origins of West Indians, which allows little scope to rely upon surnames alone to identify these brave men.

By the end of 1918 every corner of the world had finally laid their arms to rest. To mark the end of the conflict, British servicemen were awarded The British War Medal and The British Victory Medal, affectionately known as Pip and Squeak, thereby ensuring that every man that had participated bore evidence of his contribution. Badges, brooches and other memorabilia were devised for mass consumption, signifying the roles played by both civilians and the military. The West India Committee advertised these items in its fortnightly circulars, ensuring that profits went towards the costly post war effort.

As well as the living, every serviceman who lost their life during the war was commemorated by large bronze medallions known as "Death Pennies". Each bore the name and rank of the fallen, and was sent to their next of kin as a personal memorial. These classically-styled pieces were by far the largest medal struck by the British Army in its entire history and remain one of the most poignant.

Major-General Sir E.W. Chaytor decorating the 1st and 2nd Battalions of the British West Indies Regiment.

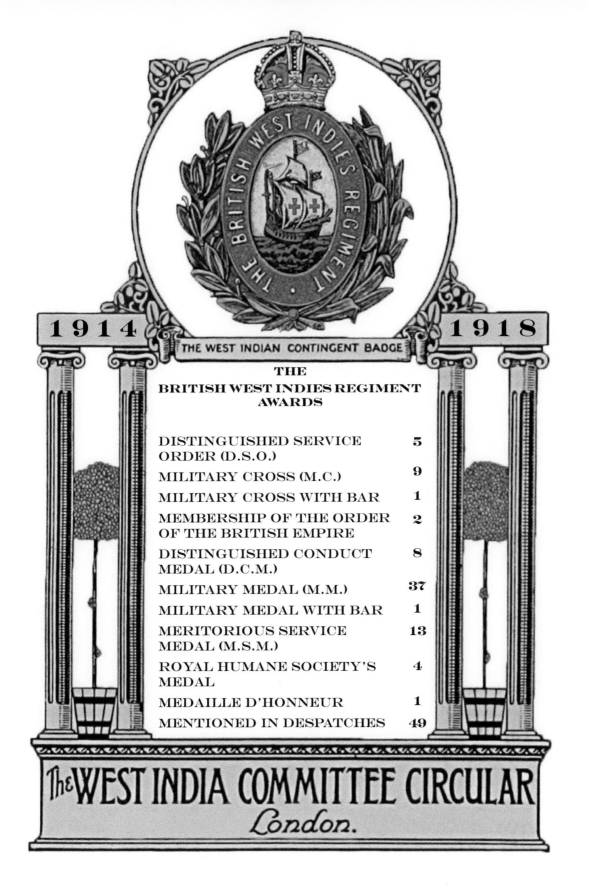

THE WEST INDIAN CONTINGENT BADGE

THE
BRITISH WEST INDIES REGIMENT
AWARDS

DISTINGUISHED SERVICE ORDER (D.S.O.)	5
MILITARY CROSS (M.C.)	9
MILITARY CROSS WITH BAR	1
MEMBERSHIP OF THE ORDER OF THE BRITISH EMPIRE	2
DISTINGUISHED CONDUCT MEDAL (D.C.M.)	8
MILITARY MEDAL (M.M.)	37
MILITARY MEDAL WITH BAR	1
MERITORIOUS SERVICE MEDAL (M.S.M.)	13
ROYAL HUMANE SOCIETY'S MEDAL	4
MEDAILLE D'HONNEUR	1
MENTIONED IN DESPATCHES	49

The WEST INDIA COMMITTEE CIRCULAR
London.

Members of the Armed Forces "mentioned in despatches" are regarded as having received a military honour in that it is an officially reported record of their gallantry or meritorious action in the face of the enemy, issued by a superior officer to the High Command. Often the subject of such a despatch may not have received a medal or decoration, and so the record of their heroism is often nothing more than a certificate recorded in a military file note. For the men and women mentioned in despatches during the First World War, this is particularly poignant as the military records held by the Ministry of Defence were destroyed in the Second World War.

As was the case for Major de Boissiere, of the 8th Battalion, mentioned in dispatches by General Cavan on 26th October 1918 leading figures of the day such as Winston Churchill, the Secretary of State for War, dispensed sentiments of appreciation for the distinguished services performed in the field, as commanded by the King.

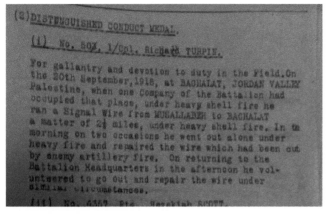

A citation for a Distinguished Conduct Medal as recorded by the War Office.

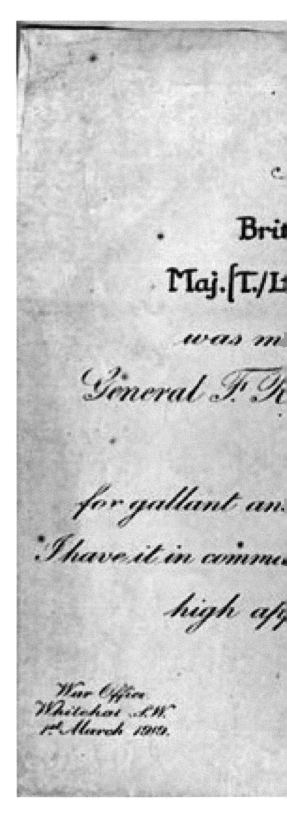

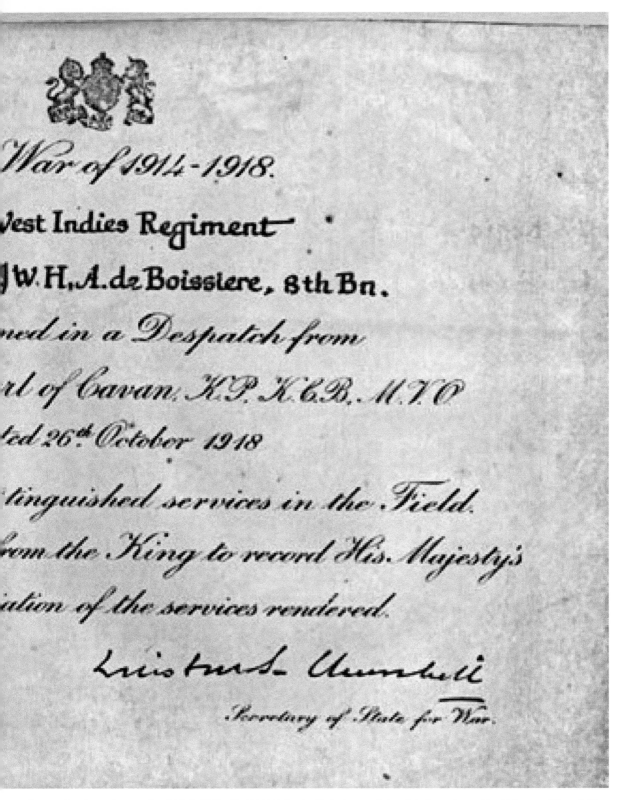

War of 1914–1918.

West Indies Regiment

W. H. A. de Boissiere, 8th Bn.

...ned in a Despatch from

...rl of Cavan, K.P. K.C.B. M.V.O

...ted 26th October 1918

...tinguished services in the Field.

...om the King to record His Majesty's

...ation of the services rendered.

Winston Churchill

Secretary of State for War.

A mention in a despatch of Maj. (T./Lt:Col.) W.H.A. de Boissiere, of the 8th Bn., signed by Winston Churchill

Distinguished Service Order (D.S.O.)

The Distinguished Service Order (DSO) was introduced in 1886 **to honour courage and initiative in battle** displayed by officers of the Royal Armed Forces. The Royal Proclamation states: *'It is ordained that the order shall consist of the Sovereign, and of such members or companions as We, Our heirs or successors, shall appoint.'*

Distinguished Conduct Medal (D.C.M.)

The Distinguished Conduct Medal was introduced in 1854 to honour non-commissioned officers and men and women of the Army **for bravery and leadership in battle.** The Conspicuous Gallantry Medal (CGM) has now replaced it.

Military Medal (M.M.)

The Military Medal (MM) was established in 1916, for non-commissioned members of the Army **who showed bravery in battle.** The Military Cross has now replaced it.

Meritorious Service Medal (M.S.M.)

The Meritorious Service Medal was a silver medal for **distinguished service or for gallantry.**

Military Cross (M.C.)

The Military Cross (MC) was established in 1914. It was given to men that ranked between major and warrant officers **to award bravery in the face of the enemy on land.**

1914-15 Star "Pip"

The 1914-15 Star is a Campaign medal of the British Empire which was awarded to officers and men by the King who was Monarch of the United Kingdom, British Dominions and Emperor of India.

British War Medal "Squeak"

The British War Medal was instituted on 26th July 1919 for award to those who rendered service from the 5th August 1914 to 11th November 1918.

Victory Medal "Wilfred"

The Victory Medal was awarded to those who mobilised for war service in the United Kingdom or the British Empire between the 5th August 1914 and the 11th November 1918.

The Death Penny

A Death Penny, or Memorial Plaque medallion was issued to the family of every serviceman who lost their life in the conflict.

THE VICTORIA CROSS
BY LORD ASHCROFT KCMG PC

A Victoria Cross.

The Victoria Cross (VC) is Britain and the Commonwealth's most prestigious gallantry award for **bravery in the face of the enemy**. It was founded by Queen Victoria through a Royal Warrant issued on 29th January 1856. This created a single decoration available to members of the Army and Royal Navy, regardless of class, colour, religion, creed or rank.

The Royal Warrant laid down fifteen "rules and ordinances", although some of these have been slightly adapted over the decades. The VC was originally instituted to reward acts of outstanding bravery during the Crimean War of 1854-6. Since then, it has been awarded more than 1,350 times.

The largest number of VCs awarded for any single conflict was for the First World War. The 1914-18 conflict led to the award of 633 VCs, 188 of them posthumously. This considerably outnumbered the figure for the Second World War when there were 182 awards of the VC, 87 of them posthumously.

As a region, the Caribbean has every reason to claim one of the Great War VC recipients as one of its own. Frank Alexander de Pass was the son of a Sir Eliot de Pass, a West Indian merchant and a President of the West India Committee. Although born in London and educated in England, de Pass never forgot his roots. As a Lieutenant in the Indian Army, he was awarded the VC for bravery in France in November 1914 when he successfully attacked an enemy trench under heavy fire and then, again under heavy fire, rescued a wounded soldier. However, the young officer, who was the first Jew to be awarded the VC, was killed in action the next day, aged twenty-seven. His decoration therefore became a posthumous award.

Furthermore, Caribbean VC heroes are very much part of the decoration's history:
Captain (later Major) Herbert Clogstoun, who was born in Port-of-Spain, Trinidad, received the VC for bravery in Chichumbah, India, in 1859. He charged the rebels with only eight men of his regiment, losing seven men and being badly wounded.

Captain (later Major-General) Henry Jerome, who was born on Antigua, received the VC for courage at Jhansi, India, in 1858. He saved, under heavy enemy fire, a lieutenant from his regiment who had been severely wounded.

Private (later Lance-Corporal) Samuel Hodge, who was born on Tortola, Virgin Islands, received the VC for bravery in West Africa in 1866. He stormed a stockaded town allowing support troops to enter, but was badly wounded in this action.

Lieutenant (later Colonel) William Chase, who was born on St. Lucia, received the VC for courage in Afghanistan in 1880. He rescued a wounded soldier and carried him for 200 yards despite being under a heavy enemy fire.
Lance-Corporal (later Sergeant) William Gordon, who was born on Jamaica, received the VC for bravery in West Africa in 1892. He saved the life of an officer who was being fired at from close range but was himself badly wounded.

Private (later Lance-Corporal) Johnson Beharry, who was born on Grenada, received the VC for two acts of courage in Iraq in 2004. He saved the lives of comrades, driving his Warrior vehicle under heavy fire but was severely wounded in the second of two ambushes.

I have had an interest in bravery for well over half a century. Gradually, this transformed itself into a passion for gallantry medals, in general, and the VC, in particular. Over the past 30 years, I have amassed the world's largest collection of VCs, which are currently on public display at the Imperial War Museum, London. My collection includes the Henry Jerome VC group gifted, in an act of great generosity, by his family in 2011. I have also had the honour to meet Johnson Beharry several times and his courage is a wonderful example of the gallantry that has been displayed by so many Caribbean-born servicemen over many decades.

DEMOBILISATION AND THE TARANTO MUTINY

The First World War armistice was signed at 11 o'clock on 11th November 1918, the 'eleventh hour of the eleventh day of the eleventh month'. Celebrations erupted in the Allied capitals of Europe and, after years of fighting, a state of war had finally ceased in Europe.

Demobilisation of the millions of servicemen scattered across the globe commenced in 1918 and, for the West Indians, was centred upon the Cimino camp in Taranto, Italy. One of the reasons that the British West Indies Regiment was assembled at Taranto was in preparation for their return journey but, due to the geography of the West Indies, it was not as simple as just sending them back on ships. The men had to be sorted and grouped in order to put them on appropriate ships so as to reach their home islands efficiently. Other questions needed to be answered as well, such as what to do with the men that had come to Britain independently of the contingents of British West Indies Regiment volunteers.

Taranto, Italy

The war had been one of the most expensive and expansive the world had ever known. This placed nations on the verge of bankruptcy and left men strewn across the globe with little prospect of returning home for months, if not years. Whilst the men of the British West Indies Regiment that found themselves on the Western Front and in Africa experienced a relatively standardised demobilisation, and returned home to the Caribbean to a rapturous welcome, this was not the case for all members of the Regiment.

The slow demobilisation did not only affect the men that had gone to war but it also affected their families and their countries of origin as well. The men were now needed at home in order to work, with the development of trade and industry being stifled by their absence. Algernon Aspinall, the Secretary of the West India Committee, wrote a letter to *The Times* complaining of the delay, whilst pointing out that many of the men were government clerks, estate managers and overseers and were needed at home for vital work.

Whilst at Taranto, the Regiment was poorly treated and the 9th Battalion refused to obey orders and filed an official complaint on 6th December 1918 owing to the harsh command of their C.O. Lieutenant Colonel Willis. The 9th and the 10th Battalions then refused to work following news of a pay increase which was made available to other Imperial Units under Army Order 1 of 1918, but not to the British West Indies Regiment; the grounds for this were that the Regiment's depot was not in the United Kingdom. Eventually the situation became violent with the 9th Battalion attacking their officer and severely injuring their commanding officer. Disobedience of a commanding officer is deemed by the military to be an act of mutiny, which is subject to severe punishment that may include the death sentence.

The Taranto Mutiny lasted for four days and, as a result, 60 men were tried with 47 being found guilty, with one being sentenced to death, although this was later commuted to a 20-year sentence. Mutinies were prevalent during the protracted demobilisation process that stretched into 1919. However, this mutiny struck a nerve with the authorities that had maintained reservations over enlisting West Indians and consequently the 8,000 men of the British West Indies Regiment were disarmed. The Taranto Mutiny had a lasting impact on the Caribbean and drove some veterans to establish organisations to bring about independence for the island nations. This sentiment was shared by the Arab nations who, like the West Indians, had fought for the Allies against the Ottoman Empire in expectation of independence from British rule. As a result of the mutiny, West Indians were not invited to join the Victory Parade in London.

In February 1919 the camp came under the command of Brigadier General Cary-Barnard, whose experience of other races had primarily been in Southern Africa, where racial divisions had been far greater than that of the Caribbean or Europe. His attitude to the black soldiers only worsened the feelings of resentment. The issue over pay was eventually rectified thanks to the West India Contingent Committee, which made representations on the men's behalf, including sending a letter to Lord Milner signed by no fewer than 7 ex-governors of various West Indian Colonies. The West India Committee Circular of 20th February 1919 reported that, *"Had it only the settlement of this question to its credit the West India Contingent Committee would have justified its existence."* Despite the fact that the 1st and 2nd Battalions had not been present at Taranto at the time of the mutiny, when they arrived in 1919 they too were subjected to discriminatory behaviour, such as being not allowed to attend the cinema or the Y.M.C.A. and being ordered to perform fatigue duties for other units. This too led to lasting resentment.

Eventually, however, demobilisation got underway and the first ship to sail for the West Indies was the Hospital Ship *Grantully Castle* on 14th April 1919. It was followed on the 16th by *SS Helenus*, carrying men to Jamaica and the Bahamas; men on this ship bound for British Honduras would also disembark at the Bahamas for later transport home.

The West India Contingent Committee saw to it that each vessel had games and cigarettes for the men on the voyage home, with the *Grantully Castle* receiving a variety of gifts, such as draughts, chess, playing cards and ring boards, as well as 50,000 cigarettes.

More ships would bring the soldiers of the British West Indies Regiment home over the coming months and, despite being accompanied home under armed escort provided by the Worcester Regiment as a consequence of the Taranto Mutiny, they received a warm welcome. When the transport ship *Ajax* arrived at Port-of-Spain on 26th May with a contingent of men from Trinidad, many people turned out to see them and they were entertained at a breakfast, following a welcome by the Mayor, Mr F.E. Scott, and Mr Mongomerie Gordon, the acting governor. The unfortunate incident when a platform on one of the barges carrying them from the *Ajax* to land collapsed, causing several men to fall into the hold and be seriously injured, apparently did little to dampen their return.

The return of a Trinidad contingent from the *Ajax* to Port-of-Spain.

A Trinidad Contingent's Return: Scene in Frederick Street, Port-of-Spain.

A triumphal arch greeted returnees to British Guiana and, as the contingents returned, legislation to offer them grants of land for their service was being passed. Plots of Crown Lands in Jamaica, 5 acres each, were also made available to former soldiers.

A triumphal arch in Georgetown, British Guiana, on the occasion of the return of the local contingent.

Return of troops to British Guiana.

The commanding officers of the 1st Battalion of the British West Indies Regiment decided to produce a copy of the War Diary to present to the West India Committee so that it would be accessible to all those interested in the Regiment. This copy was handwritten by Company Sergeant Major W.C. Mills, who also drew the maps and plans under the direction of the battalion adjutant, Captain R.H.L. Fink. Mills would also create a beautiful dedication page and the whole book was bound in red calf leather.

Return of a British Guiana contingent: Scene in Georgetown.

A victory parade outside Buckingham Palace, London in 1919, from which West Indians were excluded.

The British West Indies Regiment returning to the West Indies. A West Indian Committee photograph used as a commemorative stamp in Jamaica.

A VALUABLE WAR DIARY.
Presented to the West India Committee.

LIEUT.-COLONEL WOOD HILL, D.S.O., and the Officers, Warrant Officers, Non-Commissioned Officers, and Men of the 1st British West Indies Regiment have presented to the West India Committee the War Diary of the Battalion which was kept without intermission from August 21st, 1915, the date of the embarkation of the first unit of the West Indian Contingent at Georgetown, Demerara, to November 30th last. The diary, which gives a very complete history of the life of the battalion and of the operations in which it took such a brilliant part, was written out by Company Sergeant-Major W. C. Mills, who designed the handsome book-plate which is reproduced on this page. On a scroll worked into the design of this book-plate are the honours of the battalion, includii g Suez Canal, Gaza, Dumbell Hill, Jerusalem, Grant Hill, Jordan Valley, Es Salt, Amman, &c. The volume has several appendixes, including a series of maps to illustrate an account of the operations in the Jordan Valley, a complete list of all officers who ever served in the battalion, and a list of all the honours and awards.

The "spade-work" of the diary was carried out by Capt. R. H. L. Fink, and the excellent maps and plans were executed by C.Q.M.S. Mills under his direction.

The idea of the regiment in presenting the diary to the West India Committee was to render it accessible to all interested in the doings of the British West Indies Regiment, it being realised that the Committee was a permanent body while the West Indian Contingent Committee would presumably bring its career to a close after the completion of demobilisation. The volume is to be bound at the expense of the donors, and at their request in solid calf with the title "War Diary, British West Indies Regiment" and the regimental crest in gold on the cover.

A particularly gratifying feature of the gift is the generous reference to the services rendered to the regiment by the West India Committee during the war.

It is hardly necessary to state that this War Diary will be greatly prized by the West India Committee, to whose library it will form a most valuable addition.

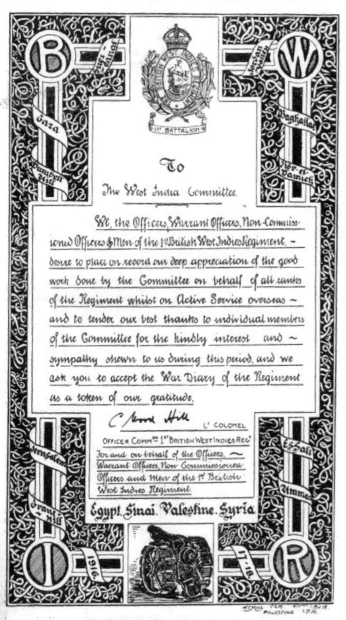

The Dedication Page of the War Diary.

The War Diary is held within the West India Committee Collection, inscribed by UNESCO as a Memory of the World.

SHOT AT DAWN
BY CAPTAIN STACEY DEHANEY

In November 2006, a pardon was given to 300 men. These men were executed by their own army and comrades for actions deemed, at the time, to be cowardice. They left families, who carried the truth of their untimely deaths, with shame. These men suffered from 'Shell Shock', a medical condition acknowledged today as a medical illness emerging from the war in the trenches, but which was unrecognised and could not be used as a defence when court-martialed during the First World War. Not all men who were executed for desertion in the face of the enemy suffered from 'Shell Shock' but it is clear that some did. The conditions of the First World War ultimately changed so much of our society, including the treatment of psychological illness.

It is not for us to question the judgements made a century ago, but rather to acknowledge that these men were victims of a type of war the world had not previously seen. Located in the National Memorial Arboretum in England is a memorial of a simple wooden post with metal tags with the names of soldiers from the British Empire who faced this end. Amongst them is Private Herbert Morris of the British West Indies Regiment, the only soldier from the Regiment to be executed for desertion and at the tender age of 17.

Private Herbert Morris was a Jamaican who volunteered to join the British West Indies Regiment. Like so many other young men from the Empire, Morris was eager to serve his King and Mother Country. He was only 16 years of age in 1916 when the 6th Battalion of the British West Indies Regiment was sent to Flanders and later Ypres in Belgium. The Battalion was tasked within the Labour Corps with the movement of ammunition and the construction of trenches. At Ypres they encountered heavy gun fire with the British attack of some 2,297 guns firing over four million shells, four times the number fired at the Somme; the Germans responded in a similar manner. The 6th Battalion experienced daily casualties. A priest in close proximity noted that some of the men became afraid of the guns and displayed signs of disorientation during the shelling, which was in the region of hundreds of tonnes of ammunition each day.

Herbert Morris was one such soldier who became disoriented by the shelling, and in response he ran away from the trenches to later be caught and arrested. After witnessing the death of some of his comrades, Herbert fled again. On his second arrest, he showed signs of battle fatigue and pleaded with the court that he could not stand the sound of the guns. He visited the doctor where he received neither medicine nor satisfaction. He was court-martialed and sentenced to be shot for desertion from active service. On 20th September 1917 he was paraded in front of his Battalion before his execution, which was to serve as an example that the Army would not tolerate cowardly behaviour.

Executed at dawn by a firing squad that included seven West Indian soldiers, he had just had his 17th birthday. Herbert Morris is buried in Belgium's Poperinge New Military Cemetery where the Commonwealth War Graves Commission faithfully maintains his grave.

The National Memorial Arboretum.

WAR GRAVES

"The Commonwealth War Graves Commission ensures that 1.7 million people who died in the two world wars will never be forgotten. We care for cemeteries and memorials at 23,000 locations, in 154 countries. Our values and aims, laid out in 1917, are as relevant now as they were almost 100 years ago."

The Commonwealth War Graves Commission was founded by Fabain Ware. He was 45 when war broke out and therefore too old to enlist. Instead he took the command of a British Red Cross Ambulance Unit, and while serving in this capacity, became dismayed by the lack of records on the final resting places of the many men he had seen die. Ware and his ambulance unit took up the task. Their work was soon given official recognition by the Imperial War Office and the unit was transferred from the British Red Cross Society to the British Army under the new title of Graves Registration Commission. By May 1916 this new organisation had registered over 50,000 graves. Relatives of fallen soldiers now had an organisation to which they could submit requests for photographs of the graves of their loved ones, and by 1917 Ware and his team had dispatched over 17,000 such photographs.

As the war continued, questions arose concerning the fate of the war-graves once Peace finally returned. With the help of Edward, Prince of Wales, Ware submitted a memorandum on the subject to the Imperial War Conference in 1917. Later that year the Imperial War Graves Commission was created by Royal Charter, with the Prince of Wales as its President and Ware as its Vice-Chairman, a role that he would hold until his retirement in 1948.

By the time that Armistice was declared in 1918, some 587,000 graves had been registered by the Commission, and a further 559,000 casualties were recorded as having no known grave. The West India Contingent Committee, upon learning in 1919 that the graves of the 300 British West Indies Regiment soldiers at Cimino camp were not being satisfactorily maintained, wrote to the Imperial War Graves Commission and the commander of the camp to complain and to give the then large sum of £50 to maintain the graves. The poor state of the graves was apparently due to the creation of an extension to the cemetery and the wooden crosses that were in place were replaced by proper headstones.

Rudyard Kipling, the Nobel Prize winner, was one of England's most famous poets and novelists. The author of world famous literature, including the much-loved 'Jungle Book', Kipling was chosen to be the literary advisor to the Commission and was made responsible for the language that would appear on the graves and memorials. The Commission also chose Sir Edwin Lutyens, Sir Herbert Baker and Sir Reginald Blomfield, three of the most distinguished and esteemed architects of the age, to design and construct the cemeteries and monuments to the dead.

The Graves of the Fallen

Imperial War Graves Commission

The Commission's activities reached a wide audience through an article written by Kipling in *The Times* in February 1919 in which he described his colleagues' designs for both the cemeteries and the individual graves. The article was popular enough to be quickly republished as an illustrated booklet, entitled "Graves of the Fallen", but there was an immediate public outcry in response, especially with regard to the decision to not repatriate the bodies of the dead, an issue which inspired a lengthy debate in Parliament. The Commission worked tirelessly through the 1920s to construct the cemeteries that would become the final resting place of the fallen of the Commonwealth. By 1921 the Commission had secured enough land from the Belgian and French authorities to establish 1,000 cemeteries. By the end of the decade most of the construction had been completed and the extended cemetery network covered over 2,400 cemeteries in France and Belgium, which contained over 400,000 headstones, 400 Crosses of Sacrifice, and 400 Stones of Remembrance. Meanwhile, the Commission built cemeteries in Italy, Egypt, Palestine, Macedonia, Mesopotamia and on the Gallipoli Peninsular.

The most prominent of these early cemeteries was Forceville in France, a walled cemetery with uniform rows of headstones that showcased the work of Britain's leading garden designer, Gertrude Jekyll. It went on to become the Commission's template for future building programmes. Each serviceman who died without a known grave was also individually commemorated by the inscription of their name upon a memorial. The first to be completed was Reginald Blomfield's Menin Gate in 1927; however, such was the death toll that a further 34,984 names had to be inscribed and could not fit. They were therefore immortalised on Herbert Baker's Tyne Cot Memorial. Further memorials were erected in the Somme, Gallipoli, and Mesopotamia. Other Commonwealth countries constructed memorials for their fallen servicemen along the Western Front, including Canada, India, Australia, South Africa, and Newfoundland.

The Imperial War Graves Commission continued its work throughout the Second World War and eventually changed its name to the Commonwealth War Graves Commission in 1960. To this day, the Commission commemorates those that have fallen in battle uniformly and equally, irrespective of race, rank or creed.

ST. JAMES MEMORIAL
AT MONTEGO BAY

ST. THOMAS MEMORIAL
AT MORANT BAY

ST. ANN MEMORIAL
AT ST. ANN'S BAY

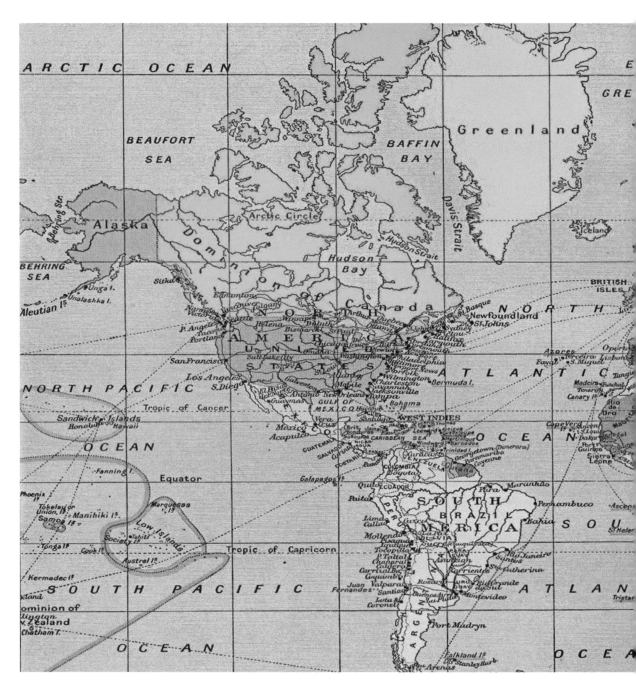

Soldiers of the British West Indies Regiment were laid to rest in the following countries:
Barbados, Belgium, Belize, Bermuda, Canada, Egypt,
France, Gibraltar, Greece, Grenada, Guiana, India,
Iraq, Israel & Palestine, Italy, Jamaica, Kenya, Malta,
St. Lucia, St. Vincent, Tanzania, UK, Sierra Leone, South Africa.

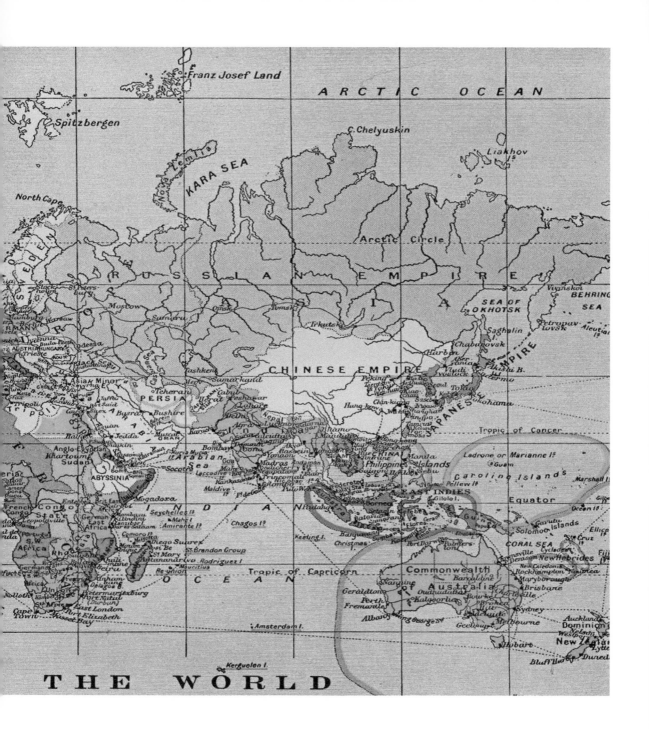

THE WORLD

WAR TAX STAMPS

War is an expensive business that has often bankrupted nations. Peoples oppressed by the conditions of war are seldom capable of remitting large sums to government in support of their war efforts. Governments have therefore adopted innovative ways to encourage the public to make financial contributions, including financial instruments, such as war bonds. In the context of the Caribbean, import duties on Caribbean goods had been a robust contributor to the Exchequer for generations. This source of revenue was lost during the conflict due to naval combat in the Atlantic. During the First World War an alternative, sustainable source of funding was devised through the introduction of War Tax stamps. Like war bonds, War Tax stamps served to reduce the level of money in circulation, thereby curbing inflation in an insecure economic environment.

The Spanish introduced War Tax stamps in 1874 during the Third Carlist War. During the First World War they were swiftly adopted by Britain for use within its Empire and Dominions, with Canada leading the way in 1915. War Tax on stamps was charged in addition to normal postage and was compulsory, enabling the Government to gauge the level of income each island could produce by this means. All post and stamped documents were eligible for the levy, making a significant contribution to Britain's war chest.

The Caribbean was particularly enthusiastic in this endeavour, each country competing with the other to demonstrate their loyalty and devotion to the Mother Country. Canada set the bar, raising over four million pounds in stamp tax, proving the effectiveness of this simple revenue system. Jamaica was the first of the Caribbean countries to issue a tax on post and in 1916 included telegrams, publicising the new tax as a *"sound investment"* for Jamaicans.

The stamps themselves were cost-effectively produced locally by overprinting existing stamps with various officially recognised terms such as 'War Tax', 'War Surtax', 'Postal Surtax', and 'Postal Tax'. Antigua, Bahamas, Barbados, Bermuda, British Guiana, British Honduras, Cayman Islands, Dominica, Grenada, Jamaica, Montserrat, St. Kitts, Nevis and Anguilla, St. Lucia, St. Vincent, Trinidad and Tobago, Turks and Caicos and the Virgin Islands all contributed to Britain's war effort through stamp tax levies. This practice continued into the 1920s, long after the war itself had concluded, until the British economy began to see signs of recovery from the huge financial drain the war had proved to be.

In addition to those stamps used to generate revenue, a series of stamps were introduced to commemorate the war effort, including two generated from the West India Committee's photographic collection.

VETERANS WHO BECAME LEADERS
BY LEAH ALEXANDER

The First World War brought about significant changes within the British Empire. West Indians from various colonies were united, in many cases for the first time, to fight alongside each other in the face of the same challenges. This environment allowed for the rapid spread of ideas, introducing many to the concepts of nationalism and trade unionism. Meanwhile, West Indian experience of racial discrimination, combined with the obvious destitution of British servicemen, did much to dispel the prevailing myth of European superiority. As a result, West Indians returned from war battle-hardened and politically conscious, with a new understanding of their role and relevance in the world. Their contributions to new political movements, adhering more closely to the needs of the Caribbean people than the interests of Britain, have established many veterans as historic figures within the region.

Arthur Andrew Cipriani (1875-1945) and Tubal Uriah "Buzz" Butler (1897-1977)

Known throughout Trinidad as the *"champion of the barefoot man,"* Arthur Andrew Cipriani, born in Corsica in 1875, was influential throughout the West Indies as a politician and labour unionist. The former cocoa farmer, promoted to the rank of Captain in the British West Indies Regiment, returned from his deployment in Egypt with a commitment to West Indian self-determination. Cipriani helped revive the Trinidad Workingmen's Association, then the country's principal workers' organisation, and in 1919 led what is considered to be Trinidad's first important industrial strike in Port-of-Spain, gaining him significant popularity. Off the back of this support, Cipriani climbed the political ranks, earning himself a seat on the City Council of Port-of-Spain and becoming Mayor of the capital in 1925. The elections of that same year, the first in Trinidad and Tobago's history, secured Cipriani a seat on the Legislative Council, where he championed issues such as workers' rights, women's rights and compulsory education.

With the formation in 1934 of Cipriani's Trinidad Labour Party, from the ashes of the recently dissolved Trinidad Workingmen's Association, the nation's first political party had a diverse membership, with members of African, European and Indian heritage. Adrian Cola Rienzi and Tubal Uriah "Buzz" Butler, two young labour advocates more radical than Cipriani, were among the members. They would become significant figures in Trinidad and Tobago's political history.

Born in Grenada in 1897, Butler had been inspired by Cipriani when he served in his British West Indies Regiment at the tender age of 17. Upon returning from war, Butler was politically active in Grenada, establishing the Grenada Union of Returned Soldiers and Grenada Representative Government Movement, the latter of which called for universal suffrage. However, the Trinidad Labour Party, which Butler joined after moving to Trinidad in search of work, proved too moderate for him and in 1935 he led a hunger march for dismissed oilfield workers. As a result of his actions, Cipriani denounced Butler, a retired oilfield worker himself. Rienzi and Butler soon broke away from the Trinidad Labour Party, and in 1936 Butler formed the British Empire Workers' and Citizens' Home Rule Party to support workers in the oil industry. It was from this platform that Butler, a rousing orator, called for the passing of trade union laws, health insurance laws, social legislation for workers and the right of blacks to reach the highest positions in the Colony.

By 1937, and in light of the effects of a Global Depression, tensions in Trinidad and Tobago had significantly increased. One grievance centred on the oil industry; Trinidad had been one of the largest producers of refined oil in the Empire until 1937, but the prosperity of the industry was not reflected in the wages of the workers. Butler's call for *"land to the people"* amplified these tensions that eventually evolved into a modern labour movement.

The attempted arrest of Butler on sedition charges by British authorities at an oilfield workers' public meeting in Fyzabad precipitated the 1937 disturbances. Cipriani, who preferred constitutional action, denounced the militancy of the strikes that followed. The disturbances came to a close at the end of 1937, a result of both militant action and concessions enacted by the British authorities; however, similar unrest manifested itself throughout the Caribbean. The strikes and disturbances, which involved workers from the domestic services to the sugar fields, are widely recognised as instituting a watershed in the political history of Trinidad and Tobago.

Though over the years Cipriani and Butler's political popularity waned, the pair left behind a strong legacy in Trinidad and Tobago. The strikes reflected the fact that the working class could organise and agitate for itself and highlighted the political consciousness of the nation, paving the way for independence to be granted by Britain in 1962.

Cipriani died in 1945 after having served as Mayor for a record 8 times. In 1959 he was honoured posthumously with a statue in Port-of-Spain, where then Chief Minister Dr Eric Williams eulogised him: *"Captain Cipriani is the pioneer of the nationalist movement of Trinidad and Tobago. With the unveiling of this statue we commemorate our own historical development, our own positive action, our own native history made by native hands, and the aspiration of our native peoples."*

Butler served on the Legislative Council during the 1950s and ran two unsuccessful election campaigns before his death in 1977. He was honoured with the Trinity Cross in 1970, the nation's highest award, and in 1973 the anniversary of the oilfield disturbances, June 19th, was declared an annual national holiday - Labour Day.

Tubal Uriah Butler, who had served in the British West Indies Regiment during the First World War.

Norman Washington Manley (1893-1969)

Born in Jamaica in 1893 to a family of mixed racial heritage, Rhodes Scholar, Norman Washington Manley established himself as one of the most iconic figures in Jamaica's political history. An athletically and academically gifted young man, in 1915 Manley interrupted his studies at Oxford University to join the British war effort, enlisting as a Private in the Royal Field Artillery and fighting in battles including the Somme and Ypres. Upon his return to Jamaica Manley became a well-respected lawyer, earning himself a place on the King's Counsel of George V.

Against the backdrop of the Great Depression and a growing labour movement developing in the West Indies, in 1938 confrontations between colonial officials and the largely black labouring class of Jamaica swept the nation. In response Manley cofounded the People's National Party, the island's first modern political party, borne out of his belief that political action was the necessary precursor to constitutional reform. In the years that followed, the People's National Party dominated labour politics in Jamaica, and their efforts were soon realised when in 1944 the British colonial government granted Jamaica universal suffrage. However, in the first general election of that same year, it was Manley's cousin Alexander Bustamante and his Jamaica Labour Party who secured victory, establishing the People's National Party as the island's first official Opposition. Having finally secured electoral victory with the People's National Party in 1955, Manley became the nation's Chief Minister. In 1958 Manley integrated Jamaica into the Federation of the West Indies, an initiative sponsored by the British government to unify its Caribbean colonies in an effort to share resources and facilitate development. The Jamaica Labour Party, however, was staunchly opposed to this, and Manley's decision to hold a referendum to decide the matter, an unprecedented move in Jamaica's history, resulted in Jamaica's departure from the Federation in 1961. Having arranged this withdrawal, Manley, with cross-party support from Bustamante, drafted the constitution for Jamaican independence from Britain, which was granted in 1962.

Elected President of the People's National Party every year from its establishment to his retirement

31 years later, Manley is credited with creating a climate in which Jamaican independence could be secured. At his last annual party meeting, Manley declared that the *"mission of my generation was to win self-government… To win political power which is the final power for the black masses of my country from which I spring… Mission accomplished"*. Manley died in 1969, the same year he was proclaimed a National Hero of Jamaica alongside Bustamante, and three years before his son Michael Manley would become the fourth Prime Minister of Jamaica, following in his father's footsteps as leader of the People's National Party.

Sir Étienne Dupuch O.B.E. (1899-1991)

Awarded knighthoods by a total of 3 different countries, Sir Étienne Dupuch O.B.E. was a distinguished Bahamian journalist and publisher of international acclaim. Born in 1899 Dupuch spent his early years supporting his father's fledgling newspaper, *The Tribune*, delivering it on foot throughout his hometown of Nassau, an experience he later described as a *"regular social tour"*. In 1916, and at only 17 years of age, Dupuch joined the British West Indies Regiment as a Private, during which time he endured the appalling conditions of service in Egypt, alongside Trinidad's Cipriani, before serving in a labour battalion along the Western Front. Shocked by his experience of racial prejudice, that he would not have encountered to such an extent in the Bahamas, as a man of European descent, and informed by his encounters with West Indians who championed social and political change for the region, Dupuch returned from war disillusioned with Europe. He later observed he was a *"changed person... after seeing the people of Europe wallowing in a cesspit of human degradation"*.

In 1919 Sir Étienne, assisted by his younger brother Eugene, took over editorship of *The Tribune* from his father, who had established the newspaper in 1903. In keeping with the newspaper's motto, *"Being bound to swear to the dogmas of no master"*, the Dupuchs used this platform to critique the governing bodies of Bahamian society, firstly the Bay Street Boys, a group of white merchants concentrated in Nassau who chiefly controlled commerce, land and politics, and then the nation's first political party, the Progressive Liberal Party. Throughout his life Dupuch continued to challenge the status quo, going over the head of the Duke of Windsor, the Governor of Bahamas during World War Two, to set up a war relief fund to support Bahamian soldiers and a canning factory to send food to Britain. The amount of food donated to the UK, gifted by the Bahamian people, was only exceeded by Zimbabwe, then named Rhodesia.

Like their father, both Sir Étienne and Eugene Dupuch served in the Bahamian government. Sir Étienne's greatest achievement was to table a historic resolution in 1956, the first comprehensive anti-discrimination legislation in the Colony, outlawing the practice of racial discrimination in hotels, theatres and other public places in the Colony. Dupuch presented an emotive case to the Select Committee, and it was later reported in *The Tribune* that he proclaimed *"The day is past in the world when classes and races can be divided by some cruel invisible line"*, refusing to cease standing until his protestations were heard. Though Dupuch's original resolution was not adopted in full, in a show of support many hotels in Nassau announced they were open to everyone, regardless of race. Dupuch lost his seat in the 1956 general election a few months later, but remained politically active, and was later appointed to the Senate.

Dupuch's record-breaking 54 years as editor of *The Tribune* came to an end when, in 1972, he passed the mantle to his daughter Eileen. Internationally recognised as a champion of the free press, Dupuch died in 1991, aged 92, entering the Guiness Book of Records as the longest serving newspaper editor of his time.

THE STORY OF THE COMMONWEALTH

BY GEORGIA TOPLEY

The West Indies were 'discovered' by Christopher Columbus in 1492 when he landed on Watling Island in the Bahamas. Drawn by talk of gold and the descriptions of the long sandy beaches, palm trees and blue skies, other European nations soon followed. The first British settlement was on St. Christopher's Island, St. Kitts in 1623; within a few years, settlements in Barbados, Tobago, Antigua and Montserrat followed. The largest British island, Jamaica, was taken from the Spanish after a failed attempt to take the colony of Hispaniola (today known as Haiti and The Dominican Republic). As the British sailors were afraid of returning home to Cromwell empty-handed, they endeavoured to capture Jamaica instead, and succeeded. Great battles were fought in the West Indies between the different European powers but Britain kept a stronghold on its islands for hundreds of years. The abolition of the slave trade in 1807 was a precursor to the independence of the British Caribbean islands which were eventually granted independence from Britain during the Nineteenth and Twentieth centuries. Those that are a part of the Commonwealth today voluntarily chose to remain in association with the British monarchy and have kept the same political structure developed by Britain, and retained the British Monarch as their Head of State, whilst becoming strong independent countries in their own right.

The British involvement in the tropics began somewhat by accident when a fleet of six ships set out for Virginia in 1609 and encountered heavy storms. The ships were separated, but through a feat of endurance the flagship, the *Sea Adventurer*, managed to stay afloat even though it was leaking in many places. After three days and three nights, and on the brink of despair, the Governor, Sir George Somers, saw something on the horizon - Bermuda. The island, although diminutive, was rich in natural resources, far beyond what had been found in Virginia. Subsequently, in 1610 the sailors returned with more settlers and in 1612 Bermuda became a British colony. In 1620, in the town of St. George, the first General Assembly gathered; this became the oldest Parliament outside Britain in the Commonwealth. This marked the beginning of the political structure shared by the countries of the Commonwealth. This framework is still in place today, a testament to the beneficial nature of a shared legal system, and to the practicality of the system itself. During its history, although a considerable distance from the West Indies, Bermuda was administered along with Britain's holdings in the Caribbean, leading to many West Indians migrating north to Bermuda. Today, like Anguilla, the British Virgin Islands, the Cayman Islands, Montserrat, and Turks and Caicos, Bermuda continues life under the Union Jack as an Overseas Territory of the United Kingdom. Despite comprising some of the earliest colonies of the British Empire, forerunner of the Commonwealth, the Overseas Territories are as yet not full, but associate, members of the Commonwealth. Partially governed by the U.K. Parliament, these countries are Britain's most distinctive presence in the Americas today.

Today, *"The Commonwealth is a voluntary association of 53 independent and equal sovereign states. It is home to 2.2 billion citizens, of which over 60% are under the age of 30. The Commonwealth includes some of the world's largest, smallest, richest and poorest countries, spanning five regions. Thirty-one of its members are small states, many of them island nations. Commonwealth countries are supported by an active network of more than 80 intergovernmental, civil society, cultural and professional organisations."* Over 23% of the membership of the Commonwealth is held by Caribbean countries.

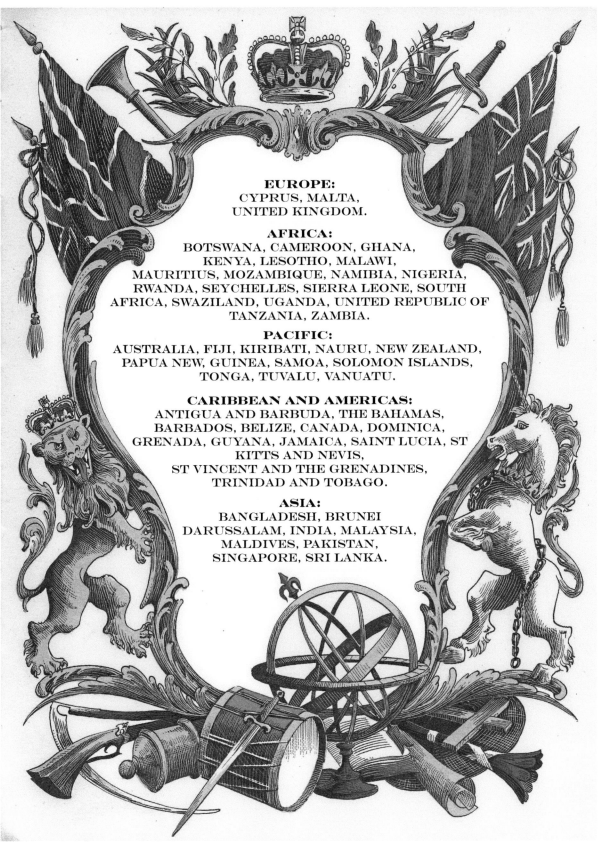

EUROPE:
CYPRUS, MALTA,
UNITED KINGDOM.

AFRICA:
BOTSWANA, CAMEROON, GHANA,
KENYA, LESOTHO, MALAWI,
MAURITIUS, MOZAMBIQUE, NAMIBIA, NIGERIA,
RWANDA, SEYCHELLES, SIERRA LEONE, SOUTH
AFRICA, SWAZILAND, UGANDA, UNITED REPUBLIC OF
TANZANIA, ZAMBIA.

PACIFIC:
AUSTRALIA, FIJI, KIRIBATI, NAURU, NEW ZEALAND,
PAPUA NEW, GUINEA, SAMOA, SOLOMON ISLANDS,
TONGA, TUVALU, VANUATU.

CARIBBEAN AND AMERICAS:
ANTIGUA AND BARBUDA, THE BAHAMAS,
BARBADOS, BELIZE, CANADA, DOMINICA,
GRENADA, GUYANA, JAMAICA, SAINT LUCIA, ST
KITTS AND NEVIS,
ST VINCENT AND THE GRENADINES,
TRINIDAD AND TOBAGO.

ASIA:
BANGLADESH, BRUNEI
DARUSSALAM, INDIA, MALAYSIA,
MALDIVES, PAKISTAN,
SINGAPORE, SRI LANKA.

The Commonwealth

Flag of the Commonwealth Nations.

THE ORIGINS OF CARICOM WITHIN THE WAR

BY BARNABAS HOWARD WALE

Whilst paying due attention to all meaningful threads, contemporary conflict analysis acknowledges the First World War as a unique historical event, and as a progenitor of significant regional and social change. The West Indian experience of the First World War, as both a Home Front of the British Empire and a contributor of troops and aid from the region, would engender a process of democratic agitation, and for many West Indian nations, the call to independence.

The perspicacity and long suffering of servicemen and officers of The British West Indies Regiment would prove to be a primary factor in the next phase of the region's development. The military experience of the Caribbean played a key role in the consecution and destiny of Caribbean regional integration.

After demobilisation, several ex-servicemen and officers continued their leadership in the civic and political life of the Caribbean, bringing with them a new sense of nation and sacrifice that had been tested on campaigns in Europe, Africa and the Middle East. The noted West Indian intellectual C.L.R James remarked in his account of the life of Captain Arthur Andrew Cipriani (1875-1945) on the great impression made by black volunteers in the British West Indies Regiment. Their grim treatment by British personnel and the War Office precipitated both bitterness and self-determination. In addition, these events occurred at a time when the vindication of Empire was both questioned and challenged at the core and periphery of its influence. Captain Cipriani amongst many others would go on to become a prominent political leader, advancing self-rule in Trinidad and contributing to a developing sense of West Indian Nationalism.

Both British and West Indian scholars of the British West Indies Regiment have commented on the role of non-commissioned officers in the formation of the Caribbean League on 17th December 1918. Over fifty West Indian non-commissioned officers founded the Caribbean League, with clear parallels to the sentiments of the League of Nations. Its aims included redressing what was considered to be racist mistreatment during the conflict, in addition to establishing regional unity, full adult suffrage and self-governance. Whilst the Caribbean League was short lived, its ideals and rhetoric are broadly acknowledged to be formative to the post-war democratic agitation in the West Indies. It can also be credited with subsequent attempts at regional self-determination through the West Indies Federation (1958-62), and the eventual founding of the Caribbean Community (CARICOM) in 1973 under the Treaty of Chaguaramas.

CARICOM is composed of the fifteen English speaking Caribbean nations, together with the UK Overseas Territories as associate members, and seeks regional integration along economic and foreign policy lines. In addition, the forming of the CARICOM common market and free movement of goods and people enables harmonisation at various levels, to the benefit of the Caribbean and Latin America. The achievements and vision of CARICOM are reminiscent of the shared identity, understood by men of all classes, colours and creeds who volunteered to serve in the British West Indies Regiment. The twelve battalions of the British West Indies Regiment were composed of men who originated throughout the region, bringing together a shared knowledge of culture and issues, which would have far-reaching implications for the region's institutions and development. In addition, the shared experience of military sacrifice and systemic discrimination would play a significant role in the forming of a Caribbean regional consciousness. Remembering that past is prologue, *The Caribbean's Great War* recalls the gallantry and achievements of West Indians throughout the global conflict whilst acknowledging their place in the history of regional development.

THE FALLEN

West Indian men of every Class, Creed and Colour went to war and many did not return home, but were remembered by those who did. All participants of the Great War are now deceased, but the memory of their patriotism and sacrifice lives on.

Of the West Indians who went to war, 178 were killed in action or died of their wounds and 1071 died of disease in Britain during training. In all 1583 soldiers were lost between 1915 and 1918 with many more unrecorded losses in other regiments, at sea and in the air.

Private Alexander Solomon of Trinidad, First Battalion British West Indies Regiment, who died 10 October 1918 from malaria.

Sergeant Albert Victor Chan of British Guiana, First Battalion British West Indies Regiment, who died 20 September 1918, two days before the attack on Damieh Bridge.

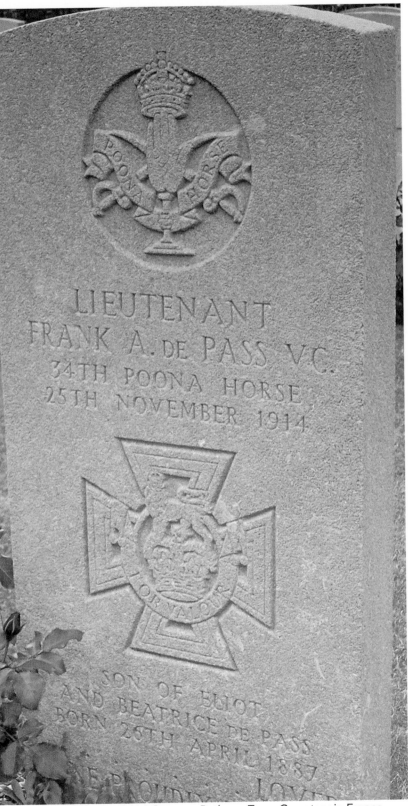

Frank Alexander De Pass' Grave at Bethune Town Cemetery in France.

It is impossible to provide comprehensive records of all the West Indians that fought in during the First World War, as so many made their own way into the conflict. Moreover, with the wholesale destruction of the War Office records during the Blitz of 1940 and 1941 official records of their contribution and experiences no longer exist. The studious record keeping of the West India Committee, that retains information on the region spanning 500 years, provides the most comprehensive record of the time. This, coupled with that of the Commonwealth War Graves Commission which lists the 1,583 men that fell between 1915 and 1918 provides us with a basis upon which personal, family accounts may be added, together with those of the Caribbean's legislative assemblies at the time. The West India Committee Circulars, that began in the 1830s and were published fortnightly throughout the conflict, were fed with intelligence from its comprehensive network of reporters, envoys and representatives both in the Caribbean and Britain and provide not only written accounts, but also pictorial records of the Caribbean's experience. The digitalisation of the West India Committee's wartime collection is now freely available to all at http://westindiacommittee.org/caribbeansgreatwar/

The recent inscription of the West India Committee's Archives as a UNESCO Memory of the World attests to the importance of the West India Committee's work as one of the preeminent institutions related to the Caribbean.

The fallen of the Caribbean are today commemorated by the poppy, a wild flower that flourished in the battlefields of the Western Front, reminiscent of the blood spilt throughout the conflict. Each year wreaths of poppies are laid throughout the Commonwealth as a reminder of the priceless contribution made by the fallen.

A wreath of poppies laid by the Chief Executive of the West India Committee at the opening of the Caribbean's Great War exhibition on 11th November 2015 held at the Museum of London Docklands, which incorporated the first named memorial in the UK to the Caribbean's fallen.

THE FALLEN
1915-1918
AS RECORDED BY THE
COMMONWEALTH WAR
GRAVES COMMISSION

Rank	Initials	Surname	Service No.				
Private	H B	ABRAHAM	537	Private	H	ANDERSON	13538
Private	Z	ADAMS	4249	Private	C R	ANDERSON	3395
Private	C	AFFLICK	15374	Private	J	ANDERSON	9645
Corporal	P	AHLSTEDT	16399	Private	D	ANDERSON	15360
Private	A U	AIKEN	2132	Private	E	ANDERSON	7772
Private	G A C	AINSLIE	6630	Private	E	ANDERSON	3851
Private	H	AITCHISON	2593	Private	I P	ANDERSON	7781
Private	U	AITKEN	11806	Private	J	ANDERSON	7780
Private	J	ALBURY	5411	Private	C A	ANDERSON	2776
Private	J	ALBURY	15475	Private	K B	ANDREWS	760
Private	W	ALCOCK	9641	Private	W	ANGLIN	11810
Private	T	ALEXANDER	10656	Lance Corporal	H B	ANGLIN	7000
Private	L	ALEXANDER	291	Private	T	APPLETON	7188
Lance Corporal	L	ALEXANDER	3209	Private	P	ARCHER	13829
Private	S T	ALLEN	9658	Private	L G	ARCHER	3742
Private	R	ALLEN	7519	Private	C	ARNOLD	6416
Private	A	ALLEN	14467	Private	J A	ARTHUR	2447
Private	M	ALLEN	16112	Private	T L	ARWIN	7520
Private	E	ALLEN	7899	Private	E	ASH	3922
Private	N	ALLEN	6403	Private	E	ASHLEY	3119
Private	J	ALLEN	11046	Private	A	ASHLEY	13528
Private	F	ALLEN	3275	Private	J	ASHLEY	15790
Private	D A N	ALLEYNE	6881	Private	A	ASHTON	16769
Private	D	ALLEYNE	10599	Private	I	ATKINSON	5706
Private	O O	ALLEYNE	9024	Private	A	AUGUSITIN	1092
Corporal	A	ALLEYNE	5187	Private	J	AUGUSTE	10458
Private	A	ALLISEN	7073	Private	A	AUGUSTIN	16617
Private	S	ANDERSON	8056	Private	B	AUSTIN	14926
Private	D S	ANDERSON	11811	Private	W	AUSTIN	7778
Private	A	ANDERSON	7629	Private	C	AUSTIN	9836
Private	T	ANDERSON	7006	Private	A F	AUSTIN	9027
Private	S A	ANDERSON	5707	Private	G	AUSTIN	11916
Private	H B	ANDERSON	3511	Lance Corporal	F	AUSTIN	536
Private	H	ANDERSON	7514	Private	L	AYER	8070
				Lance Corporal	V	BABB	1309

Rank	Initials	Surname	Number
Private	G H	BACCHUS	6428
Private	L	BAILEY	9668
Private	S	BAILEY	11829
Private	C	BAILEY	2689
Private	J	BAILEY	9788
Private	J R	BAILEY	4583
Private	I S	BAILEY	7032
Private	P E	BAILEY	2609
Private	A	BAILEY	6496
Lance Corporal	G A	BAILEY	763
Private	C N	BAKER	1865
Private	I	BAKER	5023
Private	F	BAKER	1078
Private	W	BAKER	3717
Private	S	BAKER	3774
Private	J	BALLANTINE	15574
Private	B	BALLANTYNE	10880
Private	G L	BANKS	2780
Private	A	BANTING	7020
Private	W	BAPTISTE	9240
Private	L	BAPTISTE	10878
Private	C J	BARNES	6203
Private	C	BARNETT	9772
Private	T	BARRETT	9714
Private	J E	BARRETT	4720
Private	U	BARRETT	8685
Private	S	BARRETT	9625
Private	R	BARRETT	3335
Private	E S	BARRETT	2146
Private	E	BARRETT	6542
Private	N	BARRIFFE	7046
Private	G	BARTHO-LOMEW	10932
Private	E	BARTON	3337
Private	S	BARTON	4736
Private	J	BARTON	8875
Private	P	BASCOE	6500
Private	C	BASCOM	10906
Private	C S	BASCUS	6531
Private	D	BEAUMONT	3288
Private	H	BECKFORD	9746
Private	C B	BECKFORD	2161
Private	A B	BECKFORD	15666
Private	C	BELL	3396
Private	H	BELL	6393
Private	J	BENARES	14791
Private	H	BENN	6898
Private	J	BENN	10886
Private	J	BENNET	7804
Private	H	BENNETT	11893
Private	L E	BENNETT	3762
Private	E	BENNETT	8372
Private	E M	BENNETT	5031
Private	L G	BENNETT	2159
Private	A	BENNETT	5240
Private	W	BENT	7033
Private	E	BENT	2451
Private	S	BENT	7441
Private	J E	BENWAUGH	5430
Private	R W	BERESFORD	16911
Private	J	BERNARD	13581
Private	C	BERNARD	13582
Private	R	BERRY	9763
Private	J	BERTRAM	2726
Private	F	BEST	5418
Private	E H	BEST	13573
Private	C	BETHEL	6018
Private	T J	BIGBIE	4421
Private	T	BIGGS	4422
Private		BIPHAT	16888
Private	L	BIRCH	10912

Rank	Initials	Surname	Number	Rank	Initials	Surname	Number
Private	R	BIRD	5707	Private	N H	BRAVO	5429
Private	I	BISHOP	14977	Private	A	BRAZANT	11831
Private	H	BLACK	3156	Private	V	BRIGGS	6634
Private	C	BLACK	15316	Private	A	BRIM	7044
Private	R	BLACK	6632	Private	N	BRISSETT	7293
Private	J	BLACKMAN	9789	Private	U	BROADLEY	3331
Private	A M	BLACKSTOCK	2663	Private	E V	BROOKES	2779
Private	J	BLACKWOOD	7795	Private	E	BROOKS	11847
Private	G	BLACKWOOD	8094	Private	J	BROOKS	9721
Private	T	BLACKWOOD	8338	Private	C	BROOKS	13574
Private	O	BLACKWOOD	9787	Private	J	BROUGHTON	2947
Private	I	BLAGROVE	9688	Serjeant	C	BROWN	9662
Private	J S	BLAIR	14122	Private	J	BROWN	9726
Private	W	BLAKE	5745	Private	U	BROWN	9739
Private	E	BLAKE	11866	Private	H G	BROWN	3273
Private	B O	BLAKE	6516	Private	B	BROWN	10890
Private	G	BLAKE		Private	N	BROWN	8908
Private	F	BLANCHARD	10894	Private	P	BROWN	6226
Private	J J	BLOOMENDAAL	25	Private	H S	BROWN	5044
Private	G	BOLT	3822	Private	R P	BROWN	3871
Private	A	BONNETT	311	Private	T A	BROWN	3338
Private	O	BOON	2468	Private	A E	BROWN	3121
Private	J	BOOTHE	9762	Private	G	BROWN	7011
Private	N	BOURNE	9786	Private	J	BROWN	7277
Private	S F	BOVELL	9316	Private	L	BROWN	3544
Private	O	BOWEN	14947	Private	L	BROWN	8074
Private	J	BOWEN	13569	Private	L	BROWN	15665
Private	H	BOXHILL	5420	Private	D	BROWN	8033
Private	H	BOYCE	4952	Private	H	BROWN	9760
Private	H A	BOYDE	298	Private	J	BROWN	7806
Private	A	BRADLEY	7796	Private	M	BROWN	5716
Private	H E	BRAITHWAITE	9613	Private	J	BROWN	5730
Private	H N	BRANCH	9136	Private	J W	BROWN	1880
Private	M A	BRATHWAITE	564	Private	J	BROWN	13551
Private	M	BRATHWAITE	1325	Private	C	BROWN	8687

Rank	Initials	Surname	Number
Private	N M	BROWN	9773
Private	A	BROWN	6224
Private	B	BROWN	8063
Private	G A	BROWN	4637
Private	R	BROWN	10887
Private	P	BROWN	2665
Private	A B	BROWN	2664
Private	S N	BROWN	5046
Private	G	BROWN	6225
Private	W	BROWN	5968
Private	E	BROWN	8083
Private	H	BROWN	6248
Private	W	BROWN	7522
Corporal	J T	BROWN	11865
Corporal	J L	BROWN	572
Company Serjeant Major	L G	BROWN	281
Serjeant	G	BROWNE	9667
Private	C	BROWNE	1330
Private	B	BROWNE	10888
Private	H J	BROWNE	2601
Private	C	BRUCE	3123
Private	G	BRUNO	6779
Private	J H	BRUSCH	10920
Private	N	BRYAN	2831
Private	J E	BRYAN	3218
Private	H	BRYAN	3580
Private	W	BRYAN	5793
Private	A C	BRYCE	2172
Private	A	BUCHANAN	8590
Private	U	BUCHANAN	10285
Private	T	BUCKNALL	4906
Private	E M	BUNBURY	26
Private	A W	BUNTIN	303
Private	A C H	BURGESS	5048
Private	H	BURKE	6399
Private	J	BURRELL	9724
Serjeant	G R	BURROWES	4411
Private	C	BURTON	8061
Private	H	BURTON	W/6776
Private	A	BUTLER	3816
Corporal	W V	BYER	10905
Private	P	BYLES	13576
Private	C	BYNOE	5426
Private	M	CADENHEAD	7553
Private	S A	CADLE	1590
Second Lieutenant	B R W	CAHUSAC	
Private	F A	CAINS	580
Private	R A	CALLENDER	50
Private	A	CALLISTE	6440
Private	U	CAMPBELL	14301
Private	L	CAMPBELL	7286
Private	M L	CAMPBELL	3226
Private	A	CAMPBELL	8361
Private	H	CAMPBELL	13595
Private	H	CAMPBELL	9861
Private	S	CAMPBELL	15241
Private	C	CAMPBELL	8093
Private	C	CAMPBELL	7558
Private	G S	CAMPBELL	2828
Private	D	CAMPBELL	15525
Private	E	CAMPBELL	13792
Private	J	CAMPBELL	8099
Private	P	CAMPBELL	13841
Private	S	CAMPBELL	7511
Corporal	C	CAMPBELL	9796
Private	T	CARD	13625
Private	C	CARR	9574
Private	S	CARR	14555
Private	C A	CARR	5236
Private	R	CARR	10179

Rank	Initials	Surname	Number	Rank	Initials	Surname	Number
Serjeant	J E	CARTER	5103	Private	R	CLAYTON	8359
Private	L A	CARTER	7504	Private	A	CLEMETSON	2894
Private	C	CARTER	1340	Private	J	CLERKE	3224
Private	E	CASSIUS	10979	Private	L	COATES	9799
Corporal	T N	CATO	14269	Private	O A	COATES	8115
Private	A	CHAMBERS	9802	Private	C	CODRINGTON	7555
Private	N	CHAMBERS	4166	Private	W	COHEN	8344
Lance Corporal	A	CHAMBERS	4086	Private	T	COHEN	7550
Serjeant	A V A	CHAN	46	Private	S	COKE	7076
Private	W	CHARLES	16462	Private	J	COKE	8041
Private	T	CHARLES	1343	Private	T	COKE	13608
Private	N S	CHARLES	10973	Private	E	COLE	7074
Private	T	CHARLES	16722	Private	W	COLE	16675
Private	D	CHARLTON	3821	Private	R	COLE	15801
Private	L A	CHISHOLM	9811	Drummer	J	COLLAMAN	5798
Private	H	CHRISTIANI	51	Private	W	COLLIE	5073
Private	P	CHRISTIE	7549	Private	D	COLLINGS	14560
Private	C	CHRISTIE	5139	Private	S	COLLINS	3401
Private	J	CLARK	7544	Private	M	COLLYMORE	13620
Pioneer	J	CLARK	9822	Private	C	COMRIE	
Private	C	CLARKE	6235	Private	H	CONSTANTINE	3464
Private	E	CLARKE	3587	Private	W H	COOKE	3463
Private	G N	CLARKE	2611	Private	N	COOKE	12000
Private	H A	CLARKE	4881	Private	J	COOPER	5759
Private	S	CLARKE	9872	Private	H	COVER	3517
Private	S	CLARKE	13844	Private	T	COVER	4257
Private	F	CLARKE	13624	Private	E	COWAN	6248
Private	W A	CLARKE	7069	Private	A F	COX	16561
Private	J	CLARKE	6392	Private	E T	CRAWFORD	3129
Private	T	CLARKE	8932	Private	F	CRICHLOW	10987
Private	W	CLARKE	15720	Private	L	CRITCHLOW	9315
Private	G	CLARKE	6040	Private	S J	CROOKS	1606
Private	J	CLARKE	6462	Lance Corporal	E S	CROOKS	3855
Private	L A	CLAYTON	3339	Private	N M	CROSBIE	1366
Private	M	CLAYTON	10966	Private	U	CROSS	6766

160

Lance Corporal	E	CROSS	4591	Corporal	L A	DAVIS	8011
Private	E	CROSSDALE	6239	Second Lieutenant	J V	DE BOISSIERE	
Private	S	CUKE	794	Company Serjeant Major	A	DE LA BASTIDE	11067
Private	S	CUMBERBATCH	6910	Private	H	DE SILVA	7837
Private	D	CUMMINGS	1902	Corporal	J	DE SOUZA	11063
Serjeant	W	CUNAH	9572	Lance Corporal	G F	DE-PRADINES	822
Private	E	CUNNINGHAM	16046	Private	W	DEACON	7097
Private	J	CURRIE	9620	Boy	J	DEAN	6497
Private	J M	DA SILVA	76	Private	R	DEHANEY	7095
Serjeant	H R	DACOSTA	9934	Private	A	DENNY	11080
Private	G	DACRES	8375	Lance Corporal	A	DES VIGNES	591
Serjeant	C O	DAIRE	2594	Private	J E	DIAMOND	1614
Lance Corporal	A	DAKEY		Private	E	DILLON	6613
Private	J	DALE	8385	Private	E	DIXON	7312
Private	J	DALEY	8388	Private	B	DIXON	2734
Private	J I	DALEY	4154	Private	A	DIXON	8945
Private	T	DALEY	12033	Private	J	DIXON	7089
Private	J	DANIEL	1371	Private	J	DIXON	15932
Private	W E	DANIEL	80	Private	T W	DIXON	3593
Private	P U	DAVIDS	3067	Private	E	DIXON	6213
Private	H	DAVIDSON	7305	Private	N	DIXON	5381
Private	O	DAVIDSON	13857	Private	A L	DONALD	4700
Serjeant	D S	DAVIS	2718	Private	J H	DORSET	340
Serjeant	W	DAVIS	7564	Private	J N	DOUGLAS	5767
Private	A	DAVIS	9931	Private	J	DOVE	6664
Private	T	DAVIS	4899	Private	T	DOWNER	9904
Private	E	DAVIS	12043	Private	S H	DOWNER	7092
Private	J	DAVIS	8586	Private	C	DOYLE	11045
Private	T	DAVIS	13925	Private	V	DRAKE	1137
Private	U H	DAVIS	3228	Serjeant	D A	DRAYTON	4987
Private	J	DAVIS	8119	Private	B A	DRAYTON	9150
Private	J	DAVIS	13843	Private	J	DRIGGS	2482
Private	A	DAVIS	6810	Private	J	DRUMMOND	3168
Private	J	DAVIS	15398	Lance Corporal	E	DUFFAS	3281
Corporal	A A	DAVIS	9909	Private	P	DUHANEY	9907

Rank	Initials	Surname	Number	Rank	Initials	Surname	Number
Private	J B	DUNCAN	12044	Private	C	ELLIS	9966
Private	J W	DUNCAN	11065	Private	J	ELLIS	2788
Private	C	DUNCAN	5092	Private	S G	ELLIS	15745
Private	G	DUNCAN	1385	Private	D	ELLIS	6121
Private	H	DUNCOMBE	2484	Private	E	ELLIS	3220
Private	E A	DUNKLEY	3934	Private	A	EMMANUEL	11095
Private	T	DUNN	8049	Private	A	ENNIS	3801
Private	T	DUNN	9928	Serjeant	E	ESTWICK	4935
Private	J	DUNN	9630	Private	J	EVANS	9626
Private	W	DUNN	15668	Private	E E	FACEY	15813
Corporal	F L A	DUNN	3596	Private	J	FAIRCLOUGH	14572
Private	H	DURRANT	2896	Private	F	FALKCONER	15244
Private	A	DURRANT	16741	Private	J H	FARQUHARSON	3350
Private	S C	DWYER	3990	Private	J	FARQUHARSON	4910
Private	T	DYCE	9912	Private	W	FARQUHARSON	4709
Private	E T	DYCE	4098	Lieutenant	N B	FELLOWES	
Serjeant	J	DYER	5646	Private	D	FERGUSON	7856
Private	A J	DYER	4426	Private	D	FERGUSON	10003
Private	R	DYER	6351	Private	P A	FERGUSON	3470
Private	C	EDDY	11113	Lance Corporal	H	FERGUSON	12080
Private	L	EDMONDSON	86	Private	D	FEVRIER	1149
Private	J C M	EDMUNDS	9050	Private	N	FEVRIER	1150
Serjeant	L R	EDWARDS	1619	Lance Corporal	H A	FINDLATER	6453
Private	F	EDWARDS	6043	Private	H N	FINN	7585
Private	S	EDWARDS	9976	Private	W G	FISHER	1391
Private	N	EDWARDS	12065	Private	R	FISHER	12082
Private	E	EDWARDS	8704	Private	T	FLAKE	3072
Private	B	EDWARDS	8950	Private	W S	FLETCHER	3288
Private	R	EDWARDS	8592	Private	E	FLETCHER	14386
Private	R	EDWARDS	3133	Private	I	FLORIUS	9265
Private	F E	EDWARDS	3991	Private	F	FORBES	10000
Private	P	EDWARDS	6380	Private	N	FORBES	2790
Private	J	ELCOCK	6788	Private	A	FORBES	10002
Private	J	ELLINSON	14371	Private	S	FORBES	3230
Private	A	ELLIOTT	6686	Private	J	FORDE	9266

Private	E	FORRESTER	6382	Private	R E	GARWOOD	2681
Lance Corporal	A C	FORSYTHE	3173	Private	J	GAYLE	10044
Private	A	FOSTER	7854	Private	J	GAYLE	12114
Private	A M	FOSTER	1932	Private	E	GAYLE	10063
Private	J E	FOSTER	3229	Private	G J	GAYLE	2538
Private	D	FOSTER	7329	Private	P	GAYLE	7865
Private	E	FOSTER	13804	Private	C	GEORGE	11161
Private	H	FOWLER	8596	Serjeant	C	GIBBS	11163
Private	W	FOWLING	3169	Private	E	GIBBS	7120
Private	L	FOWLS	8718	Private	W	GIBSON	8255
Private	E	FRANCIS	8141	Private	M	GIFFORD	9386
Private	I	FRANCIS	12101	Private	E	GILLESPIE	3234
Private	W	FRANCIS	2846	Private	R A	GILLING	2792
Private	E	FRANCIS	15987	Private	H	GILPIN	15516
Private	H	FRANCIS	12055	Private	L	GISCOMBE	6113
Private	L	FRANCIS	11135	Private	C	GITTENS	11174
Private	S A	FRANCIS	2789	Private	S	GITTENS	13842
Private	R	FRANCIS	6397	Private	V J	GLUIS	3046
Lance Corporal	J	FRANCIS	3585	Private	W	GOATER	11167
Private	L E L	FRANCOIS	842	Private	A	GODDARD	14108
Private	W	FRASER	15816	Private	E L A	GODDARD	849
Private	W	FRATER	12098	Private	T	GODDEN	6446
Private	N	FULLER	15878	Private	W	GOFFE	2960
Private	A	GABAY	6394	Private	S	GOODEN	12148
Private	F	GABB	5117	Private	W	GOODEN	8399
Private	S O	GABOUREL	1638	Private	A	GOODWIN	9601
Private	W E	GABOUREL	1639	Private	P	GORDAN	11194
Private	W E	GABOUREL	5119	Serjeant	D N	GORDON	5090
Private	C E	GABRIEL	624	Private	A	GORDON	7601
Lance Corporal	D N	GABRIEL	627	Private	C	GORDON	3137
Private	J	GALBRAITH	7864	Private	E	GORDON	3476
Private	H	GALLIMORE	15606	Private	P	GORDON	15753
Private	E	GARNES	8155	Private	C	GORDON	10062
Private	A W	GARRAWAY	11175	Private	S A	GORDON	4164
Private	T	GARVEY	6502	Private	R	GORDON	7454

Private	F	GOWIE	7353	Private	W	GREEN	6264
Serjeant	H S V	GRAHAM	3115	Private	J T	GREEN	3519
Private	G A	GRAHAM	4735	Private	C	GREENFIELD	13651
Private	I B	GRAHAM	2849	Lieutenant	J A	GREER	
Private	J	GRAHAM	7860	Private	F	GRIFFITH	15048
Private	E	GRAHAM	15553	Private	G	GRIFFITHS	14109
Private	J	GRAHAM	7115	Private	A	GRIFFITHS	1659
Private	J	GRAHAM	6325	Private	H C	GRUBB	2239
Private	A	GRAHAM	5780	Private	A U	GUNTER	2739
Lance Corporal	F	GRANDISON	15375	Private	O	GUSTAFF	10093
Serjeant	Z	GRANT	8734	Private	S	GUTHRIE	7116
Private	H	GRANT	15584	Private		HALEY	
Private	A	GRANT	3776	Private	A	HALL	8788
Private	A U	GRANT	10067	Private	A W	HALL	12232
Private	L M	GRANT	4138	Private	S	HALL	8611
Private	A	GRANT	11181	Private	A	HALL	4265
Private	C	GRANT	10040	Private	D A	HALL	3830
Private	N	GRANT	14446	Private	C	HALL	11251
Private	P	GRANT	8737	Private	J	HALL	14388
Private	S	GRANT	15397	Private	W	HALL	12218
Private	J	GRANT	8601	Private	V	HALL	6572
Private	J	GRANT	5796	Private	J	HALL	5557
Private	C J	GRANT	109	Private	W	HAMILTON	5154
Corporal	M	GRANT	13769	Private	J	HAMILTON	8186
Private	H	GRAVES	4544	Private	E	HAMILTON	15830
Private	W	GRAY	7605	Private	U	HAMILTON	7364
Private	B E	GRAY	2795	Private	E	HAMILTON	6066
Private	A	GRAY	6265	Private	W	HAMILTON	4166
Private	L	GREAVES	15043	Private	B	HAMILTON	5958
Private	J	GREAVES	12152	Private	E	HAMILTON	6411
Private	S	GREAVES	13661	Private	C	HAMMOND	6564
Private	A A	GREEN	10099	Private	C M	HANCHARD	2802
Private	N W	GREEN	3354	Private	I	HANDLAN	4486
Private	Z	GREEN	14242	Private	E	HANNA	6057
Private	J	GREEN	5502	Private	C	HANSON	4829

Private	F A	HARDING	5156	Private	I F	HENRY	12179
Private	M	HARDING	1416	Private	S A	HENRY	3481
Private	A M	HARPER	134	Private	C	HENRY	11222
Private	J	HARRIS	8778	Private	E	HENRY	8190
Private	L	HARRIS	4413	Private	I K A	HENRY	8192
Private	H	HARRIS	3356	Private	T N	HENRY	13800
Private	J	HARRIS	8951	Private	Z	HENRY	14391
Private	E	HARRIS	2620	Private	J	HENRY	6444
Private	E	HARRIS	14595	Private	A	HENRY	5491
Private	C	HARRIS	8787	Private	J	HENRY	9648
Private	N	HARRISON	5825	Private	J	HENRY	
Private	R	HARRISON	8609	Corporal	I	HENRY	4040
Private	W N	HART	8606	Private	R	HEPBURN	1179
Private	J	HARTLAN	7631	Private	M	HERCULES	16291
Private	T	HASSOCK	8411	Private	J A	HERCULES	11244
Private	J	HASTINGS	7311	Private	E	HESLOP	10133
Private	P H	HAUGHTON	3235	Private	R	HEWAN	9961
Private	R V	HAWKES	3477	Captain	G E	HEWETT	
Private	C	HAWKES	12198	Lance Serjeant	L	HEWITT	
Private	C	HAWKINS	15941	Private	J	HEYWOOD	15829
Private	D	HAWKINS	5514	Private	D	HIBBERT	7382
Private	J	HAWTHORNE	2276	Private	D A	HIBBERT	5527
Private	J	HAWTHORNE	3238	Private	J A	HIGGINS	10112
Private	F	HAWTHORNE	18101	Private	S	HIGGINS	10105
Private	G W	HAYNES	4905	Private	J	HILL	7622
Private	A E	HEADLEY	1418	Private	B A D C	HIND	6396
Private	A	HEAVEN	7883	Private	J	HINDS	10114
Private	J	HEMMINGS	8188	Private	J	HINDS	3078
Lance Corporal	E A	HENLON	3360	Private	J	HINDS	4434
Private	J	HENRIQUES	5816	Private	J	HINDS	6037
Serjeant	J A	HENRY	4081	Private	A	HINDS	2208
Private	J	HENRY	3623	Private	A	HINES	3264
Private	C	HENRY	8405	Private	W	HITCHMAN	7371
Private	J	HENRY	1963	Captain	H R	HOLCOMBE	
Private	C	HENRY	3141	Private	G A E	HOLDER	1420

Rank	Initials	Surname	Number	Rank	Initials	Surname	Number
Private	A A	HOLDER	16410	Private	T	JACKSON	6301
Corporal	C S	HOLDER	16848	Private	J	JACOBS	16713
Private	U	HOLTHAM	10989	Private	G H	JACOBS	385
Company Quartermaster Serjeant	J R	HOWE	1679	Private	D	JAMES	3293
Private	L	HOWELL	10150	Private	T	JAMES	1191
Private	C	HOWELL	10122	Private	H	JAMES	16621
Private	A	HOWELL	3483	Private	J	JAMES	10190
Private	A	HOWELL	5532	Private	E	JAMES	1433
Lance Corporal	S A	HOWELL	6281	Private	A	JAMES	16042
Private	L H	HUDSON	5820	Private	R	JAMES	10198
Private	J	HUDSON	12210	Private	E D	JAMES	1436
Private	L G	HUEY	3890	Lance Corporal	L	JAMES	6080
Private	S W	HUNTE	5536	Private	S	JARRETT	16145
Private	J	HUNTER	10163	Private	J	JARRETT	15991
Private	E	HURLINGTON	6262	Private	C	JARVIS	654
Private	J R	HUSBANDS	5535	Lance Corporal	E J	JARVIS	147
Private	R	HUTCHINSON	10102	Private	F	JEFFREY	6258
Private	J	HUTCHINSON	3629	Private	L	JEREMIAH	389
Private	F	HUTCHINSON	6221	Lance Corporal	A	JEROME	13924
Private	W	HUTCHINSON	12686	Private	A	JOFFIER	12265
Lieutenant	S M	HUTCHINSON		Private	D	JOHN	13950
Private	N	HYATT	8567	Private	W	JOHN	16810
Corporal	J J	HYLTON	15758	Private	H	JOHNNY	16652
Private	F L	IFIELD	1684	Serjeant	H	JOHNSON	10193
Private	G U	INGRAHAM	6079	Private	S	JOHNSON	7647
Corporal	L S	INGRAM	4414	Private	C M	JOHNSON	10196
Private	C	IRELAND	3891	Private	J T	JOHNSON	12263
Private	L	IRVING	10207	Private	W A	JOHNSON	2692
Private	A	ISAACS	14315	Private	W	JOHNSON	12259
Private	D M	ISHMAEL	9317	Private	A	JOHNSON	10192
Private	H	JACK	11267	Private	J	JOHNSON	14818
Private	A	JACK	6949	Private	A	JOHNSON	14172
Private	A	JACKSON	5832	Private	A	JOHNSON	6295
Private	L	JACKSON	14497	Private	C	JOHNSON	8738
Private	T	JACKSON	8448				

Private	R	JOHNSON	13872	Private	M	JOSEPH	15623
Private	W S	JOHNSON	3000	Private	N	JOSEPHS	10204
Private	H B	JOHNSON	9627	Private	M	KELLY	7652
Private	E	JOHNSON	7137	Private	A	KELLY	10232
Private	J	JOHNSON	5184	Private	S	KELVIN	1695
Private	A	JOHNSON	9584	Private	J	KEMIST	7389
Private	C	JOHNSON	7643	Private	G B	KENDALL	153
Private	C	JOHNSON	6089	Serjeant	F B	KENNINGTON	13771
Private	H	JOHNSON	7904	Lieutenant	F H	KING	
Private	J	JOHNSON	7644	Private	J	KNIGHT	5549
Private	F J	JOHNSON	4328	Private	E	KNIGHT	16141
Private	T	JOHNSON	2271	Private	S	KNIGHT	14080
Private	A	JOHNSON	2509	Private	N	LAIDLOW	16588
Private	J A	JOHNSTON	3545	Private	R H	LAING	1698
Private	H	JONES	3484	Private	D	LAKE	4046
Private	W	JONES	8744	Serjeant	S E	LANG	662
Private	J	JONES	9631	Lieutenant	F A S	LANSDOWN	
Private	A	JONES	11287	Private	I	LARGIE	2624
Private	E	JONES	16011	Private	A	LARMOND	15349
Private	H	JONES	10199	Private	C M	LASHLEY	1460
Private	H	JONES	12250	Serjeant	A	LATIFF	16879
Private	H	JONES	14317	Corporal	M	LAUDER	10252
Private	E	JONES	4380	Private	J W	LAWRENCE	11377
Private	H	JONES	7231	Private	H	LAWRENCE	7160
Private	S B	JONES	6013	Lieutenant Colonel	R R	LAWRENSON	
Private	C	JONES	6581	Private	N	LAWSON	8467
Private	L	JONES	10851	Private	D	LAWSON	4382
Captain	L J	JONES		Private	A	LAYNE	16316
Serjeant	O L	JORDAN	1046	Private	A	LEADER	15842
Private	J N	JORDAN	4883	Private	N	LECKEY	8298
Private	G	JORDAN	11316	Private	I	LEE	3734
Private	F W G	JORDON	1446	Private	A L	LEE	1991
Private	D	JOSEPH	11308	Private	W A	LEITH	4920
Private	E	JOSEPH	6954	Private	J	LEONCE	11365
Private	W	JOSEPH	3024	Private	W	LESLIE	14204

Private	H	LESLIE	15528	Private	F	MAIRS	14216
Private	R	LESTER	8782	Private	C A L	MAIS	2004
Private	R	LETMAN	8979	Private	R	MALCOLM	9185
Private	F T	LETT	11393	Private	H M	MANIX	16815
Private	S	LEWIS	7912	Private	H	MANNING	2915
Private	J	LEWIS	6569	Private	C	MANNS	14065
Private	A	LEWIS	10271	Lance Corporal	H C	MAPP	921
Private	S M	LEWIS	11373	Corporal	J	MAPP	16869
Private	I	LEWIS	7395	Private	C	MAPSON	6829
Private	A	LEWIS	14231	Private	N	MARCUS	8436
Private	J	LEWIS	4893	Private	J	MARK	6833
Private	D	LEZAMA	16427	Private	I	MARKS	16947
Private	R	LILLEY	12566	Private	J	MARKS	16754
Private	E	LINTON	4437	Private	D	MARKSMAN	11404
Private	R E	LINTON	3895	Private	D	MARSHALL	11425
Private	I	LLEWELLYN	9632	Private	J	MARSHALL	2525
Private	M	LLEWELLYN	7092	Private	J	MARTIN	3650
Private	A	LLEWELLYN	6364	Private	C	MARTIN	4223
Private	C	LOGAN	8969	Private	I	MARTIN	8994
Corporal	H	LONEY	5851	Private	E R	MARTIN	1224
Private	R	LOPEZ	15120	Private	T	MARTIN	1713
Private	J	LOVELL	5211	Major	A T De M	MARTIN	
Private	E	LOWE	11355	Private	J	MASON	10351
Private	M	LUGG	7670	Private	J	MASON	6309
Private	L S	LYNCH	3185	Serjeant	J	MASSON	1715
Private	A	LYNCH	897	Private	R	MATHURIN	9290
Private	J	LYNCH	7159	Private	E	MATTHEWS	16448
Private	M	LYNCH	3415	Private	M	MATTS	7427
Private	D S	LYNCH	1471	Private	S	MAXEY	7682
Corporal	A P	LYON	2000	Private	J	MAXWELL	5862
Private	R A	LYONS	10280	Private	E	McBURNIE	11443
Private	J	MACK	R/3367	Private	E	McCALLA	12330
Private	S	MAHONEY	8009	Private	C	McCARTNEY	15686
Private	C W	MAILLARD	2006	Private	H A	McCOY	3249
Private	E	MAINE	8807				

Corporal	W	McCREBIE	16120	Private	C	McPHERSON	1482
Private	A	McDERMOTT	10317	Private	L	McPHERSON	2312
Private	W	McDERMOTT	8432	Private	H R	McPHERSON	4175
Private	C P	McDONALD	7416	Private	J	McQUAY	14844
Private	L	McDONALD	14105	Second Lieutenant	R	MEEK	
Private	T	McDONALD	5463	Private	J	MELLISH	3491
Lance Corporal	C V	McDONALD	2303	Private	C	MENZIE	10228
Lance Corporal	L Z	McDOWALL	3305	Corporal	J S	MERCURIUS	11432
Private	D	McFARLANE	7988	Private	A	MESSAM	8101
Private	T	McFARLANE	12250	Private	C	MIGNOTT	10938
Private	J A	McFAYDEN	3515	Private	P	MILFORD	14795
Private	R G	McGLASHIN	7681	Private	Z	MILLAR	6537
Private	W	McGLOIRE	6838	Private	L	MILLER	15351
Private	S T	McINTOSH	3189	Private	T	MILLER	6257
Private	J	McINTOSH	11438	Private	E	MILLER	6766
Private	S	McINTOSH	7675	Private	H	MILLER	5559
Private	W D	McINTOSH	12353	Private	J N	MILLS	4012
Private	J	McINTOSH	13780	Private	E	MILLS	1227
Private	A	McINTYRE	8152	Lance Corporal	L	MILLS	13522
Private	C	McKENZIE	3365	Private	S O	MING	7435
Private	E P	McKENZIE	4673	Private	T	MINOTT	6145
Private	S	McKENZIE	6322	Private	C A	MITCHELL	5578
Private	J J	McKENZIE	14249	Private	J	MITCHELL	6485
Private	G H	McKENZIE	16148	Private	J	MITCHELL	12341
Private	W	McKENZIE	6102	Private	J	MITCHELL	9191
Private	J A	McKOY	6576	Private	D	MITCHELL	14618
Private	C	McLAUGHLIN	10308	Private	R A	MITCHELL	2529
Private	C	McLEAN	10335	Private	S	MITCHELL	11454
Private	J	McLEAN	12377	Private	S W	MOAZE	9091
Private	W	McLEAN	2309	Private	H	MODESTE	11474
Private	A R	McLENNON	2589	Private	E	MODESTE	16570
Private	S	McLEOD	6314	Private	T	MOFFATT	15958
Private	J W	McLEOD	15700	Private	J	MOLLETT	7690
Private	R	McNAUGHT	8426	Private	C	MONLOUIS	9294
Private	J	McNEIL	14836	Private	C	MOODIE	13972

Rank	Initials	Surname	Number	Rank	Initials	Surname	Number
Private	A	MOODY	8406	Company Serjeant Major	E N T	MUNN	6409
Private	W	MOORE	7929	Private	J	MURPHY	4220
Private	C	MOORE	3150	Private	S	MURRAY	9506
Private	L H	MOORE	8110	Private	L	MURRAY	3004
Private	L	MOORE	5162	Private	J	MURRAY	7422
Private	H	MOORE	5584	Private	C	MURRAY	6263
Private	J	MORALDO	680	Private	M	MYERS	7932
Captain	J W	MORAND-LEES		Private	E	MYERS	3783
Second Lieutenant	C F	MORGAN		Corporal	J	MYRIE	7109
Private	J	MORGAN	6319	Private	J	NASH	16738
Private	C	MORGAN	16248	Private	J A	NEDD	185
Private	Z	MORGAN	16204	Private	P	NELSON	10412
Private	J	MORGAN	423	Private	B	NELSON	6981
Private	A	MORGAN		Private	E S	NELSON	2697
Corporal	L A	MORGAN	3656	Private	H	NELSON	7709
Captain	H F	MORRELL		Private	W	NELSON	7937
Private	W	MORRIS	10336	Lance Serjeant	T	NELSON	5253
Private	H	MORRIS	7429	Corporal	J	NEMBHARD	10416
Private	J	MORRIS	6090	Private	N	NENTON	11427
Private	D	MORRIS	6327	Private	A	NEVERSON	6582
Private	G S	MORRIS	14248	Private	H	NEWELL	9528
Private	S	MORRIS	4914	Private	J	NEWMAN	6119
Private	C	MORRISON	4690	Private	J	NEWTON	12421
Private	S	MORRISON	10312	Private	B	NEWTON	6045
Private	S	MORRISON	10324	Private	P	NICHOLAS	15268
Private	J	MORRISON	13691	Private	J	NICHOLS	6404
Private	C W	MOSS	12414	Private	J	NOBLE	10407
Private	T	MOSS	2520	Private	A	NOBLE	15652
Private	C	MOSS	5861	Private	I	NORTHOVER	2976
Private	O	MOSS	14130	Private	B	NORVILLE	15141
Private	E A	MOULTON	4010	Private	J	O'MEALLY	2039
Private	W F	MULLIN	15136	Private	R S	OAKLEY	6398
Private	D	MULLINGS	10358	Private	R	OGITRIE	
Private	C	MULLINS	2440	Private	L	ONFROY	10422

Rank	Initials	Surname	Number
Private	M J	OROSCO	16382
Private	P	OSBORNE	5590
Private	J	OSBOURNE	12430
Private	L T	OSORIO	1745
Lieutenant	K C G	OTTLEY	
Serjeant	C	OTTO	9365
Private	L J	OUGHTON	15960
Private	H	OWEN	4959
Private	R	OWENS	12431
Private	S	PADDYFOOT	7327
Private	L	PAISLEY	6550
Private	E N	PALMER	3493
Private	F	PALMER	7182
Private	L	PALMER	4614
Private	J	PALMER	10435
Private	S	PALMER	8181
Private	D	PANTON	8964
Private	G N	PARKER	16075
Private	G	PARKER	1494
Corporal	S	PARKER	10436
Private	W	PARKES	12435
Private	J	PARKES	8462
Private	A	PARKES	8962
Private	D	PARKINS	8065
Private	C	PARKS	2750
Private	J	PARKS	
Private	J	PASCALL	16590
Private	J	PASSLEY	4278
Private	J	PATERSON	6270
Private	D J	PATRICE	1239
Private	J	PATRICK	11516
Private	J F	PATRICK	15146
Private	A	PATRICK	1493
Private	I S	PATTEN	6124
Private	S	PATTERSON	7947
Private	H	PAYNE	5600
Private	E S	PEART	5602
Private	H	PEART	3915
Private	L	PECK	15843
Private	E	PEDDIE	7187
Private	V G	PEREIRA	191
Private	E A	PERO	1241
Private	W	PERRY	
Private	A	PETERS	446
Private	E	PETERS	6595
Private	A	PETERS	16235
Private	O	PETERS	7328
Private	C	PHILBERT	11530
Private	H	PHILLIPS	14118
Private	J	PHILLIPS	10449
Private	C	PHILLIPS	11505
Private	C	PHILLIPS	4895
Private	N	PHILLIPS	447
Private	H	PHILLIPS	6160
Lance Corporal	G	PHILLIPS	1077
Private	T	PHOENIX	15150
Private	F	PIERRE	16305
Private	R	PIERRE	11549
Private	D L	PIERREPOINT	5605
Private	T	PILE	16905
Private	E	PINDER	441
Private	P	PINKNEY	4902
Private	G	PINNOCK	8638
Private	S	PINNOCK	10452
Private	C	PINNOCK	6678
Private	E	PLUMMER	12434
Private	W	PLUMMER	2150
Private	C H	POMMELLS	6358
Private	A	POMPEY	11523

Rank	Initials	Surname	Number	Rank	Initials	Surname	Number
Private	J J	PORTER	6332	Private	W	REID	9103
Private	E	POTTINGER	3722	Private	L	REID	476
Private	R A	POTTINGER	15965	Private	P	REID	6145
Serjeant	L E	POWELL	5197	Private	A	REID	8489
Private	G	POWELL	10428	Private	J	REID	4393
Private	S	POWELL	8204	Private	A	REID	14395
Private	E	POWELL	10448	Private	E	REID	14722
Private	I	POWELL	14335	Private	N	REID	15775
Private	F	POWELL	15715	Private	E	REID	4127
Private	H B	POWELL	5889	Private	F	REID	4717
Private	M	PRENTICE	707	Private	A	REID	3642
Private	D	PRESCOTT	14351	Private	D S	RENEAU	5295
Lance Corporal	H L	PRESTON	3494	Private	R	RENNIE	5911
Serjeant	J	PRICE	14027	Private	F	RENNIE	5614
Private	C	PRICE	10467	Private	C	RENNIE	960
Private	C	PRICE	15160	Lieutenant	C	REVELL	
Private	S	PRICE	12461	Private	D	REYNOLD	11570
Private	J	PRICE	15769	Private	C	REYNOLDS	3903
Private	T D	PRIMO	199	Private	N	RHODEN	12487
Private	P A	PRINCE	4559	Private	I D	RHODEN	2367
Private	A	PROSPERE	11511	Private	V A	RICHARDS	3495
Private	J	PRYCE	15646	Private	H	RICHARDS	8642
Private	R H	PUSEY	3842	Private	A R	RICHARDS	2631
Second Lieutenant	G	PYKE		Private	J	RICHARDS	6501
Private	F	RAMIEREZ	11592	Private	S R	RICHARDS	3669
Private	C	RAMSEY	6336	Private	D	RICHARDS	7195
Private	P	RAMSEY	7333	Private	C	RICHARDS	6712
Private	P	RAMSEY	6342	Private	J R	RICHARDS	5913
Private	E	RAMSON	12471	Private	J	RICHARDS	6261
Private	S J	RAPER	5635	Private	W C	RICHARDSON	14398
Private	S	REDWOOD	8469	Private	J	RICHARDSON	3563
Private	W S	REEVES	14220	Private	N	RICKETS	5903
Private	E	REID	6139	Private	D	RICKETTS	8235
Private	A N	REID	3029	Private	N L	RICKETTS	8260
Private	C	REID	5623	Private	F O	RICKETTS	5621

Rank	Initials	Surname	Number	Rank	Initials	Surname	Number
Private	T	RICKETTS	5918	Private	W	RUSSELL	12466
Private	Z	RICKETTS	6176	Private	C O	SALMON	3200
Corporal	O	RICKMAN	9628	Private	J O	SALMON	14209
Private	S	RILEY	6421	Private	C L	SALMON	2060
Private	I	RILEY	6405	Private	H	SALMON	14176
Private	H	RIVAS	5299	Private	J	SALMON	8088
Private	E	ROACH	10484	Private	C A	SAMMS	3675
Private	D	ROACHFORD	11578	Serjeant	A F	SAMPSON	3749
Serjeant	R	ROBERTS	8651	Serjeant	S	SAMUEL	4958
Private	R	ROBERTS	8847	Private	U	SAMUELS	2638
Private	J E	ROBERTS	12465	Private	D	SAMUELS	3496
Private	R R	ROBERTS	15508	Private	B	SAMUELS	8656
Private	B E	ROBERTS	6137	Private	J	SAMUELS	5002
Lance Serjeant	D S	ROBERTS	5271	Private	J	SAMUELS	9590
Corporal	J	ROBERTS	3101	Private	W	SAMUELS	5944
Serjeant	A	ROBINSON	7191	Private	C	SAMUELS	5540
Private	C	ROBINSON	4966	Private	E	SAMUELS	12491
Private	N L	ROBINSON	3671	Lance Corporal	T R	SAMUELS	10562
Private	J	ROBINSON	16766	Lance Corporal	L	SAMUELS	15611
Private	N J	ROBINSON	15892	Private	G	SANDY	16312
Private	T A	ROBINSON	2379	Private	J	SAUNDERS	6157
Private	W	ROBINSON	2375	Private	J	SAUNDERS	2567
Drummer	S	ROBINSON	5417	Private	J	SAUNDERS	8230
Private	F	ROCQUE	1262	Private	N	SAUNDERS	15969
Private	F A	ROJAS	1514	Private	E	SAUNDERS	2559
Private	D	ROLLE	6144	Serjeant	A R	SAVAGE	5100
Private	S	ROLLE	15478	Private	A	SAVAGE	6548
Private	I	ROMNEY	1087	Private	L	SAVARY	492
Private	G	ROSE	5631	Private	E V	SCARBOROUGH	9004
Private	P	ROSE	12505	Private	C	SCARLETT	9629
Private	D	ROSS	8857	Private	C	SCARLETT	10058
Private	A B	ROUSE	1059	Private	C	SCHOLES	4061
Private	W	ROY	8262	Lance Corporal	H A	SCIPIO	11646
Private	H	ROY	15967	Private	R	SCOTT	13948
Private	J M	RUDDOCK	3431				

Private	E	SCOTT	10641	Private	R A	SLUSHER	1784
Private	J H	SCOTT	1778	Private	F W	SMALL	4562
Lance Corporal	J	SCOTT	6345	Private	C	SMALL	12570
Private	L A	SEACOMBE	1780	Private	W	SMALLING	9520
Private	J A	SEALES	11651	Private	C	SMALLING	6355
Private	G S	SEALY	5640	Private	W	SMART	221
Private	S A	SEARS	233	Private	N F	SMART	12550
Private	J A	SEARS	12537	Private	I	SMART	239
Private	A	SEATON	2389	Private	C	SMITH	10609
Private	F A	SEAVERS	2752	Private	R A	SMITH	7225
Private	C	SEVERIN	11626	Private	A	SMITH	8261
Private	Z	SHAND	4448	Private	J Z	SMITH	5927
Private	S	SHARP	3364	Private	C	SMITH	5326
Private	S A	SHAW	2981	Private	C	SMITH	8244
Private	R	SHAW	15970	Private	J	SMITH	4451
Private	G	SHAW	2997	Private	C	SMITH	8251
Private	R	SHERWOOD	6348	Private	C J	SMITH	16892
Private	B	SHRIMPTON	10602	Private	M	SMITH	14400
Second Lieutenant	L G	SILVERA		Private	C	SMITH	11640
Private	O S	SILVERA	2076	Private	E	SMITH	14174
Private	D	SIMMONDS	3433	Private	R	SMITH	7461
Private	F	SIMMONDS	3787	Private	W	SMITH	7219
Private	G	SIMMONDS	6862	Private	M	SMITH	8232
Private	P	SIMMONS	11620	Private	P A	SMITH	6402
Private	W	SIMPSON	10554	Private	J E	SMITH	13951
Private	J	SIMPSON	7222	Private	A	SMITH	10614
Private	H A	SIMPSON	3318	Private	B	SMITH	2560
Private	P	SIMPSON	3309	Private	C	SMITH	14678
Private	J	SINCLAIR	12563	Private	J	SMITH	490
Private	E	SINCLAIR	3527	Private	O	SMITH	7736
Private	F	SINCLAIR	14383	Private	J E	SMITH	2394
Private	G	SINCLAIR	10643	Private	R S	SMITH	5113
Private	A	SKEETE	240	Private	N	SMITH	5391
Private	C	SKEETE	13956	Private	N	SMITH	4287
Private	C	SKYERS	7203	Private	J H	SMITH	3882

Corporal	A C	SMITH	2924	Private	A	STEWARD	12529
Private	C	SNAITH	3317	Private	H	STEWART	3432
Private	W	SNOW	6281	Private	T	STEWART	10595
Private	A	SOLOMON	719	Private	C	STEWART	12527
Private	H A	SOMMERS	5948	Private	E	STEWART	8653
Private	S	SONGSTER	484	Private	T	STEWART	5923
Lance Serjeant	C S	SPARKMAN	6164	Private	E	STEWART	6153
Private	A	SPARKS	8240	Private	H	STEWART	14221
Private	I	SPEARIN	15416	Private	S	STEWART	6400
Corporal	D	SPEID	10573	Private	D	STEWART	5835
Private	J	SPENCE	12532	Private	M	STODDART	3260
Private	G	SPENCE	10561	Private	J N	STONE	12522
Private	J	SPENCE	15971	Private	E	STORR	2569
Private	C J	SPENCE	8874	Private	R	STRACHAN	9818
Private	T	SPENCE	6165	Private	G	STRAKER	9114
Private	J	SPENCE	13946	Private	A	STREET	8535
Private	R N	SPENCER	11621	Private	H	SULLIVAN	4945
Private	L R W	SPENCER	11617	Corporal	F C	SULLY	11631
Private	T	SPENCER	6181	Private	R	SUTHERLAND	15712
Private	G B	SPRINGER	5652	Private	D	SUTHERLAND	5949
Private	A	SQUIRES	6746	Private	C H	SWABY	12559
Private	H	St. BERNARD	16579	Private	M L	TAITT	704
Private	M	St. PHOR	11623	Private	J A	TAITTE	1530
Private	W	STAPLETON	11614	Private	O	TATE	7373
Private	C	STEINBERGER	12578	Private	J C	TAYLOR	12626
Private	L	STEPHEN	488	Private	D	TAYLOR	6752
Private	A	STEPHENS	12533	Private	A	TAYLOR	9011
Private	W	STEPHENS	16190	Private	J	TELESFORD	6514
Serjeant	J	STEPHENSON	4135	Private	J	TELFORD	5668
Private	J A	STEPHENSON	5646	Private	J	TELFORD	5669
Private	A J	STEPHENSON	16123	Private	G A	THANKS	3790
Private	W	STEPHENSON	9633	Major	H W	THELWALL	
Private	J	STEPHENSON	15430	Serjeant		THOMAS	8316
Private	A	STEPHENSON	5935	Private	J	THOMAS	8562
Private	D	STERLING	7221	Private	E	THOMAS	5674

Rank	Initials	Surname	Number	Rank	Initials	Surname	Number
Private	V	THOMAS	6867	Private	E J	TYNE	2988
Private	F	THOMAS	16813	Private	J	ULETT	6505
Private	H	THOMAS	13718	Serjeant	G E P	USHER	1813
Private	A	THOMAS	11708	Lance Corporal	B A	VAN GRONIGEN	1534
Private	S E	THOMAS	3437	Private	J	VARGAS	5356
Private	L	THOMAS	743	Private	L A	VASSEL	7252
Private	J	THOMAS	15270	Private	A J	VASSELL	14690
Private	U	THOMAS	11257	Private	S	VASSELL	7239
Lieutenant	C L	THOMAS		Lance Corporal	J A	VAUGHAN	988
Serjeant	C C	THOMPSON	13893	Private	W	VICKERS	10714
Private	L	THOMPSON	10673	Private	S F	VIDAL	2201
Private	R	THOMPSON	14003	Private	F	VIEARA	11719
Private	E	THOMPSON	10701	Private	A	VINCENT	11720
Private	E	THOMPSON	16022	Private	D	WAITE	6402
Private	C	THOMPSON	10671	Private	C	WAITE	11660
Private	W	THOMPSON	8827	Private	G	WAITH	10582
Private	S U	THOMPSON	8665	Corporal	S	WAITHE	15204
Private	H	THOMPSON	10662	Private	J	WALDEN	3505
Private	N	THOMPSON	6391	Private	C	WALDRON	11787
Private	J A	THOMPSON	2576	Private	J	WALKER	7489
Private	C E	THOMPSON	5268	Private	R	WALKER	7765
Lieutenant	A E	THOMPSON		Private	J	WALKER	10799
Private	W	THOMSON	6166	Private	L	WALKER	6159
Private		THORPE		Private	Z	WALKER	4243
Private	L P	TIMPSON	3502	Private	J	WALKER	5369
Private	N	TODD	9611	Private	P	WALKER	12663
Private	W	TOMLINSON	15369	Private	J	WALKER	5631
Private	R	TOUSSAINT	6754	Private	J	WALLACE	6187
Private	M	TRACEY	6395	Private	N	WALLEN	10778
Private	A	TRESTAN	10445	Private	A	WALSH	6287
Private	L	TUCKER	8490	Private	A	WALTERS	8304
Private	S A	TUCKER	9634	Private	Z	WALTERS	3440
Lance Corporal	R R	TURNBULL	6388	Private	J	WALTERS	10925
Private	E	TUSLIN	12611	Private	W	WARD	5983
Lieutenant	G S H	TYNDALE					

Rank	Initials	Surname	Number	Rank	Initials	Surname	Number
Private	G	WARD	996	Private	N S	WILLIAMS	3020
Private	A U	WARREN	3696	Private	I	WILLIAMS	9311
Private	G	WASHINGTON	2655	Private	W	WILLIAMS	5984
Lance Corporal	A A	WASHINGTON	263	Private	E H	WILLIAMS	12689
Lance Corporal	R H	WASON	1070	Private	A	WILLIAMS	5981
Private	L O	WATERMAN	11761	Private	A	WILLIAMS	11794
Private	J J	WATSON	4674	Private	S	WILLIAMS	8536
Private	S	WATSON	10818	Private	J	WILLIAMS	12641
Private	E	WEBB	15913	Private	R	WILLIAMS	14505
Private	A	WEBBER	7162/8512	Private	R S	WILLIAMS	3382
Private	A	WEDDERBURN	7278	Private	E	WILLIAMS	11736
Private	J	WEEKLEY	10781	Private	G	WILLIAMS	9535
Private	A	WELLINGTON	5879	Private	L	WILLIAMS	8279
Private	R	WELLS	9305	Private	N	WILLIAMS	10766
Private	V	WENT	11772	Private	N A	WILLIAMS	10742
Corporal	P S	WHEATLEY	3698	Private	S A	WILLIAMS	7998
Private	C	WHILBY	6183	Private	D	WILLIAMS	7241
Private	D C	WHITE	6377	Private	C A	WILLIAMS	3507
Private	R T	WHITE	1285	Private	C	WILLIAMS	10825
Private	J	WHITE	4075	Private	F	WILLIAMS	14222
Private	C	WHITE	7163	Private	S	WILLIAMS	8540
Captain	H C	WHITELEGG		Private	E M O	WILLIAMS	11732
Private	F A	WHITELOCKE	4407	Private	E	WILLIAMS	9014
Private	J	WHITLEY	8520	Private	J	WILLIAMS	10807
Private	T J	WHITTAKER	3516	Private	T	WILLIAMS	5989
Private	J	WHITTINGHAM	5781	Private	S	WILLIAMS	8005
Private	W B C	WILLIAM	2430	Private	E	WILLIAMS	5695
Serjeant	E W	WILLIAMS	4360	Private	D	WILLIAMS	7276
Serjeant	L	WILLIAMS	4977	Private	E	WILLIAMS	10804
Regimental Serjeant Major	E	WILLIAMS	4749	Private	R	WILLIAMS	6401
Private	D	WILLIAMS	8305	Private	A	WILLIAMS	3524
Private	J	WILLIAMS	10817	Lieutenant	A J De C	WILLIAMS	
Private	R	WILLIAMS	10733	Lance Corporal	S N	WILLIAMS	2879
Private	J E	WILLIAMS	3444	Company Serjeant Major	P N	WILLIAMS	10813
Private	C G	WILLIAMS	1838	Private	J	WILLIS	3506

Rank	Initials	Surname	Number	Rank	Initials	Surname	Number
Private	D	WILLOCK	5867	Private	J H	WRIGHT	3703
Private	H B	WILSON	10834	Private	A	WRIGHT	14767
Private	J	WILSON	14828	Private	C	WRIGHT	6185
Private	J	WILSON	2126	Private	S	WRIGHT	7050
Private	W G	WILSON	1834	Private	W R	WRIGHT	4841
Private	D	WILSON	13991	Private	H	WRINGER	10492
Private	J	WILSON	7990	Private	G	WRITTEN	11185
Private	G O	WILSON	3383	Private	W	WYNTER	14280
Private	T M	WILSON	10780	Private	E	WYNTER	14385
Private	W	WILTSHIRE	11777	Private	L	YARD	15223
Private	S	WINES	7242	Private	H W F	YAW	1073
Private	T A	WINT	2994	Private	E	YEARWOOD	14412
Lance Corporal	J A	WINTER	2937	Second Lieutenant	L B	YOUNG	
Private	J A	WISDOM	10757	Private	L	YOUNG	8282
Private	J T	WITTER	2823	Private	S	YOUNG	16411
Serjeant	E W	WOOD	1546	Private	I	YOUNG	6622
Private	A J	WOODLEY	2127	Private	D	YOUNG	5429
Private	J	WOOLERY	14179	Private	I	YOUNGSOME	10848
Private	N	WOOLERY	3203	Soldier			
Private	R L	WOOLWARD	1293	Soldier			
Lance Corporal	R B	WRIGHT	6398	Soldier			
Serjeant	D	WRIGHT	15217	Soldier			
Private	Z	WRIGHT	10810	Soldier			
Private	A F	WRIGHT	3385	Soldier			
Private	U	WRIGHT	2824	Soldier			
Private	C A	WRIGHT	749	Serjeant			

For more information please see westindiacommittee.org/caribbeansgreatwar/

EPILOGUE

The Caribbean's Great War was in many ways similar to that of the rest of the world. The sheer scale and technological nature of this global event baffled and shocked millions, taking the lives of over 15 million people as its gloom and terror engulfed the world. With Colonialism rife at the time of the conflict, it is far too easy to portray the West Indian men and women who strove to secure victory for their King and Mother Country as people who were misled or in some way forced to participate, manipulated by a colonial machine that held them captive long after the infamous era of slavery had passed. It is true that the administration of the British Caribbean was centralised, with the Colonial Office in London sitting at its hub, fed into by the various legislative councils throughout the region. These administrations were led by successful white and mixed race men, and influenced by their commercial interests. It is also true that the prospects of the average black man in the region had never attained the same level as white and mixed race Creoles. As a heavily agricultural region, the fate of West Indians as a whole lay not only in the hands of Mother Nature, but those of the Mother Country too, being economically dependent upon its trade relations with her and her support in recovering from the perpetual natural disasters that beset the region. The successful introduction of European sugar beet had ripped the heart out of the Caribbean sugar industry, an industry that had placed them at the pinnacle of global economic growth, for centuries making the Caribbean one of the richest economies the world had ever known. As is the way of mankind, this wealth was concentrated in the hands of a few, and harvested from the sweat of many according to the social edicts of the Plantocracy. This situation had to end, and did almost a century before the first traces of the First World War became evident.

As the shots rang out from Gavrilo Princip's gun in Sarajevo on 28th June 1914, fatally wounding Archduke Franz Ferdinand and his beloved wife Sophie, unbeknown to the men and women of the West Indies, this proved to be the starting pistol of their race towards the second and most powerful episode of their liberation. This war, the worst the world had ever known, was seen by some as a territorial struggle between the progeny of their beloved Queen Victoria, each jostling for more power and land in Europe. From this perspective, it is easy to construe the thousands of West Indians who rallied to the aid of their King and Country as being misdirected and manipulated by the colonial power that was all too influential in their lives. Whilst these men and boys had insisted on fighting, they were not well briefed and may not have fully appreciated, nor understood, the circumstances of the war, nor the consequences their personal sacrifices would have for their people in the Caribbean. Most simply pursued a better life for themselves and their families in the guise of regular pay and a pension. Instead they saw the Mother Country in the raw, Edwardian Britain, where class division was at its worst. Whilst training in Britain, and serving alongside their British comrades, they experienced first-hand the plight of the working classes - their poor housing, sanitation, dismal health and lack of prospects. West Indians of every hue began to question the order of things and, like other members of the Empire that had come to Britain's aid, began to question their place within a colonial system whose very existence they now challenged. It was clear that they had a healthier lifestyle, and by and large fared better than their British counterparts. This led them to question why they should rank beneath them socially. The benefits of this biased arrangement were now scrutinised as was its duration – measured in centuries. These questions were all the more pertinent to the Caribbean, a region racked by annual natural disasters, whose economy had been undermined by the success of the European sugar beet, and decimated by trade embargoes imposed during the war.

Inevitably those with investments in the status quo were keen to impose a structure that secured their position at the top, but now those very same people needed help from the masses that for centuries had languished beneath them. This was no new story, but one repeated for centuries throughout mankind. What was different in the case of the First World War was the velocity in which change progressed, forcing people together without time to carefully choreograph their interactions to ensure each remained blind to the weakness of those above them in the artificial edifice of colonialism. For once the realities were glimpsed, the whole sham could and did so easily unravel.

Ad hoc military punishments far too inhumane to record in this book, but prevalent throughout the conflict and administered to all lower ranking personnel throughout the British Army, served to remind men of their 'place' in the Army and the Empire it served. Racism reflected in unequal pay and benefits and deployment to native labour corps to undertake the lowliest of tasks placed the West Indians at the bottom of the colonial pile. The entire experience served to encourage these men to assess their place, and to interrogate the rules of entitlement.

The story of West Indian liberation is not one confined to that of slavery, but one that encompasses the experiences of the Caribbean's Great War. Here, like so many shifted from one end of the globe to the other by the colonial powers that clashed in Europe, West Indians experienced their first taste of citizenship of the wider world, a place strangely familiar to creoles that had originated from the four corners of the Earth. Like women in Britain that had taken up employment left vacant by the troops, it would prove too much for society to demand that they resume their pre-war subservience whereby their human rights and individual potential were thwarted.

With the Representation of the People Act 1918, that resulted from a step change in people's political awareness and expectations, all men over the age of twenty-one gained the vote in Britain, as did those aged nineteen at the time of their service in the conflict. Women over the age of thirty also gained the vote, provided they were married, owned property or were graduates voting in their university town. Until that point in British history, the vote was reserved for the privileged few; upper class white men. In the Caribbean, the 16,000 'Huge and Mighty Men of Valour' of every class, colour and creed received no such recognition. This failure to appreciate their vast contribution to the security of their Sovereign and Mother Country gave rise to a plethora of political activism that took the region by storm. Not only were they indignant at the treatment of their heroes in the lead up to Taranto, but this now close-knit multiracial band of brothers of every class and creed saw little justification for the continued inequality that had for centuries been dictated by race. For them, it was no longer acceptable to be administered by Legislative Councils comprising whites, and their mixed race relations, albeit punctuated by the few affluent blacks whose social positions had slowly evolved since the abolition of slavery generations before. Instead the veterans of the First World War, like their comrades in Britain, expected and were to demand a 'Land Fit for Heroes' in the Caribbean. In so doing, they recognised their ability and the opportunity to shape their own destiny, and seized it with both hands.

Despite an heroic contribution to the Caribbean's Great War, although their slave ancestors had become the first women in the then British Empire to receive female suffrage in the settlement of Freetown established for freed slaves in Sierra Leone, West Indian women were forced to wait until the 1960s for that right, being among the last British women to receive the vote.

At the end of the war, the world was awash with millions of servicemen and women failed by countries bankrupted by the war effort that could no longer afford the pay, transportation, welfare, pensions or medication the veterans and their families had been promised. Displaced troops, situated thousands of miles away from home and their loved ones who had also suffered from the attrition of war, found themselves living in unacceptable conditions during a prolonged demobilisation that appeared endless for people exhausted from years of conflict and its inevitable hardships. Many tested barriers that they no longer accepted as pertinent or necessary given victory had been accomplished. Succumbing to behaviour that challenged military authority, particularly as that authority compromised what we now regard as their human rights, men were found guilty of 'mutiny'. Pay cuts, loss of benefits, poor living conditions and little hope of returning home agitated the troops and undermined military authority. The racial bias displayed by men, such as Barnard and his command, was fuel to the fire and men tired of war and the oppressive nature of military service, provoked by a command keen to remind them of their inferior status within the traditional colonialist scheme of things, were soon branded mutineers. This overshadowed their contribution to the war, leading to the British West Indies Regiment being excluded

M. Sowerby

THE · WEST · INDIES
Oh, don't you hear my bugle blow?
For when it sounds "revally",
All the West Indies wake, you know,
And to the flag they rally!

from the honour of participating in the Victory Parade in London on 19th July 1919 and virtually erased from history. Amongst these men the move towards liberation accelerated rapidly. On returning home, they received a rapturous welcome from people who had suffered from having their markets shut down by the war. Reunited, these West Indians began to review the conditions, position and prospects of the British West Indies, and to question whether the pre-war status quo should continue. Now Europe was weak, and had little appetite or resources to challenge detractors from the colonial regime. Now was the time for change. Out of the ashes of the colonial hierarchy, undermined by the avarice and jealousies of fellow empires, a phoenix arose, embodying the search for equality that was so sadly lacking in the Caribbean, advancing its people beyond mere liberty and closer to their goal of mutual respect with those that had for centuries belittled them.

When the call to arms once again echoed across the British Empire with the advent of the Second World War in 1939, the response from the Caribbean was made by a people whose consciousness had been awakened by the Caribbean's Great War and it was different.

TIMELINE OF THE HISTORY OF THE CARIBBEAN

Christopher Columbus becomes the first known European to 'discover' the Caribbean.

English privateer Sir Francis Drake begins a lengthy assault on Spanish ships and ports in the Caribbean.

British colony founded on Barbados.

1612   **1623**

1492   **1500**   1585   **1600**   Britain colonises Bermuda.   Britain colonises St. Kitts.   **1627**

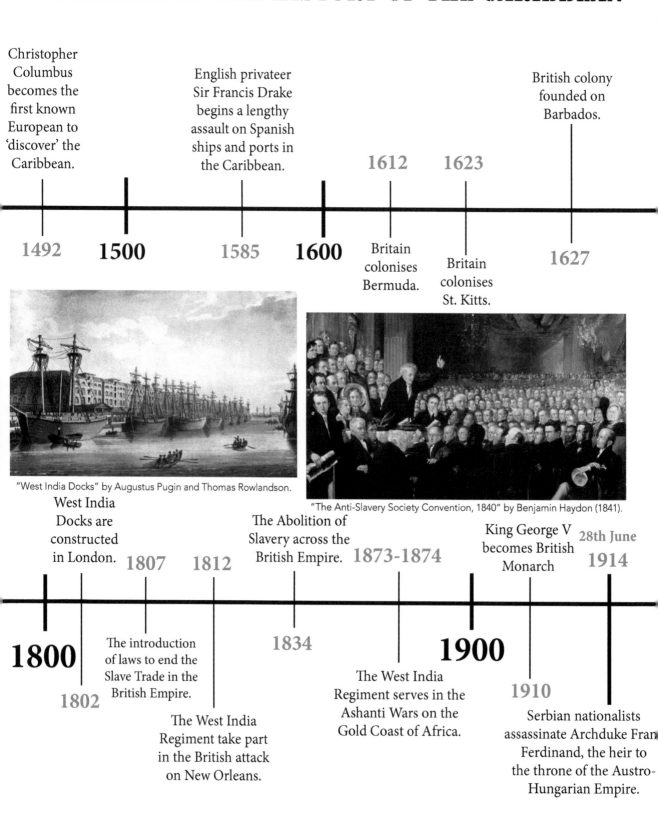

"West India Docks" by Augustus Pugin and Thomas Rowlandson.

West India Docks are constructed in London.

"The Anti-Slavery Society Convention, 1840" by Benjamin Haydon (1841).

The Abolition of Slavery across the British Empire.

King George V becomes British Monarch

28th June

1807   **1812**   **1873-1874**   **1914**

1800   1834   **1900**

1802

The introduction of laws to end the Slave Trade in the British Empire.

The West India Regiment take part in the British attack on New Orleans.

The West India Regiment serves in the Ashanti Wars on the Gold Coast of Africa.

1910

Serbian nationalists assassinate Archduke Fran Ferdinand, the heir to the throne of the Austro-Hungarian Empire.

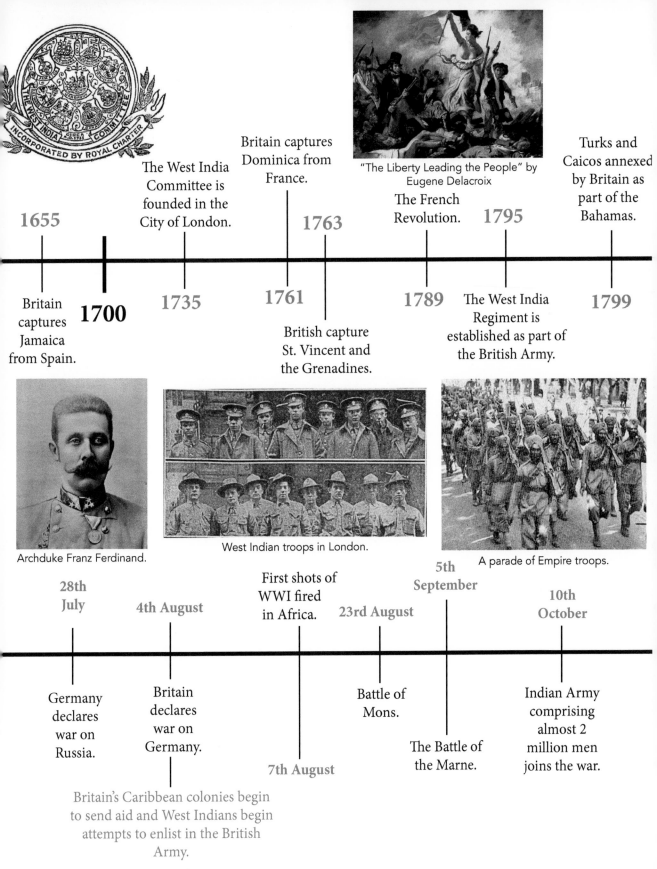

1655

Britain captures Jamaica from Spain.

1700

The West India Committee is founded in the City of London.

1735

Britain captures Dominica from France.

1761

British capture St. Vincent and the Grenadines.

1763

"The Liberty Leading the People" by Eugene Delacroix

The French Revolution.

1789

1795

The West India Regiment is established as part of the British Army.

Turks and Caicos annexed by Britain as part of the Bahamas.

1799

Archduke Franz Ferdinand.

West Indian troops in London.

5th September

A parade of Empire troops.

28th July

Germany declares war on Russia.

4th August

Britain declares war on Germany.

First shots of WWI fired in Africa.

23rd August

Battle of Mons.

The Battle of the Marne.

10th October

Indian Army comprising almost 2 million men joins the war.

7th August

Britain's Caribbean colonies begin to send aid and West Indians begin attempts to enlist in the British Army.

The British West Indies Regiment on Parade.

Gallipoli Campaign: The Allied Forces attack Germany's allies, the Ottoman Turks, in The Middle East.

3rd January

Sir Douglas Haig replaces Sir John French as the Commander-in-Chief of the British Expeditionary Force.

26th October

1915

25th April

The British West Indies Regiment is established with the approval of George V. 16,000 West Indians volunteer

10th December

First use of poisonous gas.

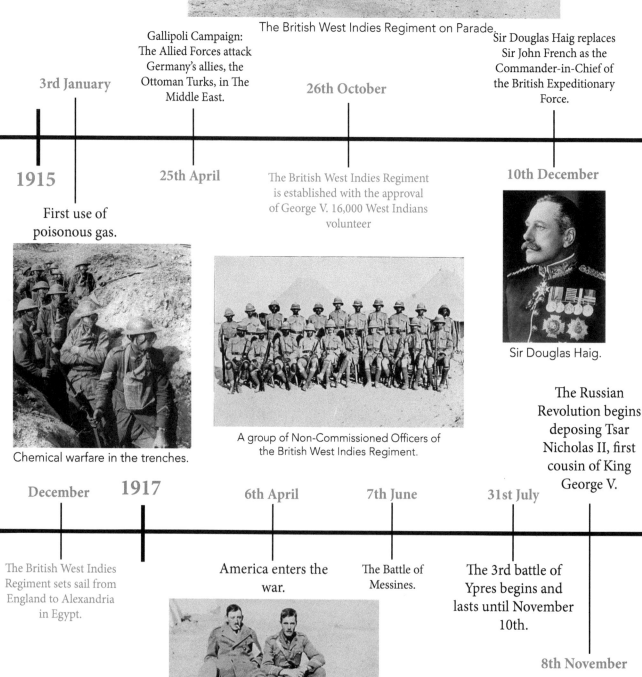

Chemical warfare in the trenches.

A group of Non-Commissioned Officers of the British West Indies Regiment.

Sir Douglas Haig.

The Russian Revolution begins deposing Tsar Nicholas II, first cousin of King George V.

December

1917

6th April

7th June

31st July

The British West Indies Regiment sets sail from England to Alexandria in Egypt.

America enters the war.

The Battle of Messines.

The 3rd battle of Ypres begins and lasts until November 10th.

8th November

West Indian officers in the Middle East.

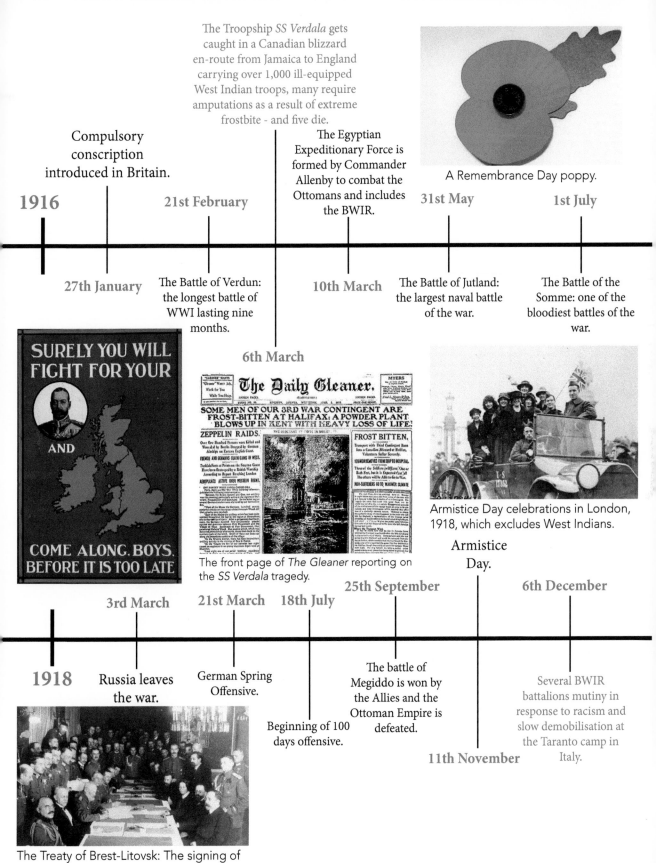

The Troopship *SS Verdala* gets caught in a Canadian blizzard en-route from Jamaica to England carrying over 1,000 ill-equipped West Indian troops, many require amputations as a result of extreme frostbite - and five die.

Compulsory conscription introduced in Britain.

The Egyptian Expeditionary Force is formed by Commander Allenby to combat the Ottomans and includes the BWIR.

A Remembrance Day poppy.

1916

21st February

31st May

1st July

27th January

The Battle of Verdun: the longest battle of WWI lasting nine months.

10th March

The Battle of Jutland: the largest naval battle of the war.

The Battle of the Somme: one of the bloodiest battles of the war.

6th March

The front page of *The Gleaner* reporting on the *SS Verdala* tragedy.

Armistice Day celebrations in London, 1918, which excludes West Indians.

Armistice Day.

25th September

6th December

3rd March

21st March

18th July

1918

Russia leaves the war.

German Spring Offensive.

The battle of Megiddo is won by the Allies and the Ottoman Empire is defeated.

Several BWIR battalions mutiny in response to racism and slow demobilisation at the Taranto camp in Italy.

Beginning of 100 days offensive.

11th November

The Treaty of Brest-Litovsk: The signing of armistice between Russia and Germany.

185

"As we recall the Caribbean's
Huge and Mighty Men of Valour
who fell during the Great War of 1914 to 1918
whose numbers have now swelled to the fullest
with the passage of time,
let us remember that their Caribbean sunset,
one of the most beautiful spectacles of this, our world,
was in truth, our dawn."

Blondel Cluff
11th November 2015
Museum of London Docklands
West India Quay

BIBLIOGRAPHY

Anthony M. (1986), Heroes of the People of Trinidad and Tobago, Port-of-Spain, Circle Press.

Anthony M. (1997), Historical Dictionary of Trinidad and Tobago, New York, Scarecrow Press.

Appiah A. & Gates, Jr. H. L. (eds.) (1999), Africana: The Encyclopedia of the African and African American Experience, New York, Basic Civitas Books.

Bennett G. (2005), Naval Battles of the First World War, Barnsley, Pen & Sword Maritime.

Bruce A. (2002), The Last Crusade: The Palestine Campaign in the First World War, London, John Murray.

Burchall L. (2014), "100 Years Ago: First Bermudian Dies in WWI", Bernews, http://bernews.com/2014/09/100-years-ago-first-bermudian-dies-in-wwi/ [accessed 20 January 2016].

Cecil H. & Liddle P. (1996), Facing Armageddon: The First World War Experience, London, Leo Cooper.

Callo J.F. & Wilson A (2004), Who's Who in Naval History: From 1550 to the Present, London, Routledge.

Field Marshal Lord Carver (2004), The National Army Museum Book of the Turkish Front 1914-1918, London, Pan Books.

Caribbean Roll of Honour [online], http://caribbeanrollofhonour-ww1-ww2.yolasite.com, [Accessed 2 February 2016].

Craton M. (1998), Islanders in the Stream, A History of the Bahamian People, Athens (Georgia), The University of Georgia Press.

Sir Julian S. Corbett (1938), Naval Operations Vol. I (second edition), London, Longmans Green and Co.

Cundall F. (1925), Jamaica's past in the Great War 1914-1918, London, The West India Committee.

Davies J.G.M. (2009), War Tax Stamps of the British Empire First World War The West Indies, London, The Royal Philatelic Society

De Lisser H.G. (1917), Jamaica & the Great War, Kingston

Doherty R. (2015), Churchill's Greatest Fear: The Battle of the Atlantic 3 September 1939 to 7 May 1945, Barnsley, Pen & Sword Military.

Dupuch E.J. (1967), Tribune Story, London, Ernest Benn Limited.

Elkins, W.F (1970), "A Source of Black Nationalism in the Caribbean: The Revolt of the British West Indies Regiment at Taranto, Italy" in Science and Society 34 (1) pp. 99-103.

Forbes K.A., Bermuda's Royal Navy Base at Ireland Island from 1815 to the 1960s [online], http://www.bermuda-online.org/rnd.htm [accessed 20 January 2016].

Fryer P. (1984), Staying Power: The History of Black People in Britain, London, Pluto Press

Garton S. (2014), "The Dominions, Ireland and India" in Empires at War:1911-1923 (Gerwarth R. & Manela E. eds.), Oxford, Oxford University Press, pp.152-178

Grant R.M. (2003), U-Boat Hunters: Code Breakers, Diver and the Defeat of the U-Boats, 1914-1918, Penzance, Periscope Publishing Limited

Gray W. (2009), War memoirs: Corporal William Dale and the Boys of Stewart Town, Browns Town, St. Ann, Jamaica

Harris E.C. (2011), "The second destruction of the–HMS Aboukir", The Royal Gazette [online], http://www.royalgazette.com/article/20111022/ISLAND09/710229979/-1&source=RSS, [accessed 7 April 2016]

Holmes F. (1924), The Bahamas during the Great War, Nassau, The Tribune

Horner A. E. (1919), From the island of the sea: glimpses of a West Indian battalion in France, Nassau, Guardian Office

Howe G. (2002), Race, War and nationalism: A social history of West Indians in the First World War, Kingston (Jamaica), Ian Randle

James, C.L.R (1932), The Life of Captain Cipriani: An Account of British Government in The West Indies- The Case for Self- Government, Durham & London, Duke University Press

Johnson H. & Watson K. (1998), The White Minority in the Caribbean, Kingston (Jamaica), Ian Randle

Joseph C.L. (1971), 'The British West Indies Regiment 1914-1918' in Journal of Caribbean History (Vol. 2), May 1971, pp. 94-124

Kelleher Storey W. (2014), The First World War: A Concise Global History, London, Rowman & Littlefield Publishers

MacDonald S.B. (1986), Trinidad and Tobago: Democracy and Development in the Caribbean, Santa Barbara, ABC-CLIO

Mansergh R. (2015), Barrow-in Furness in the Great War, Barnsley, Pen & Sword Books Limited

Marder A.J. (2014), From the Dreadnought to Scapa Flow Volume IV 1917: Year of Crisis, Barnsley, Seaforth Publishing

Mendez S., Cueto G. & Rodríguez Deynes N. (2003), Notable Caribbeans and Caribbean Americans: A Biographical Dictionary, Santa Barbara, ABC-CLIO

Muir Jr. M. (2014), Falklands, 'Battle of the (December 8, 1914)' in Germany at War: 400 Years of Military History (Zabecki D.T. ed.), Santa Barbara, ABC-CLIO LLC

Myles T.W. & Morris L.M. (eds.) (1929), The Journal of the Royal Naval Medical Service, (vol.15), London, John Bales, Sons & Danielsson Limited

Noppen R.K. (2015), German Commerce Raiders 1914-18, Oxford, Osprey Publishing

Parry J.H. and Sherlock P. (1971), A Short History of the West Indies, New York, St. Martin's

Payne A. (2008), The Political History of CARICOM, Manchester, Manchester University Press

Pearce W.J., We fought disaster on the Glatton [online], http://www.doverwarmemorialproject.org.uk/Information/Articles/Incidents/Glatton.htm [accessed 26 January 2016]

Pocock, M.W. (2008), Daily Event for July 31, 2008 [online], http://www.maritimequest.com/daily_event_archive/2008/07_july/31_ss_belgian_prince.htm, [accessed 2 February 2016]

Reynolds A. (2011), "Atkinson, Edward Leicester (1881–1929)" in Oxford Dictionary of National Biography (Matthew H.C.G., Harrison B. & Goldman L. eds.) [online], http://www.oxforddnb.com/view/article/37133, Oxford, Oxford University Press [accessed 26 January 2016]

Richard J.W. (1977), "The Politics of Protest in Trinidad: The Strikes and Disturbances of 1937", in Caribbean Studies 17 (1/2), Institute of Caribbean Studies, pp.5-54

Richardson B.C., The Caribbean in the wider world 1492-1992, Cambridge University Press, 1992, Cambridge

Roberts P., Black Oxford: The Untold Stories of Oxford University's Black Scholars, Signal Books Limited, 2013, Oxford

Rutherford Young D. (2005), 'Great Britain, Colonies' in Encyclopedia Of World War I: A Political, Social, And Military History (Tucker S. & Roberts P.M. eds.), Santa Barbara, ABC-CLIO

Saunders G. (1987), "The Role of the Coloured Middle Class in Nassau, Bahamas, 1890-1942" in Ethnic and Racial Studies, vol. 10, no. 4, Oxford, Routledge, pp.448-465

Spencer I.R.G. (1997), British Immigration Policy Since 1939: The Making of Multi-Racial Britain, London, Routledge

Smith R. (2004), Jamaican Volunteers in the First World War: Race, Masculinity and the development of the national consciousness, Manchester, Manchester University Press

Lieutenant-Colonel J.C. Smuts' Dispatch in The London Gazette (second supplement) no.29906, 16 January 1917, pp.687-702

Starling J. & Lee I. (2014), No Labour, No Battle: military labour during the First World War, Stroud, Spellmount

Strachan H. (2004), The First World War in Africa, Oxford, Oxford University Press

Stranack I. (1990), The Andrew and the Onions: The Story of the Royal Navy in Bermuda 1795-1975, Old Royal Navy Dockyard (Bermuda), Bermuda Maritime Museum Press

Teelucksingh J. (2012), "Political ambitions and contributions to trade unionism: Tubal Uriah 'Buzz' Butler during the 1930s and 1940s" in Caribbean Journal of Labour and Co-Operative Studies vol. I, Issue 1 pp.1-15

Tennant A.J. (2006), British Merchant Ships sunk by U-Boats in World War One, Penzance, Periscope Publishing Limited

The British West Indies Regiment War Diary, 1st Battalion, The West India Committee Archive, London

The British West Indies Regiment War Diary, 2nd Battalion (W0 95/4732), The National Archive, London

The British West Indies Regiment War Diary, 4th Battalion (W0 95/409), The National Archive, London

The British West Indies Regiment War Diary, 6th Battalion (W0 95/495), The National Archive, London

The British West Indies Regiment War Diary, 7th Battalion (W0 95/409), The National Archive, London

The Commonwealth War Graves Commission website, http://www.cwgc.org/ [accessed 26 February 2016]

The London Gazette no. 31013, 15 November 1918, p.13497

The London Gazette (supplement) no. 31974, 12 July 1920, p.7422

The London Gazette no.32998, 2 December 1924, p.8783

The London Gazette no.35187, 10 June 1941, p.3322

The Times 11 August (1967), OBITUARY: AIR VICE-MARSHAL C. Mcl. VINCENT, p.8

The Tribune (2014), It's Now Time For Bahamian Society To Heal Itself [online], http://www.tribune242.com/news/2014/mar/18/its-now-time-bahamian-society-heal-itself/, 03/18/2014, [accessed 8 June 2016]

The West India Committee Circular 1914, The West India Committee Archive, London

The West India Committee Circular 1915, The West India Committee Archive, London

The West India Committee Circular 1916, The West India Committee Archive, London

The West India Committee Circular 1917, The West India Committee Archive, London

The West India Committee Circular 1918, The West India Committee Archive, London

The West India Committee Circular 1919, The West India Committee Archive, London

Tucker S.C. (ed.) (2005), World War I: A Political, Social and Military History, Santa Barbara, ABC-CLIO

ACCREDITED IMAGES

INDEX